The Realist Case for Global Reform

THE REALIST CASE
FOR GLOBAL REFORM

WILLIAM E. SCHEUERMAN

polity

The right of William E. Scheuerman to be identified as Author of this
Work has been asserted in accordance with the UK Copyright, Designs and
Patents Act 1988.

First published in 2011 by Polity Press

Polity Press
65 Bridge Street
Cambridge CB2 1UR, UK

Polity Press
350 Main Street
Malden, MA 02148, USA

ISBN-13: 978-0-7456-5029-6 (hardback)
ISBN-13: 978-0-7456-5030-2 (paperback)

A catalogue record for this book is available from the British Library.

Typeset in 10.5 on 12 pt Times
by Toppan Best-set Premedia Limited
Printed and bound in Great Britain by MPG Books Group Limited,
Bodmin, Cornwall

The publisher has used its best endeavors to ensure that the URLs for external
websites referred to in this book are correct and active at the time of going to
press. However, the publisher has no responsibility for the websites and can
make no guarantee that a site will remain live or that the content is or will
remain appropriate.

Every effort has been made to trace all copyright holders, but if any have been
inadvertently overlooked the publisher will be pleased to include any necessary
credits in any subsequent reprint or edition.

For further information on Polity, visit our website: www.politybooks.com

CONTENTS

PREFACE

[T]he argument of the advocates of the world state is unanswerable: There can be no permanent international peace without a state coextensive with the confines of the political world.

(Morgenthau, 1954: 477)

What follows is an unabashedly contrarian book by an author who – or so I have been told by those closest to me – exhibits a strong streak of intellectual stubbornness. The conventional wisdom is that Realist International Theory offers an institutionally complacent vision of global politics, wedded to the existing state system and congenitally opposed to far-reaching global reform. To be sure, some Realists have spoken out powerfully against irresponsible foreign policies like those which produced the Vietnam and Second Gulf Wars. Yet Realists supposedly remain a cautious and even pessimistic bunch, defenders of the thesis that in global affairs

> states are the only major actors, and no structure of power or authority stands above them to mediate their conflicts; nor would they peacefully consent to such a structure, even if it could be shown to be workable. States act according to their power interests, and these interests are bound at times to conflict violently. Therefore, even if progress toward community and justice is possible *within* states, the relations *between* them are doomed to a permanent competition that often leads to war. However deplorable, this permanent competition remains an unavoidable reality that no amount of moral exhortation or utopian scheming can undo. (Smith, 1986: 1)

Though initially attracted to this interpretation, I have decided that it is not only misleading, but also gets in the way of formulating an international theory properly attuned to the moral and political imperatives of globalization. What ensues is an openly revisionist view of significant strands in mid-century Realism, in which I counter the standard portrayal of Realism as intellectually and institutionally conservative.

Admittedly, this must initially seem like an odd and indeed implausible endeavor, given the unabashedly anti-reformist instincts of prominent Realists like Henry Kissinger, Kenneth Waltz, or John Mearsheimer. Contemporary Realists have indeed closed ranks around a stodgy and rather self-satisfied defense of the international status quo. However, its most important mid-twentieth-century representatives – E. H. Carr (1892–1982), Hans J. Morgenthau (1904–80), Reinhold Niebuhr (1892–1971), as well as some unfairly neglected secondary figures: John Herz (1908–2006), Frederick Schuman (1904–81), Georg Schwarzenberger (1908–91), and Arnold Wolfers (1892–1968) – developed a forward-looking reformist Realism very different from that now pervasive in both the academy and halls of government. Those whom I dub *Progressive Realists* typically were situated on the political left during some juncture in their long careers. Most were influenced by the experiences of the interwar European (and especially German) left. With many left-leaning refugees among its ranks, mid-century Realism indeed drew on a so-called "Germanic tradition" – of Weimar reformism, and not as commonly asserted, reactionary Bismarckian *Realpolitik*.

Starting from the assumption that the nation state was increasingly anachronistic, Progressive Realists engaged in a fierce debate with proponents of global transformation, including the "one-world" global federalist movement which briefly flourished in the aftermath of the Second World War. Unfortunately, the debate's heated character masked important programmatic overlap; the comparatively conservative predilections of more recent Realists encouraged them to ignore it as well. Like global federalists, Progressive Realists sought extensive international reform. They argued, however, that many of its proponents neglected the centrality of *supranational society*, or what they occasionally called *world community*: any desirable as well as viable system of postnational governance would need to rest on a corresponding postnational society capable of exercising basic integrative functions akin to those regularly achieved by successful national political communities. From this standpoint, dramatic global reform and perhaps even world statehood constituted admirable goals, but they were only achievable if reformers figured out how the necessarily thick societal background for a prospective postnational political order might be constructed. Global liberal democracy remained for them a distant goal, albeit one having immediate consequences, whose social preconditions would have to be constructed in a gradualist and reformist spirit.[1]

The volume's first half thus offers a critical-minded revisionist intellectual history of mid-twentieth-century Realism. Yet its aims are by no means chiefly antiquarian: intellectual history can help shed fresh light on conventional disciplinary divides and shake up ossified ways of thinking. As such it remains an indispensable component of any international theory aspiring to counter present-day fashions or the widespread "presentist" bias which dogmatically posits that contemporary modes of thinking are necessarily more advanced than those of our historical predecessors. Unfortunately, such presentism is ubiquitous among scholars of international politics; it needs to be challenged. Without a creative retelling of the history of twentieth-century Realism, we simply miss its most provocative and surprisingly relevant ideas.

I begin by briefly revisiting the complex intellectual and political universe in which mid-century Progressive Realists came of age, along the way explaining why existing attempts to define "Realism" mask core elements of the story. In particular, the conventional category of "classical Realism" gets in the way of serious discussion more than it helps ignite it. Chapter 1 shows how Progressive Realists, while defending refreshingly nuanced theses about international law and morality, interpreted some of the conceptual mainstays of their intellectual tradition – the national interest, balance of power, and security dilemma – so as to leave open extensive possibilities for international reform. Most important perhaps, their sophisticated and surprisingly demanding political ethics underscored the *necessity* of changes to the global status quo. Chapter 2 then reconsiders their appreciative but ultimately critical views about the nation state, while Chapter 3 turns directly to Progressive Realism's lively internal debate on global reform, and especially its discussion of the pros and cons of David Mitrany's competing *functionalist* theory of international change. There I also outline why attempts by contemporary Realists (including Kissinger, Waltz, and Danilo Zolo) to transcend the reformist impulses of their mid-century predecessors ultimately founder.

The second half of the volume then shows why and how contemporary defenders of global reform can gain from a serious engagement with Progressive Realism. Chapter 4 argues that the commonplace dichotomy between Realism and Cosmopolitanism is overstated: more common ground is shared by the two intellectual tendencies than is widely presupposed. To be sure, some Cosmopolitan ideas remain vulnerable to Progressive Realist criticisms. When properly interpreted, however, the Progressive Realist critique is by no means exclusively destructive in character. On the contrary, Realist insights can be welded effectively to the present-day Cosmopolitan argument for democracy "beyond the nation state." In particular, Progressive Realist ideas about the centrality of supranational society remain vital for present-day Cosmopolitans, as does the Realist defense of robust statehood as ultimately essential to successful global governance. Realism, in short, offers powerful untapped intellectual resources for criticizing the presently fashionable idea of "global governance without government." Even a recent editor of the journal *Global Governance* has begun to acknowledge the limits of this concept: Progressive Realism can help us see why such skepticism remains pertinent (Weiss, 2009: 215–33). Cosmopolitans can strengthen their arguments by reintegrating some forgotten Realist ideas. They should join Progressive Realism in seeking ways to deepen supranational society; they would also do well to abandon their kneejerk hostility to world statehood.

Chapter 5 examines other notable recent attempts to further global reform – as advanced by Liberal Transgovernmentalism, the English School, Republicanism, and Constructivism – from the standpoint of Progressive Realism. Notwithstanding their many virtues, each of these competing approaches is found wanting. At the very least, each can learn something from the reform-minded Realism of Carr, Morgenthau, Niebuhr, and others. Chapter 6 argues that Realists were right to argue that even if world statehood represented a long-term aspiration manifestly unachievable in the foreseeable future, a properly conceived model of it remains a suitable goal. I defend this unfashionable and seemingly far-fetched intuition by responding to the most commonly voiced criticisms of world statehood, most of which turn out to rely on intellectual caricature. Even hardheaded rational choice legal scholars now concede that "problems of global collective action have multiplied and increased in seriousness" and will probably continue to do so (Posner, 2009: 38).[2] Progressive Realists were justified in viewing global government as ultimately the best way to tackle them. Finally, I reflect briefly on US President Barack Obama's apparent sympathies for Reinhold Niebuhr, perhaps the most important figure in mid-century Progressive Realism, considering the possibility that Obama's policies may be shaped to some degree by Progressive Realism.

Global reform today seems at a standstill, with the United Nations unable to pursue minimal yet overdue changes, and the European Union mired in internal divisions about how best to deal with the ongoing economic and financial crisis. For reasons to be described below, this situation should worry us. Yet the momentarily frozen character of some present-day global institutions perhaps provides a useful opportunity to re-think many of the increasingly tired clichés that dominate thinking about global-level change. A reconsideration of the neglected reformist legacy of Progressive Realism can help us do so.

ACKNOWLEDGMENTS

Thanks are owed to many who helped in the pursuit of this project. My editor at Polity, Louise Knight, enthusiastically supported it, while audiences at Cornell, University of Iowa Law School, Ohio State University, Prague Conference on Philosophy and the Social Sciences, and Yale offered critical feedback on its main arguments. In particular, I thank Seyla Benhabib, Peter Hohendahl, Alexander Somek, and Alexander Wendt for gracious invitations to present parts of the project. Joohyung Kim helped locate articles and essays, and the wonderfully competent staff at the Indiana University Wells Library was generous with its time. I should also thank the Indiana University Institute for Advanced Studies, where I served as a resident fellow while writing it.

Some sections of the manuscript previously appeared in *Ethics and Global Politics*, *International Politics*, *International Theory*, and *Transnational Law and Contemporary Problems*, to whom I am grateful for allowing me to integrate them here.

The book is dedicated to my most important undergraduate and graduate teachers – Seyla Benhabib, Ingeborg Maus, as well as the late George Schrader and Judith Shklar – in gratitude for their patience with an ignorant and stubborn student who under their tutelage became a marginally less ignorant and stubborn scholar.

INTRODUCTION

Meet the Progressive Realists

Ernest (alias "Ernie") had studied hard for his final written examination in international relations theory. When the test instructions asked for a concise definition of *Realism*, he was happy to be able to display his new knowledge. During the course of the semester, Ernie had carefully read the assigned texts on Realism (few of which, however, were original sources), and his professor had also lectured twice on Realism's core theoretical attributes; he had conscientiously taken good notes. Confident that this was a question he could easily "ace," Ernie wrote:

Realism denies morality any meaningful role in international politics. It takes this hostility to "moralism" from the political theories of Machiavelli and Hobbes, who exerted a substantial influence on Realism. Machiavelli argued in favor of discarding traditional moral norms in order to ensure self-preservation in a dangerous political universe; Hobbes believed that shared ideas about justice presuppose a system of shared sovereignty. Realists point out that because there is no sovereignty or state at the global level, interstate affairs are characterized by a perilous "state of nature" in which no common moral framework operates. Realism affirms *Realpolitik,* meaning that individual states can legitimately pursue their vital power interests even when doing so conflicts with morality. Realism's skepticism about international law stems from the same roots. As Machiavelli and Hobbes asserted, binding law requires sanctions backed up by a coercive state apparatus. Because interstate affairs remain characterized by anarchy, the regular enforcement of law there inevitably is plagued by massive deficits. More often than not, international law – like many appeals to a shared moral code – serves as little more than the political instruments of powerful global interests or Great Powers. When international morality or international law operates effectively, it does so only because big power interests at the global level happen to decide that it is in their interest for it to do so. But in a Hobbesian world, their support necessarily remains fragile. This is why Realists are hostile to what they call "moralism" and "legalism."

Because the essay question also asked of Ernie that he outline one of the main flaws of Realism, he added that

Realism's main flaw is its institutional conservatism. Because of international anarchy, Realists say, states can do little more than pursue their parochial national interests. International organizations always represent fragile creatures, dependent on the cooperation of power units whose interests may conflict. The basic dynamics of an international system in which rival states compete for power and security render utopian any attempt to establish ambitious varieties of global governance. This is why Realists even today remain committed to maintaining the primacy of the nation state, despite evidence that globalization is undermining it. They discount even modest attempts at international reform. Rather, they believe that peace is best preserved by the realities of the "balance of power," on which they sometimes offer a backwards-looking and nostalgic gloss. Their dogmatic view of international anarchy makes them skeptical of attempts to reform international politics in the direction, for example, of "cosmopolitan democracy," as advocated by some writers. Such skepticism also partly derives from the pessimistic (and highly dubious) view of human nature endorsed by some early or "classical" Realists. But even among Realists who do not base their views in ideas of human nature, skepticism about global reform is widespread. Such Realists often focus on the "security dilemma," which basically says that because no state can feel perfectly secure in a world with competing autonomous political units, each state is driven to acquire as much power as possible. Even these Realists miss the need today, in the face of globalization, to develop new forms of political organization. Consequently, Realism cannot make sense of the rapid growth of international organizations, appearance of new political systems like the European Union, or the emergence of a global system of human rights, all of which have already transformed so-called anarchy. Realism's main nemesis, Cosmopolitanism, probably does a better job understanding the emerging realities of globalization.

Ernie's instructor, Professor Conventional ("Connie") Wisdom, read his essay and quickly rewarded Ernie with a high grade. The answer, she determined, not only covered most of the main points relevant to Realism, but also successfully identified its most striking flaws. Of course, more could have been said about Realism's different variants and the ways in which recent Neorealism breaks with the "classical" Realism of writers like E. H. Carr and Hans J. Morgenthau, or the disagreements between contemporary "offensive" and "defensive" Realists (Layne, 2006: 15–25). Yet given the examination's time constraints, Connie fair-mindedly acknowledged, no answer could conceivably cover every feature of Realist theory. As she was well aware, Ernie's response meshed nicely with the account of Realism found in a great deal of the secondary literature. In particular, his interpretation of Realism overlapped at most junctures with that of Cosmopolitanism, which – as Ernie accurately noted – probably represents Realism's most important rival in present-day international thought.[1]

Based on his hard work and strong academic record, Ernie successfully finished his studies and ultimately earned a doctorate in political science. Only a few years after having completed the international relations theory exam, he found himself administering a similar test to his own eager (and not-so-eager) students, from whom he expected a parallel assessment of Realism.

Realism: A Second Look

Now if this were the final word on Realism, you could put this book down and return to whatever activity you were contentedly doing just a few minutes ago. I would have gone back to that detective novel I was reading while comfortably ensconced on my back deck overlooking the woods. We could all go on happily repeating the conventional interpretation of Realism, enveloped in a smug sense of the certainty of our knowledge. And for those among us (like Ernie and perhaps Connie, as well as this author) sympathetic to Cosmopolitanism, we could also rest assured in the superiority of our theoretical and political preferences. Realism, we might again tell ourselves, is a conservative and outdated international theory, poorly suited to the social and political realities of our rapidly globalizing world. It may once have captured, albeit somewhat one-sidedly, some key elements of the traditional state system, when relatively discrete nation states faced off in a nasty struggle for power. Yet it becomes ever more outdated as the Westphalian system fades into the past.

For better or worse, I will have to ask you to stay with my somewhat polemical little book for just a while longer. Too much present-day international theory seems disturbingly reminiscent of shadow boxing, with participants directing their punches at imaginary antagonists outfitted with crudely stylized arguments, but rarely in fact landing a real punch on an actual opponent. Comfortably ensconced in the disciplinary subfield of

"IR" and committed to the systematic empirical study of international politics, Realist political scientists, for example, hardly take notice of the remarkable recent revival of Cosmopolitanism, most of whose representatives hail from the ranks of normative political philosophy. Caught up in their own internecine methodological battles, Realists occasionally seem oblivious to the efforts of their colleagues (many of whom can be found just down the departmental hallway) in constructing ambitious accounts of global justice, for example, or global democracy.

Yet Realists are by no means alone in their preference for shadow boxing. Cosmopolitans and many other critics of Realism have made things too easy for themselves by embracing a simplistic and occasionally caricatured interpretation of Realism. They regularly ignore versions of Realist international theory – and especially sound normatively minded variants of mid-century Realism, described in the present volume as *Progressive Realism* – which rest on more sophisticated and politically appealing ideas than those pretty much universally ascribed to it. Although continuing to recycle conventional wisdom would certainly offer us all an easier path, anyone committed to intellectual integrity has a responsibility to do better.

For the modest purposes of this chapter, let me just try to convince you that Realist international theory potentially offers a more supple starting point for reflecting on the challenges of global politics than perhaps you, like Ernie and many others, are presently willing to concede. If I can succeed, you might then also consider the contrarian claim that at least *some* Realists not only have developed a surprisingly sound vision of far-reaching global reform, but that present-day global reformers can in fact strengthen their case by building on Realism.[2]

Will the Real Realists Please Stand Up?

So what then *is* Realism, and how might we best describe its main features?

Since one purpose of this book is to challenge the conventional portrayal of Realism, we cannot simply return to standard interpretations mirroring Ernie's examination answer. How then might we proceed? At first glance, the problem seems daunting: an unusually diverse variety of thinkers – ranging from the Italian political philosopher Danilo Zolo to US political scientists like John Mearsheimer and Kenneth Waltz – presently describe themselves as Realists. Henry Kissinger, an architect of conservative US foreign policy in the late 1960s and 1970s, embraces the label, while some scholars have also characterized Noam Chomsky, the radical critic of US foreign policy, as a Realist (Osborn, 2009). Some Realists are chiefly philosophical and normative in their approach; others are hard-headed social scientists who eschew normative analysis. Some are ensconced comfortably on the political right, many would describe them-selves as centrists or (in US terms) moderate liberals, and a rare few are linked to the radical left. Realist or at least Realist-type arguments appear in the pages of both the radical *New Left Review* and neoconservative *The National Interest*.

Fortunately, there is already a rough scholarly consensus about *who* the most influential voices in modern English-language Realist theory were during the mid-twentieth century, when it exploded onto the intellectual scene and rapidly reshaped discourse about international politics. Although hardly an unproblematic starting point, since any attempt to characterize a thinker as "Realist" depends on how we ultimately define it, revisiting those who have been described – and sometimes *self*-described – as the framers or "founding fathers"[3] of modern Realist theory gives us one way of figuring out what Realism has been about, at least in the English-speaking intellectual world (to which this inquiry is limited). Of course, we will need to keep in mind that Realism, like any great theoretical tradi-tion, has undergone decisive changes since the mid-twentieth century. (In Chapter 3, we discuss the implications of such shifts.) Yet initially it makes sense to return to those mid-century thinkers who by any account deter-mined the outlines of what quickly became known as "Realist" interna-tional theory.

So who were the mid-century "classical" Realists?[4] First and foremost, we encounter three towering figures: the British historian and scholar of international politics, E. H. Carr (1892–1982), political scientist Hans J. Morgenthau (1904–80), and last but by no means least, theologian Rein-hold Niebuhr (1892–1971), famously described by another important mid-century Realist, the US diplomat and political commentator George Kennan (1904–2005) as "the father of us all," and unquestionably a tremendous influence on every major as well as minor representative of mid-century Realism (cited in Thompson, 2007: 1). No discussion of the history of Realism legitimately omits the pivotal role of the "big three" in intellectual and political life at mid-century. Not surprisingly, a vast amount of scholar-ship has been devoted to their ideas.[5] Like any serious intellectual or political movement, Realism has its own canonical texts, to which its disciples (and critics) regularly turn. If one were asked to come up with such a list, Carr's *The Twenty Years' Crisis, 1919–1939* (1939), Morgen-thau's *Scientific Man vs. Power Politics* (1946), *Politics Among Nations: The Struggle for Power and Peace* (1948b, 1st edn), *In Defense of the National Interest: A Critical Examination of American Foreign Policy*

(1951), as well as Niebuhr's *Moral Man and Immoral Society* (1932) and *The Children of Light and the Children of Darkness* (1944) would surely be placed atop it.

In this first generation of Realist international thinkers, born roughly around the turn of the century, many other secondary figures come to mind. Any sensible categorization would necessarily have to include three more prominent postwar US political scientists, relatively neglected today but widely respected at mid century – John H. Herz (1908–2006), Frederick Schuman (1904–81), and Arnold Wolfers (1892–1968) – as well perhaps as the pretty much totally forgotten UK teacher of international law, Georg Schwarzenberger (1908–91), who influenced generations of law students at the University of London. Schuman wrote what arguably was the first identifiably Realist university textbook, *International Politics: An Introduction to the Western State System* (1933, 1st edn), widely adopted in classrooms and reissued, like Morgenthau's influential *Power Among Nations*, on numerous occasions over the course of many decades. At mid century Schuman was a prominent public intellectual who popularized Realist ideas, with a major intellectual historian aptly describing him as the *"New Republic's* resident specialist in Realpolitik" in light of his vocal role as a foreign affairs commentator for the leading (then) left-wing political journal (Pells, 1985: 38; also, Bucklin, 2001; Oren, 2003: 116–21; Pells, 1973: 64, 77, 301–2, 308, 322). Herz coined the influential term "security dilemma" in his *Political Realism and Political Idealism* (1951), while Wolfers penned a set of influential essays, the most considerable of which were collected in his classic *Discord and Collaboration: Essays on International Politics* (1962). The title of Schwarzenberger's massive *Power Politics: A Study of International Society* (1st edn, 1941), a book also frequently revised and widely used in the classroom by law professors, speaks for itself.[6]

One might also categorize the US journalist Walter Lippmann (1889–1974), Dutch-born US political scientist Nicholas Spykman (1893–1943), and religious-minded British philosopher of history Herbert Butterfield (1900–79) as "classical Realists." Although his views often meshed with those of Morgenthau and other Realists, Lippmann was chiefly a journalist and political commentator whose original contributions to Realist theory were ultimately modest. Spykman is best described as a defender of geopolitics and a geographically deterministic view of politics, whose ideas also sometimes overlapped with those of Realists, but whose thinking differed substantially from theirs. A case can also be made for including Butterfield. Yet – like another major mid-century British thinker, Martin Wight[7] – one places him under the "Realist" label only with difficulty: at the very least, Butterfield's impact (like that, by the way, of the

Frenchman Raymond Aron) on postwar Realist *empirical* political science was limited. Though widely read and consulted by Realists of a theological and philosophical bent, Butterfield did not help reshape the study of international politics along the lines, for example, of Morgenthau.[8] Sometimes Henry Kissinger (born 1923) is classified as a "classical" Realist, though for reasons to be outlined in Chapter 3, he is in some respects better grouped alongside other members of the same generational cohort (e.g. Kenneth Waltz [born 1924]), who joined him in redirecting the course of Realist thought (and, in Kissinger's case, Realist *practice* as well) away from the critically minded aspirations of an earlier generation born between 1890 and 1910.

Lawyers, Believers, and Socialists

So the terms "Realism" and even "classical Realism" have been employed to describe a broad variety of thinkers and ideas. Now that we have narrowed our inquiry a bit, however, some striking biographical and intellectual commonalities immediately jump out, at least as far as a significant subset of Realist thinkers is concerned.[9] For reasons that should become clear in the following pages, I have opted to use the term *Progressive Realist* to describe especially Carr, Morgenthau, Niebuhr, as well as Herz, Schuman, Schwarzenberger, and Wolfers. Admittedly, none of these writers ever employed the category; one might perhaps include others under this rubric as well. Nonetheless, they remain the dominant figures in what I consider to be an almost universally misconstrued variety of normatively and politically sensible mid-century Realism.[10] At least to some extent, they saw themselves as constituting a coherent group: they learned and borrowed from each other, corresponded and argued (sometimes heatedly) with one other, cited and reviewed each other's work, and sometimes cooperated on shared projects. The category of *Progressive Realism* not only aptly sets this group of mid-century Realists apart from the politically and institutionally conservative Realism of, say, Butterfield or Kissinger, but it also properly highlights the neglected institutionally reformist and oftentimes left-leaning political character of their rich body of thought.[11] Unlike the conventional – and somewhat misleading – category of "classical Realism," which lumps together a range of inconsonant thinkers in potentially misleading ways, it allows us to zero in on a group of intellectuals possessing a shared political background and roughly parallel political aspirations.

Mid-century Progressive Realists developed a prescient critique of the existing international state system and advocated far-reaching changes (see

Chapters 2 and 3). Although they built on – and indeed sometimes helped formulate – otherwise familiar Realist ideas and concepts, they interpreted them in an institutionally open-ended and sometimes expressly reformist fashion (Chapter 1). Progressive Realism constitutes a fruitful source for fresh thinking about the challenges of global change, as well as a powerful corrective to influential contemporary versions of reform-minded international theory (Chapters 4, 5). The following pages undertake to salvage its core components for more than purely historical reasons: it has something important to tell us. Its neglect comes at a high price not simply to the intellectual history of international thought, but also to contemporary debates about global politics.

So what were the most striking commonalities among Progressive Realists? Most obviously, many of them were trained as lawyers. Both Herz and Morgenthau early in their careers were tied to the prominent legal theorist and international lawyer, Hans Kelsen, central Europe's most important legal positivist and erstwhile defender of a system of seamless and strictly enforceable global law. The youthful Wolfers gained a legal training in his native Switzerland, before going to Berlin and then fleeing Nazism for the US. Schwarzenberger was a protégé of one of Weimar Germany's most famous socialist jurists, Gustav Radbruch, before also having to escape fascism and becoming a law professor in the UK. Although by the late 1930s they had become sensitized to the fragilities of the international legal order, their early (and in many cases still untranslated) legal writings evince surprising sympathy for the League of Nations.[12] Even their later English-language contributions demonstrated an undeniable mastery of the intricacies of international law.

Progressive Realism began to a great extent as a movement of disappointed and displaced ex-lawyers who – traumatized by the disintegration of the League of Nations – struggled to make sense of why the twentieth century's first great experiment in postnational governance fell apart like a house of cards, disastrously paving the way for the rise of Nazism and the Second World War. On the basis of the League's demise they concluded that many influential ideas about international law, and especially the brand of legal positivism endorsed by Kelsen, occluded the centrality of real-life power relations in distorting and undermining international law's otherwise noble attempt to preserve peace. To make sense of the frailties of international law one would have to undertake an empirical – or what Morgenthau and Schwarzenberger both initially described as a "sociological" – analysis of how law operates in the context of explosive relations of power and inequality (Morgenthau 1940; Schwarzenberger, 1941: 15–53; also, Herz, 1951: 97–102; Herz, 1984, 106–15). Whereas Kelsen had argued for a strict separation between legal science and empirical analyses of the law, his Realist offspring insisted that any worthwhile theory of international law would have to situate it within a hardheaded "realistic" analysis of social and political power.

In fact, "Realism" at first primarily entailed a critical-minded, empirical analysis – based in the social sciences – of international politics and especially international law. Although Carr never received a legal training, this was the view of Realism he advanced, and whose roots he located in the ideas of critical social thinkers like Karl Marx and Karl Mannheim. Their theories, he argued, provided the requisite basis for understanding the collapse of the interwar international system. Relying heavily on Mannheim's *Ideology and Utopia* (1936; also, Jones, 1998), Carr's Realism offered a critical autopsy of power relations and real-life inequalities which generated delusional and ideological ideas veiling the unpleasant realities of global politics (Carr, 1964 [1939]: 15, 45, 63–88; also Schwarzenberger, 1941: 19–25, 353–60). Absent Carr's recourse to Marx or Mannheim, Wolfers' rival account of the demise of the interwar European state system similarly jettisoned a narrowly legalistic approach in favor of a rich and multifaceted empirical analysis of interstate power struggles (1966 [1940]). In an analogous vein, the Chicago-trained Schuman undertook "to interpret political forms and forces against the background of the whole social and economic order of the Western world," in which the dynamics of a crisis-ridden capitalism in the 1930s had abruptly taken center stage (1933: viii).

Progressive Realists observed the League's demise from close quarters. Herz and Morgenthau spent formative years in the early and mid 1930s in Geneva, the League's main institutional site, where they quickly gained a sense of its fragility. Carr had been Assistant Advisor on League Affairs for the British Foreign Office, which sent him to observe some of the League's most important meetings, on the basis of which he soon surmised that it "was dangerously out of touch with reality" (cited in Haslam, 1999: 49). While based in the 1930s at the London-based New Commonwealth Institute,[13] a reform-minded think tank and advocacy group sympathetic to the League and international reform, "Schwarzenberger traveled, on behalf of the Society, as an observer to sessions of the League of Nations." At close hand he witnessed its destruction under the combined weight of democratic incompetence and ruthless fascist *Realpolitik* (Steinle, 2004: 670).

A second striking commonality were the deep religious commitments of a number of Progressive Realists, most evident in the case of the Protestant theologian Reinhold Niebuhr, but clearly discernible among others as well (Epp, 1991). When Niebuhr first embraced the term "Realism," it chiefly signaled his alliance with an emerging theological tendency, pioneered by a younger generation of Protestants frustrated with mainstream

Christianity's insufficient political radicalism (Horton, 1934; Macintosh, 1931; Meyer, 1988; Thelen, 1946; Voskuil, 1988). The "Christian Realism" they advocated fused the struggle for far-reaching social change with a creative attempt to salvage orthodox Christian ideas about original sin and humankind's fallen state.[14] As with Carr, Morgenthau, and Schwarzenberger, the endorsement of "Realism" was partly a call for a hard-headed and critical analysis of social power relations; Marxism played a major role in Niebuhr's thinking during the 1930s (Niebuhr 1932; 1934). Yet it also referred to a theological acknowledgment of (supposedly) "realistic" verities about humankind's congenital pride, selfishness, and hubris. Here the decisive influence was exercised by the left-wing theologian Paul Tillich, who similarly sought to synthesize Marxism, radical politics, and a creative reinterpretation of Christian (and especially Protestant) orthodoxy, as part of what he described as "belief-ful Realism," and whom Niebuhr helped bring to the United States when Tillich was stripped of his German passport by the Nazis in 1933.[15]

Niebuhr was hardly the only Christian Socialist who contributed to mid-century Realism. Arnold Wolfers had also been a leading activist in Tillich's Weimar-based religious socialist movement, remaining close to Tillich even after both landed in the United States because of Hitler's ascent.[16] Wolfers wrote in the 1920s for the movement's journal, *Blätter für Religösen Sozialismus*, as well as for allied left-wing Christian journals.[17] A certain religious sensibility can sometimes also be detected in the writings of Morgenthau, a Jewish refugee who admired Niebuhr, whom he enthusiastically described at one point as "the greatest living political philosopher in America" (Morgenthau, 1962c: 109; also, Mollov, 2002; Rice, 2008). Schwarzenberger, another German Jew, ultimately converted to Christianity: he similarly admired Niebuhr, appreciatively citing the Protestant theologian at the conclusion to the first edition of his *Power Politics* when calling for a return to the Christian "springs from which our civilization grows" (1941: 433; also, 1939).

Two further commonalities deserve attention. One of them, namely the fact that so many mid-century Realists were German–Jewish refugees, or at least were influenced by German political and intellectual trends, has already been widely noted in the secondary literature. That biographical overlap can only be properly contextualized, however, if we simultaneously recall that the ranks of mid-century Realism were disproportionately populated by left-wingers.

Most – including Herz, Niebuhr, Schuman, Schwarzenberger, and Wolfers – were all at some point outspoken socialists, deeply versed in leftist social and political ideas, and sometimes having extensive histories of left-wing activism.[18] As noted, some were linked to Tillich's band of (non-Marxist) "religious socialists," Protestant and Jewish leftists who built on Marx's critique of capitalism while astutely pointing to the normative gaps of classical Marxism. Prior to 1933, Wolfers regularly defended democratic socialism while eviscerating capitalism for its "anti-spiritual" pathologies (1924).[19] Niebuhr not only sympathized with Weimar religious socialism but arguably helped translate its core ideas into terms comprehensible to a mainstream US religious audience. A consistent leftist critic of FDR's New Deal and longstanding member of the Socialist Party, Niebuhr did not support Roosevelt until 1940 when he broke with the Socialists over their pacifism and opposition to US military support for Britain (Merkley, 1975: 63–125). Schwarzenberger was forced to leave Germany not only because of his Jewish background, but also because he had been a leader in the youth wing of the Social Democratic Party (SPD). Herz, another German Jew forced to flee Nazism, was involved in émigré socialist politics during the 1930s. Morgenthau had been a left-leaning Weimar labor lawyer and protégé of Hugo Sinzheimer, the architect of the Weimar Constitution's expressly social democratic provisions. Although never a socialist, he at least sympathized briefly with core elements of an identifiably left-wing critique of capitalism (Scheuerman, 2009: 11–39).

Like his fellow US-born Realist Niebuhr, Schuman was also a left-winger and outspoken anti-fascist in the 1930s who traveled widely in Europe and was shocked by the Nazi takeover of a country for which, as a first-generation German–American he may have preserved some sense of filial attachment. Alongside Carr, and Niebuhr, he advocated a synthesis of economic collectivism – e.g. some variety of economic planning – with the preservation of core elements of the Western political tradition. He vehemently attacked the failure of the Western liberal democracies to join forces with Soviet Russia in aiding the anti-fascist cause, interpreting fascism as embodying the latest and perhaps final crisis of liberal capitalism. Schuman also shared the view that capitalism was probably on its death bed: the only real question was whether fascism could be countered by a novel political and social order successfully synthesizing socialist economics with core liberal political ideals (Carr, 1942; Niebuhr, 1932; 1934; Schuman, 1933; 1941a; 1941b).

At least some of the members of this first generation – most notably, Carr and probably Schuman – remained life-long radicals. Carr devoted much of his postwar academic career to a controversial fourteen volume study of the Soviet Revolution (1950–78).[20] In contrast, others (for example, Wolfers) quickly toned down their youthful radicalism and joined the political mainstream. In particular, those among them who were Jewish refugees from a Nazi Germany now engaged in an existential struggle with their adopted homes, outsiders subject to anti-Semitism and pervasive wartime suspicion, faced strong pressures to acclimatize themselves to a political climate quite different from that of the left-wing Weimar milieu in which they had matured.[21] The fact that even the US-born (and Gentile) Schuman could be made subject to the hostile pillorying of the infamous House Un-American Activities Committee, which he successfully escaped but only at the cost of a tarnished reputation, could not have gone unnoticed.[22] Growing awareness of the horrors of Stalinism, the New Deal's successes, and the apparently steady expansion of the welfare state, contributed even more significantly to their postwar deradicalization.

Yet even for Wolfers, who seems to have resolutely abandoned his youthful socialist dreams and whose postwar views can be justifiably described as "Cold War liberal," sympathy for a basically left-liberal domestic reform agenda remained the norm.[23] Although rejecting mainstream socialist models of state planning, in the 1950s and 1960s Morgenthau, Niebuhr, and Herz stayed committed to the further extension of the welfare state and the construction of what postwar social democrats and welfare state liberals typically described as a "mixed economy" with a large public sector and far-reaching state intervention (Morgenthau, 1960; 1970; Merkley, 1975: 169–226; Niebuhr, 1952; 1953b). Morgenthau's *The Purpose of American Politics* praised America's democratic experiment, for example, but argued that it risked coming unraveled in the face of massive social, economic, and technological changes: the United States desperately required a second and even more far-reaching bout of New Deal-type reformism (1960; also, 1970). Not surprisingly, Morgenthau and Niebuhr were both prominent members of a host of left-liberal political organizations.[24] With other Progressive Realists they vocally criticized US racism, sympathized early on with the civil rights movements, and then opposed the Vietnam War and remained active in peace and anti-nuclear movements.[25] The commonplace depiction of them as "Cold War liberals" captures *some* features of their views. Yet it distorts the extent to which their positions were often to the left of the mainstream Democratic Party, as well as the numerous ways in which they attacked Cold War foreign policies and the emerging national security state (Kleinman, 2000; Lebow, 2011; Scheuerman, 2009).[26]

Many sound reasons can be identified for recalling Realism's socialist background. Most significantly, it casts mid-century Realism's political agenda in a new light. Offspring of a radical tradition supportive of far-reaching political and social reform, theirs was not enmity to global reform *per se*, but instead to what they took to be *superficial* and potentially counterproductive reform ideas which, as they thought the disastrous inter-war experiment with the League of Nations had unequivocally demonstrated, grappled insufficiently with the harsh realities of global power relations. Schooled as socialists, their occasionally rather harsh assessment of liberal-minded global reform rested on the powerful insight that meaningful change would have to attack the structural roots of the international system's pathologies: the "utopianism" they railed against was seen as representing a pseudo-radicalism which put the cart before the horse and potentially derailed constructive reforms.

Progressive Realism's radical roots also give its widely tasted "Germanic" flavor a different taste. German and German–Jewish émigrés (i.e. Herz, Morgenthau, Schwarzenberger, and Wolfers), as well as two first-generation German–Americans, both of whom spoke fluent German and traveled extensively in Germany (i.e. Niebuhr and Schuman), indeed dominated its ranks. According to one popular interpretation, classical Realists forcefully formulated a hard-headed response to so-called interwar "Idealists" who, or so the conventional scholarly account goes,[27] downplayed the tenacity of traditional power politics. On this reading, classical Realism merely imported the tradition of continental and even Germanic *Realpolitik* into English-speaking intellectual and political discourse, ultimately updating it in accordance with Cold War political conditions, when Realism's political impact reached its apex. Bismarck, Max Weber, and maybe even Carl Schmitt, were its key theoretical sources (Haslam, 2002; Honig, 1996; Koskenniemi, 2001; Scheuerman, 1999; Smith, 1986; Söllner, 1987).

The conventional wisdom is right to emphasize mid-century Realism's Germanic tenor. Even among those who were not émigrés, Niebuhr was versed in German philosophy and theology, while Carr was influenced profoundly by left-wing German sociology. All of them closely followed political events in interwar Germany.[28] Progressive Realists indeed drew on Weber and sometimes even – in the case of Morgenthau – the reactionary Schmitt. And the conventional story indeed accurately captures core features of Kissinger's conservative Realism (Dickson, 1978; Hoffmann, 1978: 33–104; Kissinger, 1957). Yet it misconstrues the intellectual and political context in which Progressive Realism came to fruition, reproducing a caricatured portrayal of German thought and culture that says more about Anglo-American provincialism than the facts at hand. The specifically German background out of which Progressive Realism emerged was at least partly that of the contradictory yet vibrant Weimar Republic, where a radical intellectual and cultural avant-garde challenged powerful forces of cultural and political reaction. The most important "Germanic" influences on the Realists (i.e. Kelsen, Mannheim, Radbruch, Sinzheimer, and Tillich) were figures on the interwar German *left*. In any case, it seems misleading to draw a straight line from Bismarckian *Realpolitik* to Realism.

Against Intellectual Caricature

The biographical details recounted above should raise eyebrows among those committed to the conventional view of Realism as institutionally conservative and backwards-looking, indebted theoretically to Machiavelli, Hobbes, and Teutonic *Realpolitik*, but poorly suited to the challenges of globalization and the imperatives of global governance. It would prove quite surprising if a group of left-leaning intellectuals, many of whom had been lawyers and defenders of the League of Nations, as well as longtime advocates of domestic social reform with strongly religious sensibilities, suddenly embraced amoral Machiavellian power politics and altogether abandoned their youthful political dreams. Nonetheless, if we are successfully to challenge the conventional portrayal of Realism, we need to take a closer look at Progressive Realist ideas and arguments.

1 WHY (ALMOST) EVERYTHING YOU LEARNED ABOUT REALISM IS WRONG

Realism comes in many different shapes and sizes. We should avoid being too hard on Ernie. Not only did he concisely summarize the dominant scholarly view of Realism, but influential variants of Realist theory do neatly fit his definition. Even the relatively small world of so-called classical Realism had more than its own fair share of internal disagreements. For example, much of what Ernie had to say accurately captures the ideas of George Kennan, an important figure in the Realist pantheon, especially as formulated in the influential *American Diplomacy, 1900–50* (1951). Ernie's remarks also offer a useful preliminary guide to Realists like Henry Kissinger and Kenneth Waltz, whose impact has been massive.

Nonetheless, core tenets of *Progressive Realism* conflict with Ernie's examination answer. To be sure, Progressive Realists worried about the limitations of international law and international morality, argued about the ways in which political action might clash with morality, and theorized about the national interest, balance of power, and security dilemma. Yet they interpreted such familiar Realist theoretical tropes in a reformist and politically progressive fashion. Progressive Realists did not express unmitigated hostility to international law or international morality, advocate moral skepticism or amoral *Realpolitik*, offer a fundamentally Machiavellian or Hobbesian international theory, or depend on an unduly pessimistic view of human nature. Nor did they promulgate a cramped view of the national interest, embrace a backwards-looking and institutionally conservative model of the balance of power, or see the security dilemma as an insurmountable barrier to international change. The former lawyers, religious believers, and socialists who made up the ranks of Progressive Realism did not simply sacrifice their youthful humanitarian and reform-oriented views. Progressive Realism offers a more subtle account of international politics than typically acknowledged. It also provides impressive resources for those of us dissatisfied with the international status quo.

International Morality and Law

What should we make of the widespread criticism that Realists have badly downplayed the constructive roles played by international morality and law in the existing global order?

Morgenthau probably offered the most concise statement of the Progressive Realist position. Like most of his peers, he worried that the Hobbesian metaphor of an international "state of nature" was misleading: it closed our eyes to the myriad ways in which ethics, mores, and law regulated state action even absent world government (1948b: 169, 397). International affairs were not characterized by a norm-less anarchy, but instead by a complex intermeshing international "society of nations" resting on a rich variety of shared moral, legal, and social norms and practices (1954: 479). He argued emphatically against not only what he took to be exaggerated expectations about international morality and international law, *but also* in opposition to dismissive assessments of their accomplishments: "during the four hundred years of its existence international law has in most cases been scrupulously observed" (1954: 251). Even during moments of extreme crisis or emergency, nation states typically have abided by an international moral code: "the fact of the matter is that nations recognize a moral obligation to refrain from the infliction of death and suffering ... despite the possibility of justifying such conduct in the light of a higher purpose, such as the national interest" (1948c, 82).

In the immediate aftermath of the Second World War, Morgenthau understandably worried that modern total war was destroying both international law and international morality. "Nationalistic universalism," driving individual political units arrogantly to identify "the standards and goals of a particular nation with the principles that govern the universe," was working disastrously to weaken those features of international morality and law which traditionally had mitigated the dangers of international politics (1958: 176). Even a seemingly uncontroversial shared moral or legal norm consequently might mean something "different to an American, a Russian, and an Indian" since it was "perceived by, assimilated to, and filtered through minds conditioned by different experiences" (1954: 240). This resulted from disparities in everyday social existence, but also from parochial national frameworks by means of which most moral and political events were still digested: nation states continued to fill the "hearts and minds of men everywhere" with narrow "standards of political morality" (1954: 244).

Progressive Realists thus hammered away at the simple but telling point that apparent agreement on abstract moral and legal matters often masked explosive disagreements. People everywhere should and increasingly do condemn war and violent aggression, for example. Yet even apparent consensus on the relevant moral and legal prohibitions veiled explosive tensions.

They rejected a crude instrumentalist account of morality and law, which interprets them as easily manipulated playthings of the Great Powers, a passive "superstructure" determined willy-nilly by the "base" of global power relations. Such one-sided views of law and morality – including orthodox Marxism – only captured some facets of a more complex social reality (Carr, 1964 [1939]: 176–7). Even Great Powers were sometimes forced to obey norms which they otherwise would have preferred to violate: powerful "[g]overnments must at least outwardly conform to the standards which they have invoked for their own benefit" (Schwarzenberger, 1951: 227).

Nonetheless, international law and morals suffered from considerable weaknesses. In the context of a deeply divided international society, the decentralization of legislation, adjudication, and enforcement too often rendered international law subject to "vicissitudes of the distribution of power between the violator of the law and the victim of the violation" (Morgenthau, 1954: 270). This undermined law's requisite generality: powerful states were treated differently from their weak rivals. To be sure, parallel dilemmas could be readily identified at the domestic level, where law could also prove subject to inconsistent application and enforcement. Yet such trends were badly aggrandized in the international system since it lacked "the unity and coherence of communities of more limited size."[1] Unable to fulfill basic integrative functions accomplished more-or-less automatically by successful nationally based polities, international society remained embryonic and underdeveloped. The requisite "world community," Carr confessed, was increasingly a concrete lived social reality (1964 [1939]: 162). Yet it remained plagued by fragilities – most notably, stunning power inequalities – that had been minimized at least to some degree at the national level. Not surprisingly, its moral and legal instruments were unable to operate as effectively as those on the national scene, where privileged political and social interests often obeyed burdensome moral and legal norms.

Not surprisingly given Progressive Realism's socialist background, this view echoed key features of conventional leftist legal thinking.[2] Even when the law appeared to treat all parties equally, de facto power inequalities meant that it favored those possessing superior power resources. To be sure, the socialist and especially Marxist tradition typically prescribed an ambivalent conception of law: while emphasizing the virtues of the rule of law and civil liberties *within* capitalism, many Marxists thought that a postcapitalist social order could simply expend with basic rights and fundamental legal protections. Fortunately, most Progressive Realists acknowledged law's admirable normative aspirations *along with* its tendency to mirror power inequalities. They generally recognized law's institutional and normative complexity, even if they were forced to admit that a model of it as chiefly serving the interests of the powerful and privileged provided a more fruitful analytic starting point for making sense of global than domestic legal realities: in contrast to the domestic setting, where meaningful possibilities for peaceful social change could be readily identified, international law constituted a relatively static system offering few opportunities for weak states to challenge the status quo. Absent a developed system of global legislation, its static contours stymied peaceful reform (Morgenthau, 1929; Schwarzenberger, 1951). The nearest analogy to interstate conflict between "have" and "have not" powers, and thus "by far the most instructive," was found between and among representatives of labor and capital (Carr, 1964 [1939]: 212; also, Schwarzenberger, 1951: 202). That social conflict, Carr observed, was an exceptionally explosive one and thus posed major challenges even to relatively well integrated national communities. While the explosiveness of tensions between labor and capital made them something of an *exception* in domestic politics, it vividly illustrated the *normal* state of affairs in international affairs, where inequalities between "have" and "have not" states regularly threatened existing legal and moral devices.

Progressive Realists were only able to pull off this creative reworking of the old socialist critique of formal law by abandoning Marxism's economistic theory of power. Although acknowledging power's economic roots, they argued that an adequate account of international relations also needed to identify alternative sources, including relatively tangible forms of military power, but also intangibles along the lines of what Carr called "power over opinion," or even "national character" and "quality of government" as described by Morgenthau (Carr, 1964 [1939]: 102–45; Morgenthau, 1954: 93–152; Wolfers, 1962: 103–16). In striking contrast to more recent Realists who regularly envision military force as playing a predominant role in international affairs, mid-century Progressive Realists outlined a multisided analysis in which power was properly understood as deriving from a multiplicity of sources (Schmidt, 2005).

Realist Political Ethics

What then of the accusation that Realism "finds moral considerations unfit for the necessities that characterize politics, especially international politics," as well as the closely related charge that Realism endorses amoral power politics or *Realpolitik?* (Doyle, 1997: 106).

To be sure, Progressive Realists sometimes polemically and confusedly attacked "moralism," which meant a number of different things to them (Coady, 2008). And at least some of their formulations risked rendering morality's status in international affairs unnecessarily murky. Yet the religious believers and old-fashioned moralists who dominated Progressive Realism were typically not trying to cleanse international politics of moral concerns, even if they undoubtedly worried about the tendency in recent political (and especially) international thinking to overstate the transformative possibilities of moral persuasion in the face of deep political antagonisms and power inequalities. Although sometimes unfairly caricaturing the views of their opponents, they thought that too many defenders of international reform, for example, deep down believed that all that was needed to bring it about was to convince opponents of the fundamental rightness of their cause; far-reaching action would then automatically ensue. Moralism, in this view, suffered from a failure to make sense of why human beings fail to achieve that which they otherwise consider desirable and praiseworthy. Too often allied to a naive rationalism, it downplayed the existence of irrational forces at work in human beings as well as society and especially in international affairs.

Progressive Realists endorsed a robust brand of political ethics. So Herz and Wolfers, for example, turned to Max Weber's ethic of responsibility, following the German social thinker in contrasting it favorably to an "ethics of conscience." The latter demanded that political actors follow moral principles regardless of the costs or consequences, whereas the former insisted that they grapple with the great paradox of all moral and political action: moral aims can sometimes result in counterproductive and even evil results, whereas actions otherwise universally condemned (e.g. the employment of force) may sometimes prove necessary to minimize greater moral evils (Herz, 1951: 143; Wolfers, 1962: 47–65, 81–102; also, Weber, 1994 [1919]: 309–69)). Rigid fidelity to the Christian Sermon on the Mount, Wolfers followed Weber in observing, was a recipe for political disaster: the call to lay down one's arms would merely aggrandize moral evil in a world where not everyone was ready to do so. Yet Wolfers simultaneously lambasted amoral Machiavellianism, linking it directly to cynical

Nazi power politics: Machiavellian *Realpolitik* was the enemy's tool (1962: 48, 60, 82).[3] While consistently assailing *Realpolitik* and what he described as an irresponsible German intellectual tradition that minimized morality's place in international affairs, he insisted that political actors were obliged to "make the best moral choice that circumstances permit" (Wolfers, 1962: 50).[4] This nonperfectionist political ethics supposedly provided plenty of room for morally sensible political action.

Nonetheless, this version of Realist political ethics still risked leaving the status of the fundamental moral values to which political actors were expected to subscribe unclear. In his original formulation, Weber endorsed moral relativism: our ultimate moral choices cannot be grounded in a universally ascertainable manner. They represented ultimate or final values among which moral and political actors simply decided in ways that lacked the cognitive soundness of scientific verities. Like Weber, Herz and Wolfers not only sometimes seemed ambivalent about how to ground basic moral values, but their political ethics also risked opening the door to an oddly dualistic political ethics: strict morals might be appropriate outside politics, but in politics so-called nonperfectionist standards were apparently tolerable.

It fell to Morgenthau and Niebuhr to provide a more robust moral vision. They not only adamantly rejected Weber's moral relativism, but also worried deeply about the implications of a dualist political ethics.

Morgenthau relied on a theory of human nature to argue that human beings inevitably sought power over their peers. At the same time, however, he forcefully claimed that moral action requires "respect for man as an end in himself," and hence that even in the context of explosive conflicts potentially requiring some sacrifice of moral standards (e.g. the universal condemnation of killing) actors must heed the call of conscience and reduce ethical compromises to an absolute minimum (1958: 247). In this view, "the test of a morally good action is the degree to which it is capable of treating others not as means to the actor's ends but as ends in themselves" (1946: 196). The tragic contours of human existence stemmed in part from the fact that political action necessitated the instrumentalization of other human beings and thus violations of the moral imperative to treat other persons as ends in themselves. Yet because humankind was fundamentally *both* a moral *and* power-seeking creature political actors were always obliged to minimize the resulting evils.

The key attribute of admirable political leadership was the capacity to fuse a far-sighted assessment of the oftentimes deplorable realities of political struggle and power politics with a principled commitment to moral imperatives: both Hitler and Churchill were masters at the game of power politics, but only the latter deserved our praise and admiration. For

Morgenthau, as for Wolfers, it was the terrible figure of Hitler who consistently practiced amoral *Realpolitik* (1954: 206). Political life was always deeply agonistic; a perfectly harmonious political or social community could never be achieved. Yet those, like Hitler, who reduced the tension between power conflict and morality simply by abandoning the latter rebelled against the West's greatest moral and religious traditions. Instead, in the spirit of Churchill's stirring wartime leadership, we should aim for a "combination of political wisdom, moral courage, and moral judgment," and at least try to reconcile our "political nature with moral destiny" (1946: 203). Morgenthau conceded that most likely the results would be a frustrating "*modus Vivendi*," an "uneasy, precarious, and even paradoxical" state of affairs (1946: 203). Political and moral action typically left participants with a sense of unease, anxiety, and even guilt. Rather than interpret such emotions as an atavistic leftover from which modern education or advanced psychology ideally should liberate us, Morgenthau considered them a necessary and potentially fruitful force: even if we sometimes followed a nonperfectionist code, we could never rest satisfied with having done so. Our conscience would bother us; we might be encouraged to change political conditions so to minimize prospective moral trade-offs. Even if in practical terms Morgenthau's political ethics overlapped with Herz's and Wolfers' more orthodox Weberian account, the differences remained consequential. Those who compromised morality would have a hard time sleeping soundly: they might get up in the morning motivated to change those features of social life which required unpalatable ethical compromises.

Morgenthau's *Scientific Man* thus quite consistently attacked Machiavelli and Hobbes as well as the "reason of state" tradition to which they helped contribute, while also rejecting a dualist political ethics according to which "there is one ethics for the public sphere and another ethics for the private sphere" (1946: 179). Machiavelli and Hobbes were also accused of having irresponsibly abandoned Western political thought's praiseworthy aspiration to tame the exercise of power by moral means (1946: 33, 169, 174, 174–6; 1945a: 145–7). Even if the ugly realities of politics prevented perfect fidelity to the far-reaching demand to treat others as ends in themselves, a non-instrumentalist moral vision remained binding: setting up a separate (and less demanding) moral code for political action potentially meant caving into its ugliest features.

As Morgenthau periodically admitted, his political ethics had been directly inspired by Niebuhr's. The key difference was that Niebuhr built overtly on Christian foundations, while Morgenthau appealed more ecumenically to what he dubbed "Judeo-Christian morality," and even Kant and Marx, whom he read as having "decried the use of man by man as a means to an end" (1946: 184).[5] Both thinkers also sought to ground basic moral values in what they considered universally valid ways. Like both Wolfers and Morgenthau, Niebuhr doubted that a rigorous ethical stance could always be consistently realized in the political realm, accusing Christian pacifists who believed in the self-sufficiency of an ethic of love of succumbing to a well-meaning but ultimately counterproductive political naivety (1940, 1–33; 1935: 153–80). Politics might involve getting our hands dirty, for example, by employing force when necessary to avoid even greater evils. So in Niebuhr's eyes 1930s pacifists disastrously ignored the need to counter fascism by violent means, and they ignored legitimate reasons why oppressed social groups sometimes chose to take up arms. Gandhi's enthusiasts, for example, conveniently downplayed the ways in which his actions were at least indirectly destructive of human life: economic boycotts endangered working class British children (1932: 169–230, 241–56).

In sync with Morgenthau, Niebuhr built on philosophical anthropology, but of an unabashedly Christian variety. Given the foibles of human nature, and especially our congenital vanity, selfishness, and pride, Saint Augustine had been right to argue that human affairs necessarily required power, force, and coercion to secure basic order and justice. Acknowledging the accuracy of this Augustinian insight, Niebuhr claimed, hardly required buying into the political pessimism and passivity that had long plagued mainstream Christianity (1934; 1941; 1943; 1953a: 119–46). To be sure, a demanding ideal of selfless Christian love, the centerpiece of Niebuhr's moral philosophy, could never be completely realized. The best mortals could hope for was a measure of "equal justice," which Niebuhr interpreted broadly as entailing political and social as well as legal-formal justice.

At least initially, Niebuhr thus seemed to endorse a nonperfectionist political ethics. This position was also the basis, in good reformist fashion, for his critique of communist utopianism: any dream of a perfectly harmonious social order where human nature had been altogether cleansed of its familiar foibles remained unrealistic. Yet in tension to both Weber and Wolfers, he simultaneously asserted that political actors ultimately "stand under judgment from a higher ethic (for which [Christian] love is the norm)" (McKeogh, 1997: 137). As in Morgenthau's parallel political ethics, a demanding moral vision remained the *ultimate* standard for all political action. The eminently earthly ideal of equal justice remained parasitical on Christian love: though less demanding, it called for the realization of moral reciprocity and mutual respect in social relations. It therefore could not

be relegated simply to the world of transcendence. It offers immediate possibilities of a higher good in every given situation. We may never realize
[perfect] equality, but we cannot accept the inequalities of capitalism or any
other unjust social system completely. (1935: 135)

Fidelity to Christian love would spur us to eliminate avoidable forms of
legal, political, and social injustice. Even though the hubristic dream of
a perfect society resting directly on Christian love remained unrealizable,
those who followed its dictates might work to reduce unnecessarily compromised forms of equal justice. Progress was by no means assured. Yet
sound reasons remained for believing that Christian morality might effectively motor political and social change. While Herz and Wolfers
seemed to rest more or less satisfied with a nonperfectionist political
morality, Niebuhr interpreted the gap between the (oftentimes unavoidable) moral compromises of political life and the (transcendent) ideal of
Christian love as a fertile field in which movements for reform might
flourish. Guilt and unease in the face of moral compromise provided, as
in Morgenthau's parallel formulations, the requisite motivational basis
for action.

The tensions between politics and morality were most apparent in international politics since it was especially difficult there to pursue power in
morally acceptable ways. Yet such tensions merely constituted one mani-
festation of deeper enigmas deriving from the contradictory imperatives
of human existence. Humans are vain, excessively proud, and power-
hungry. Yet we are always simultaneously obliged to tame our less noble
attributes by moral means. In Morgenthau's characteristically blunt formulation of the same idea, "[m]an is a political animal by nature" but *also* "a
moralist because he is a man": the struggle for power is built into human
nature, yet the quest for principled moral action constitutes an equally
pivotal facet of the human condition (1946: 168). A sound Christian view
of human nature recognized our uglier side, but also – on a more optimistic
note – paid homage to humanity as a creature made in the image of God,
and thus fundamentally a free being possessing what Niebuhr sometimes
described as a capacity for "self-transcendence" (1941: 12–18; Lovin,
1995).

A pivotal category, self-transcendence referred in part to human creativity and the capacity to reshape our relationship to nature as well as other
human beings in ways better corresponding to a stringent ideal of Christian
love. Self-transcendence meant that we might "envision ways in which our
world and ourselves could be better than they are," including new forms
of social cooperation and the possibility of profound alterations to the

status quo (Lovin, 1995: 17). The term also captured the special human capacity to stand beyond the concrete realities of human existence and survey them from the outside, a process by which "the subject makes itself its own object" and gains some sense of its finitude. Self-transcendence pointed to humankind's "essential homelessness," which Niebuhr considered a wellspring of humanity's religious sensibility. Throughout history, self-transcendence had fruitfully prompted great cultures and philosophies to grapple with their mortality and necessary limits and "seek for the meaning of life in an unconditioned ground of existence" whose roots transcended humankind (1941: 14).

Not surprisingly, Niebuhr followed Morgenthau in regularly criticizing the political legacies of Machiavelli and Hobbes, whom he similarly accused of offering one-sided and even cynical interpretations of the human condition blind to the ways in which human beings regularly transcend harsh power and social realities.[6] Theirs was a one-sided or too consistent Realism that captured only the ugliest facets of the human condition (1932: 232). For neither Niebuhr nor his secular-minded ally Morgenthau, did recourse to a foundational theory of human nature entail a pessimistic ideal militating against potentially ambitious struggles for social and political reform. If they occasionally appeared to dwell on its pessimism, they justified doing so by pointing to certain tendencies in contemporary thought to mask unpleasant verities about human nature. With some justification, both emphasized the ways in which theirs was a balanced and multi-sided account of human nature that aptly captured its contradictory imperatives and by no means rigidly predetermined political and social conditions. Niebuhr associated self-transcendence with the quest for ever more inclusive and just forms of social organization, while Morgenthau similarly noted how the existing international system undermined the West's highest moral ideals: since humanity was a moral as well as political creature, we justifiably aspired for reforms that potentially reduced ethical compromises. *Pace* the fantasies of many utopians, political and social conflict remained permanent features of the human condition. Yet even humankind's least attractive traits might better be tamed by changes to the social climate

> which is [potentially] capable of containing the evil tendencies of human nature within socially tolerable bounds; conditions of life, manifesting themselves in a social equilibrium which tends to minimize the psychological causes of social conflict, such as insecurity, fear and aggression, and finally, the moral climate which allows man to expect at least an approximation to justice here and now, and thus eliminates the incentive to seek justice through strife. (Morgenthau, 1945b: 437)

Because man was a moralist as well as a power-seeking political creature, he – and she – would, when at all possible, have to endeavor to alter existing conditions to provide greater room for the full realization of moral impulses. The difficulty at hand was to make sure that reform could mitigate the unnecessary brutality and violence of political and social affairs rather than simply aggrandize them, as so often had happened in history.

So much for the amorality of Realist politics ethics and for heavy-handed attempts to link Realism to Machiavelli, Hobbes, or a one-sidedly bleak philosophical anthropology. As we will see, other commonplace attacks on Progressive Realism are similarly off base.

Machiavellianism Without *Virtu*?

Before we respond to them, however, we need to address the complicated position of E. H. Carr, whose support for Chamberlain's appeasement policies and apparent enthusiasm for key elements of the Soviet experiment left a bad aftertaste with even his Progressive Realist allies. In a justly famous 1948 *World Politics* critique, Morgenthau described Carr as a "lucid and brilliant" thinker, grouping him just behind Niebuhr among contemporary intellectuals for recognizing "the essential defects of Western political thought" (1948a). Yet he also promptly accused Carr of succumbing to "a relativistic, instrumentalist conception of morality." Carr lacked a "transcendent point of view from which to survey the political scene," and this led him to conflate *is* and *ought* and "worship at the altar of power." It was this moral relativism, Morgenthau angrily declared, that unwittingly transformed Carr into a tragic "utopian of power" who had offered a terrible apology for Chamberlain's appeasement policies, condoned the swallowing up of Europe's small states by their big neighbors, and now exhibited excessive admiration for Soviet collectivism. For Morgenthau, Carr was a "Machiavelli without *virtu*" (1948a:128, 133–4; also, Dunne, 2000).

Indeed, Carr was relatively uninterested in matters of political ethics, he lacked Niebuhr's religious sensibilities, and his enthusiasm for Karl Mannheim's sociology of knowledge (which led him to highlight the dependence of moral ideas on social conditions) made him vulnerable to critics who worried about his moral credentials.[7] Revealingly perhaps, Mannheim was also widely censured for moral relativism; key parts of *Ideology and Utopia* represented an attempt to ward off the accusation (1936; also, Jones, 1998). Unfortunately, Carr too often failed to pose tough moral questions about the avowedly instrumentalist – and arguably disastrous – political morality of interwar appeasement or, for that matter, some of the Soviet leadership's truly terrible actions.[8]

Yet Carr's views still remained indebted to Niebuhr. He similarly rejected any "divorce between the spheres of politics and morality," and at one juncture endorsed Niebuhr's view that uneasy compromises resulted when political actors tackled power realities while heeding the call of conscience (Carr, 1964 [1939]: 100). Even though Carr described Machiavelli as a forerunner to Realism, Marx and Mannheim always remained for him its paradigmatic representatives.[9] He credited them with doing proper justice to utopianism, in Carr's view an indispensable component of political science and necessary complement to Realism: "Sound political thought and sound political life will be found only where both have their place" (1964 [1939]: 10). Without the utopian's dream of a better world, Realism became a conservative and cynical theory overstating the staying power of existing social and political realities. Utopianism, by the same token, required a Realist antidote: without the Realist's grasp of power realities and tragic sense of the ways in which politics sometimes required ethical compromises, political or social reformers were destined to become reckless and irresponsible. Utopianism was to be condemned only when it failed to take basic Realist insights into consideration. Despite his warm words for Machiavelli, Carr was offering no easy endorsement of amoral power politics.

Yet Carr (and probably Schuman as well)[10] remained significantly more hesitant than either Morgenthau or Niebuhr to endorse a "transcendent point of view" or a timeless system of morality as an anchor for political ethics. In a 1950 essay penned perhaps partly in response to Morgenthau's jeremiad, Carr announced his fidelity to a rigorous interpretation of ultimate moral values, openly declaring his belief in the existence of "an absolute good that is independent of power." However, he quickly added, "the individual man's conception of the good is highly relative and therefore always apt to be fluctuating, uncertain, and tainted" (1949: 66–7; also, 1962: 97–109). More indebted to Mannheim than (Niebuhr's) old-fashioned Christian ethics or (Morgenthau's) appeals to the moral fundaments of the West, Carr again reverted to the sociology of ideas: because of the manifold ways in which political and social conditions inexorably determined consciousness, none of us could ever be perfectly sure that our views overlap sufficiently with the "absolute good."

All Progressive Realists worried about the perils of moral hubris. Yet Carr went a step further: he sometimes suggested that the sociology of knowledge precluded a strict ethical standpoint. Not surprisingly, his political ethics looked relativistic to some critics.

In fairness, one might worry that Niebuhr's Christianity, and even Morgenthau's occasional appeals to the leading lights of Western moral thinking, always raised difficult questions for any attempt to ground moral and political action in our pluralistic and morally disenchanted world, whereas Carr's emphasis on the social determination of morality tried to do justice to the complexities of the modern ethical condition. Yet the fact remains that the traditionalistic political ethics sketched out by Morgenthau and Niebuhr, whatever its philosophical demerits, helped immunize them against some of the most disturbing political illusions of the last century. Even if Morgenthau's critique of Carr was overheated, it successfully identified his Realist ally's conceptual Achilles' heel.

National Interest

The idea of the "national interest" is now widely associated with Realism. A major US-based Realist journal calls itself *The National Interest*, countless political organizations devoted to various foreign policy causes integrate the term into their names, and politicians, pundits, and scholars employ it to emphasize the sober content of their policy preferences, in contrast to so-called idealistic foreign policy positions (for example, attempts to give priority to human rights or disarmament) allegedly inconsonant with the demands of power politics. The term serves as a handy battering ram against so-called legalists (who seek to strengthen international law) and utopians (who desire a new and more just global order). To be sure, some of the intellectual sources of this usage can be found in the writings of mid-century Realists like Kennan (1951) and Morgenthau (1951).

Nonetheless, Progressive Realist political ethics places the idea of the national interest in a different light. Some Progressive Realists – most notably, Morgenthau – did declare periodically that the chief aim of responsible political leaders could only be the pursuit of vital or national interests, aptly defined by one of his most prominent students, Kenneth Thompson, as the view

> that every nation by virtue of its geographic position, historic objectives, and relationship to other power centers possesses a clustering of strategic interests each more or less vital to its security. At any point in time, a rational foreign policy must attend to the safeguarding of these claims. The national interest stands above and absorbs the limited and parochial claims of subnational groups, even though such groups seek to interpret the national interest in their own terms ... It so happens that the present era in international relations compels statesmen to put first the interests of the territorial nation state. (1960: 36)

In a state system characterized by power rivalry, the primary task of responsible statesmen (and women) was the protection of the wellbeing of their country and its members. It might be morally appealing, for example, if political leaders sacrificed national power and privilege for altruistic reasons. In a divided international system with competing and oftentimes antagonistic political units, however, could one plausibly require them to do so if their own peoples suffered? A principled commitment to global social justice demanded massive economic redistribution between and among nation states. Yet any political leader in a rich country who undertook to do so immediately would get driven from office. The pursuit of the national interest constituted a *moral* imperative to the extent that if statesmen failed to abide by its dictates even greater evils might result: morally appealing unilateral disarmament, for example, might counterproductively ignite a horrific war. The category also served as an *empirically* useful device for those struggling to make sense of the history of international politics: because successful political leaders presumably had relied on it to secure the wellbeing of their political compatriots, the national interest proffered a conceptual yardstick by means of which one could understand and help explain their actions (Morgenthau, 1951).

Yet even Morgenthau ultimately conceded that the purported primacy of the national interest was historically transitory. He and other Progressive Realists anticipated key elements of what more recent analysts of "globalization" have placed under its rubric.[11] Consistently skeptical of harmonistic accounts that downplay the ways in which rapidly increasing cultural, economic, and technological interdependence potentially generates new sources of conflict, they noted that in an ever more interconnected globe, the clear division between national and global interests becomes porous, and hence that "nations now have new and expanded moral responsibilities to each other" (McKeogh, 1997: 137). Writing in *The New Republic* in 1975, Morgenthau asserted that a sensible interpretation of the US national interest entailed "support of supranational institutions and procedures capable of performing the functions that in view of modern technological developments the individual nation states are no longer able to perform" (1975: 21). This included working towards constructing an international agency outfitted with far-reaching authority to regulate nuclear energy and the production of nuclear weapons, an idea which he had enthusiastically endorsed as early as 1960 and considered indispensable to human survival (1960: 169–73, 308–9). Niebuhr similarly observed that the national interest was ever more inextricably related to "a web of mutual and universal or general interests" (1965: 79). In an interdependent world, national and universal interests increasingly overlapped; the pursuit of a narrow national interest might prove as politically counterproductive as policies which ignored it.

Just as significantly, Morgenthau's huge – albeit rather selective – impact on postwar political science has helped veil the fact that other

Realists were exceedingly skeptical about drawing *any* clear implications from appeals to the national interest. In mid-century Realism's *Ur*-textbook, Schuman's *International Politics*, its left-wing author bluntly posited that "the specific purposes in terms of which the national interests of the State are expressed" were typically shaped by the economically dominant classes (1941b: 264; also, 1952b, 27–9). It was not only privileged social interests which imposed their view of the national interest upon society, but any notion of an objective interpretation of it able to serve as a lodestar for policy making was fantastic as well. Also in a critical vein, Wolfers argued that the empirical utility of the concept of the national interest was narrowly circumscribed since a vast range of competing foreign policy options could be plausibly described as corresponding to it. Even seemingly "idealistic" policies sometimes advanced it: the Marshall Plan, for example, succeeded precisely because it served the security and economic needs of a broad range of countries (1962: 77). As a normative admonition the idea of the national interest was inadequate since it mistakenly obscured the tough moral and political choices always facing policy makers. Even if national security was a legitimate policy goal, its pursuit left many unanswered questions: what degree of security could be realistically gained, and at what cost? When frugally interpreted as mandating that politicians should make the preservation of national independence their main goal, historical situations could be identified under which they might sensibly act otherwise: "There are circumstances when such sacrifice of independence has justified itself in the eyes of almost everybody, as when the thirteen American states federated successfully" (1962: 64–5).

Niebuhr also worried that Morgenthau's views served as an inappropriate normative justification for a cramped national egoism. Although the concept of the national interest potentially offered a useful analytic device for cutting through the moral hypocrisies of foreign policy, it obscured "the residual capacity for justice and devotion to the larger good," which any morally sensible political actor should try to abide (1965: 71).[12] A rigid endorsement of the national interest potentially betrayed the deep moral ideals of love and equal justice against which it would have to be judged. Those ideals often spoke powerfully against national parochialism. The idea of the primacy of the national interest pointed the way to precisely that problematic dualistic political ethics Morgenthau himself had so effectively criticized: Morgenthau had forgotten that any attempt to outfit the national interest with moral credentials downplayed its character as a tentative and uneasy compromise occasioned by ambiguous political and social realities which might need to be changed.

By the end of the day, relatively little remained of Morgenthau's original high expectations for the national interest. As Progressive Realists grasped, the apparent homily that most national leaders would and typically should hesitate before sacrificing national interests engendered difficult political and moral questions. Even uncontroversial appeals to the priority of national survival opened up a normative Pandora's box (Wolfers, 1962: 73).

Balance of Power

Few facets of Realist theory have garnered as much attention as its embrace of the idea of the "balance of power" (Claude, 1962). For Realists, the balance of power has served a number of analytic functions. Most immediately, it helps explain how international politics tends to operate. As Realists never tire of explaining, whenever an existing equilibrium of power is disturbed there will appear a countertendency to recreate the original or at least achieve a new equilibrium. When a prospective Great Power suddenly appears on the scene, for example, competing states typically join arms and cooperate in countering its rise. Alongside this idea of the balance of power as an *empirical* or sociological regularity, it has also been widely interpreted as providing useful *normative* or policy advice. Anyone hoping to survive in a potentially violent universe in which rival political units face off against each other ignores the balance of power at her own risk. Those confronting the ascent of a destabilizing revolutionary power – for example, the nineteenth-century British statesman Castlereagh, who cooperated with Austro-Hungary and Russia to counter Napoleon – should join forces with others to prevent it from gaining hegemonic status (Kissinger, 1957). In this sprit, just as the Second World War was breaking out Wolfers announced that the "one and only way" to limit the growth of German power, despite the fact that many people might be sorely "disappointed to think that Europe may have to go on with the dangerous game," remained the balance of power. "As long as there are many great sovereign powers in Europe, a balance of power is the only available alternative to the domination of one nation or group of nations over the others" (Wolfers, 1964 [1940]: 389–90).

As Wolfers and other Realists noted, policy makers sometimes opt to ignore the exigencies of the balance of power. Yet to an even greater degree than business people violating basic economic laws, they do so at an exceedingly high cost: lives may be lost. In sharp contradistinction to global reformers who posit that recent legal and institutional innovations (e.g. the League of Nations or United Nations) render the balance of power fundamentally obsolescent, Realists have regularly underscored its continuing relevance, mocking comments like President Wilson's "that the balance of power itself can be abolished together with its instruments, such as alliances" (cited in Claude, 1962: 32). Even if the UN, for example, has altered global political life, balance of power-style politics still shapes it when, for example, the US employs its Security Council veto to oppose measures directed against close allies like Israel. The international system operates in ways that would have been recognizable to classical practitioners of balance of power politics.

Of course, Realist ideas about the balance of power are vastly more complex than this simple summary suggests; some of the best work in recent international theory has tried to unpack its nuances (Little, 2007). For our purposes here, two neglected features of the story are crucial. Even if many Realists made the concept of the balance of power serve backwards-looking and institutionally anti-reformist purposes, *Progressive Realists* sometimes employed it in a significantly more creative – and unabashedly reformist – manner. Their rendition of the balance of power did not consistently entail historical nostalgia or a fundamental commitment to the international status quo.[13]

First, when the term initially appeared in Progressive Realist writings at mid century, it served primarily as a conceptual accessory to radical social reform. In the mid 1930s Niebuhr initially employed it in order to defend the need to

> destroy the [existing] accumulation of social power and to bring the irreducible minimum under the strongest possible social check. In modern society this means that economic power must be dealt with rigorously because it is the most significant power. (1934: 235)

Economic power rested disproportionately in the hands of the owners of the means of production; reform required checking their power by bringing about a more equitable distribution of material resources. In an illuminating chapter of *Reflections on the End of an Era* (1934) devoted exclusively to "The Balance of Power in Politics," Niebuhr dealt primarily with the task of realizing a rough equilibrium of social forces at the domestic level, which first and foremost meant determining how to mobilize state power to counterbalance capitalists. The balance of power required dispersing power resources – most importantly, those based on control over property – in order to ensure the possibility of some acceptable minimum of equal justice at the domestic level. In this view, socialism might successfully bring about the requisite equilibrium if it could circumvent dangers apparent in the Soviet Union: there a new (state-based) ruling group had monopolized political and social power in disastrous ways (1934: 245–6).[14]

Niebuhr's analysis quickly glided from a discussion of the domestic to the international features of the balance of power: just as a rough balance of social forces buttressed the drive for greater justice *within* the nation state, so too was a balance *between* and *among* nation states essential to peace and international justice. While "the peace of Europe before the [First] World War rested upon a balance of power," in the interwar years no effective balance had been established, and thus the interwar peace, Niebuhr presciently predicted in the early 1930s, was destined to prove unstable (1934: 246).

Regularly moving back and forth between a discussion of its domestic and its international attributes, Niebuhr generally referred to the balance of power in this admittedly loose manner. Throughout his career, he seems to have thought that it best expressed the straightforward but fundamental intuition that greater equal justice was only possible if power resources were in fact relatively equalized, or – stated somewhat differently – competing social and political interests each possessed enough power so as to be able to prevent rivals from disproportionately shaping the course of political and social life. As with other Progressive Realists, his theory of power was in fact relatively open-ended: the ability to influence and potentially coerce others rested on a rich variety of social, political, and economic sources. Not surprisingly perhaps, Niebuhr shifted abruptly from discussing the balance of power in the context of domestic class conflict to international affairs: the fact that the sources of power differed somewhat on the international from those operating on the national scene mattered less than the imperative of achieving a balance or equilibrium as a basis for stability and justice. Even though perfect social and political harmony remained an impossible and indeed unacceptably hubristic utopia, human beings could always achieve ever more satisfactory balances of power both at the domestic and international levels, each of which might come closer towards living up to Christianity's rigorous ideal of universal love. Even after the Second World War, when Niebuhr jettisoned traditional socialist views in part because he thought that the welfare state might be capable of instantiating a satisfactory balance of domestic social forces, he interpreted the notion of an equilibrium or balance of social power as integrally related to the quest for justice (Niebuhr, 1952: 101; 1953b).

Whatever the demerits of Niebuhr's sometimes imprecise reflections, for him the idea of a balance of power chiefly provided guidance as to how we might advance reform: by no means was it institutionally conservative or historically nostalgic. Nor was its primary addressee diplomats or elite-level political actors, as later became the case among more conservative Realists, but instead social reformers and ordinary people trying to figure out how to achieve greater justice. By implication, the balance of power was congruent with a broad range of institutional variations at both the national and global levels. Linked at the hip to the struggle for equal justice, it strongly suggested that we experiment with ever more egalitarian distributions of social and political power both nationally and internationally.

Second, Niebuhr's illuminating early discussion emphasized that every balance or equilibrium of power could easily become imbalanced not only "by the fortuitous or necessary creation of new disproportions of power" but also by "the underlying conflict of interest which is basic to it." Balances of power always rested on a tentative constellation of social forces, roughly "coaxed into a momentary chaos," and destined to be undermined by new political and social forces spawned by it (1934: 245). Even the most attractive attempts to equalize power resources and bring about superior ideals of justice would someday prove fragile: new forms of injustice and inequality would typically rear their heads, and fresh generations of social critics and political activists would understandably seek redress.

The simple idea that the balance of power typically provided at best a relatively *temporary* stabilization of social and political conflict soon became a Progressive Realist mainstay. Even Morgenthau's sometimes unduly nostalgic gloss on the role of the balance of power in international politics ultimately focused on its limitations as a method for preserving peace. Under normal conditions, it was difficult for competing nations to calculate effectively their power resources compared to those of antagonists. The resulting "uncertainty of all power calculations" made "the balance of power incapable of practical application" (1954: 189). Because no country could rest secure in the view that it possessed enough power in relation to its rivals, each would inevitably seek to maximize power: the dream of a perfect equalization or balance of power inevitably proved chimerical. Despite its achievements, Morgenthau questioned whether in the final analysis the balance of power could sufficiently counter the specter of war. The balance of power remained an empirical regularity as well as a normative guidepost. Yet those who sought lasting peace would have to do better (1954: 184–201).

As in Niebuhr's 1930s reflections, Morgenthau never envisioned the balance of power as a political cure-all. This is partly why he joined other Progressive Realists in considering the possibility of deep institutional changes able to compensate for its intrinsic limitations. Such changes might prove desirable as long as they paid heed to the core intuition underlying the balance of power: stability and a measure of justice could be achieved when power was made to check power and was properly (and hence relatively widely) dispersed: "nothing in the Realist position militates against the assumption that the present division of the political world ... will be replaced by larger units of a quite different character" (1954: 9). In principle, as long as it rested on a sufficient sharing of power resources and an institutionalized system of checks and balances, even a world state might prove congruent with the basic idea of the balance of power (Morgenthau, 1954: 156–60; Scheuerman, 2009: 111–14). As Richard Little has noted in a parallel vein, nothing in Morgenthau's view of the balance of power rendered his account of global politics fundamentally "fixed and unchanging" (2007: 124).

Security Dilemma

Herz's landmark *Political Realism and Political Idealism* (1951) introduced the pivotal concept of the "security dilemma" into mainstream Realist discourse. Unfortunately, here as well a certain tendency to overstate its institutional conservatism can be detected. When properly interpreted, however, the idea of the security dilemma is consistent with global reform.

In one of the most widely cited passages from mid-century Realism, Herz argued that

> [p]olitically active groups and individuals are concerned about their security from being attacked, subjected, dominated, or annihilated by other groups and individuals. Because they strive to attain security from such attack, and yet can never feel entirely secure in a world of competing units, they are driven toward acquiring more and more power for themselves, in order to escape the impact of the superior power of others. It is important to realize that such competition for security, and hence for power, is a basic situation which is unique with men and their social groups. (1951: 14)

Supposedly, the resulting security dilemma mandated recourse neither to philosophical anthropology nor a belief in a congenital lust for power, though Herz's allusions to fundamental psychological propensities occasionally blurred the divide between his views and those of Morgenthau and Niebuhr.[15] Faced with the imperative of survival, and burdened with the knowledge that others easily posed threats while never being able to know for sure what potential rivals might intend, individuals and social groups were likely to be suspicious of others. Consequently, they possessed strong incentives to accumulate power resources in order to guarantee security. Since prospective foes inevitably did the same, and since no one could ever be certain that others' intentions were pacific, individuals and social groups were always "driven toward acquiring more and more power."

Herz's formulation indeed initially recalled Hobbes' bleak description of the state of nature. Not surprisingly, institutionally complacent varieties of Realism have relied on it for support. John Mearsheimer, for example, uses the idea of the security dilemma as a building block for his brand of self-described "offensive" Realism, which posits that "the best way for a state to survive in anarchy is to take advantage of other states and gain power at their expense. The best defense is a good offense" (2001: 36). Security competition calls for states to maximize their power in relation to others. Interstate affairs are subject to never-ending power and especially military competition. Faced with uncertainty, states need to assume the worst about their rivals, and even those states not wanting to compete for security will be forced to do so.

Mearsheimer's employment of Herz has already spawned some impressive retorts (Booth and Wheeler, 2008; Glaser, 1994–5; Snyder, 2002; Stirk, 2005: 299). Rather than repeat them, let me suggest ways in which Herz's ideas were always more institutionally open-ended than first seems evident.

Revealingly, Herz's famous opening analysis of it refers to social (and "politically active") groups and individuals, but *not* to states or nation states. His examples are in fact of social conflicts occurring at the subnational level between and among individuals, social classes, and other groups over myriad power sources, including economic goods and prestige. The security dilemma can concern rivalry for "food, clothing, or other goods necessary for safeguarding life" just as much as strictly security-related objects (1951: 3–4). The rubric of politically active individuals and groups turns out to be astonishingly broad, potentially including nation states, but also many other social entities fighting over an equally diverse range of objects.

Why does it matter? Herz's own formulations suggest that we should avoid prematurely marrying the concept of the security dilemma to the existing state system. Even if it offers a useful analytic starting point for understanding why existing states engage in ruthless military competition, the particular ways in which the security dilemma becomes socially and historically instantiated seem subject to wide variations. In short, the concept remains normatively and institutionally more indeterminate than Mearsheimer and others acknowledge. One might quite logically accept its central status without being forced to conclude that it requires a state system along present-day lines. Keep in mind that for Herz the security dilemma represented an attempt to work out the implications of a deep paradox at the core of the human condition: we depend on others for survival, yet necessarily remain uncertain about their intentions in relation to us. Human beings seek self-preservation; simultaneously, we are creatures with a sense of pity and even compassion for those who suffer (1951: 6–7). Yet this view of human beings – reminiscent, by the way, of the cosmopolitan-minded reformer Kant's claim that "social unsociability" was central to human existence (1970) – assuredly leaves open the door to multiple institutional possibilities.

Even Mearsheimer admits that the security dilemma only obtains "as long as states operate in anarchy" (2001: 36). Although doubtful that a world state will ever be built, he concedes that the security dilemma could in principle be mitigated by an alternative to the international status quo. In *International Politics in the Atomic Age* (1959), Herz argued that the invention of nuclear weaponry raised difficult questions for any institutionally quiescent defense of the existing state system: nuclear weaponry suggested the necessity of humanity gradually moving towards a universal political order. The territorial state could no longer secure its citizens against the awesome destructive power of atomic weapons. The normal game of power and security competition between and among existing nation states increasingly threatened humanity with self-destruction; a new protective unit beyond the existing nation state would have to be constructed. Herz observed that political leaders who grasped the dynamics of the security dilemma might in fact be able to circumvent some of its more disturbing initial implications: "Both sides might even profit from the security dilemma itself, or, rather, from facing and understanding it," since awareness of it could productively counter "that inability to put oneself into the other fellow's place and to realize his fears and distrust" which has always constituted a main source of fear and security competition (1959: 249). Potentially dangerous psychological uncertainty about a rival's intentions could be mitigated. Policy makers might prove able to identify a shared basis for cooperation, and perhaps even pursue reform.

Kenneth Booth and Nicholas Wheeler have relied on this suggestive facet of Herz's argument to explain how political leaders have sometimes avoided the security dilemma's seemingly fatalistic implications. What they aptly dub "security dilemma sensibility" proved crucial, for example, in Gorbachev's winding down of the Cold War: the Soviet leader's astute sense of the pressures faced by his rivals led him "to reassure others by successful signaling," and ultimately by "encouraging reciprocal actions" (2008: 168). They rightly interpret the idea of the security dilemma as by no means congenitally opposed to efforts to mitigate its dangers or even the possibility of significant global change. Even if uncertainty about the goals of potential power rivals remains unavoidable, "in the house of uncertainty there are many rooms" (2008: 295). Uncertainty remains ubiquitous in political life, yet it can be managed – in part by institutional means – more or less effectively. Like many constant features of political life, it remains subject to a measure of human control and therefore hardly necessitates fundamental mistrust or potentially self-destructive fear. In postwar Europe, for example, institutional reforms gradually embedded trust in normative practices as well as institutional mechanisms that broke with "the vicious circle of security and power competition predicted by fatalist thinking" (2008: 297; also, 190–200). Although the history of postwar Western European security cooperation remains extraordinarily complex, an institutionally conservative reading of the security dilemma, according to which independent states can never free themselves from unceasing military and security competition, hardly does justice to the dramatic changes that have occurred.

The security dilemma provides no easy empirical or normative defense of the international status quo, even if it helps explain some of the huge hurdles faced by would-be reformers. Herz's *Political Realism and Political Idealism* indeed rejected the view that the security dilemma demanded sacrifice of the "idealistic" quest for reform. However misguided and politically naive, political idealists remained "the salt of the earth. Much of what has been achieved, in various stages of history, at various times in various civilizations, has been due to their thinking and to the use, in actual political history, of the concepts and ideals developed by them" (1951: 39). Reformers had repeatedly struggled to improve social and political life both at the domestic and international levels. Like other Progressive Realists, Herz not only manifestly sympathized with their efforts, but he interpreted them as no less basic to the human condition than respect for the imperatives of security competition. Even if the security dilemma sometimes confined the scope of our activities, at times preventing us from immediately achieving humanitarian political goals, it remained humankind's unfulfilled task to mitigate and civilize power and security competition.

Echoing Carr's call for a fusion of utopianism and Realism, Herz believed that the guiding star of political action should be a quest "that moves man to try to push developments in a different direction" than the status quo. However, such efforts "should be built, not on the sands of wishful thinking, but on the rock of reality. On the other hand, they should not be left where the inertia of things would carry them. Within the limits of the attainable, a combination of Political Realism and Political Idealism thus seems to be the political ideal" (1951: 131–2). As reformers fought to alter political and social conditions to advance humankind's struggle for lasting security and freedom, they needed to remain aware of the ways in which power competition circumvented their efforts. By no means did proper attention to the laws of security competition, however, necessitate "the ultimate ethical victory of the 'Machiavellian,' power-political, fascist, and related values over those of liberalism, humanitarianism, pacifism, etc." (1951: 131). Herz similarly assailed the so-called Hobbesian view of international affairs as subject to unchanging power politics, and thus "not amenable to any change in the sense of reform or basic alteration of structure" (1951: 203). His own self-described brand of Realist Liberalism rested on a normatively and institutionally flexible interpretation of the security dilemma. Herz wanted to strengthen the hand of reformist movements by helping them overcome the political naivety which had previously undermined their endeavors. They needed to be reminded of the tough realities and paradoxes of political life, not because their dreams should be jettisoned for conservative *Realpolitik*, but instead because it was due time for politically mature reformers to master the rules of power competition. Otherwise they would once again face defeat at the hands of opponents who not only better understood the dictates of the security dilemma, but who employed their wisdom at the behest of morally and politically quiescent goals.

This chapter has tried to paint a suitably multifaceted as well as sympathetic portrayal of some of the main tenets of mid-century Realism as interpreted by its main left-leaning theoretical figures. *Progressive* Realists provided a relatively balanced view of the place of both law and morality in the existing international order, endorsed a demanding political ethics while rejecting amoral *Realpolitik*, and when sometimes building on assumptions about human nature, aspired to do so in a way that paid heed both to humankind's appealing and somewhat less appealing traits. They generally rejected narrow ideas of the national interest as a proper guide for policy and envisioned the balance of power and the security dilemma as consistent with sensible efforts to bring about global change.

Even if I have perhaps partly succeeded in convincing you of the virtues of a different gloss on Realism than what Ernie learned from his teachers, some pressing questions still face us. First, why did Progressive Realists think global reform was necessary? In what ways was the existing international system obsolescent? Second, how did they hope to bring about global reform, and in which respects did their model differ from that of the purportedly naive Idealists and Utopians whom they criticized?

2 REALISTS AGAINST THE NATION STATE

The political theorist David Held has recently restated the claim that for Realists "the modern system of nation states is a 'limiting factor' which will always thwart any attempt to conduct international relations in a manner which transcends the politics of the sovereign state" (1995: 74–5; also Deudney, 2007: 70–7). When Ernie emphasized Realism's sympathies for the nation state, he was drawing on views of this type. According to the dominant interpretation, Realists stubbornly refuse to acknowledge the nation state's increasingly obsolescent character. Their dogmatic fidelity to an anarchical international system in which it remains the dominant political organization makes them congenitally hostile to global reform. Rather than treating nation states as limiting factors preventing reform, the cosmopolitan-minded Held (alongside countless others, including Ernie and his teacher Connie) asserts, we must see the nation state for what it is: a contingent product of historical circumstances and thus subject to far-reaching changes. Like the city-states of classical antiquity and Renaissance Europe, the nation state is increasingly ill adapted to the tasks of governance in the context of intense globalization.

This criticism ignores how Progressive Realists similarly deemed the decay of the nation state among the most significant institutional trends – and political challenges – of the contemporary era. As Morgenthau put it with his usual bluntness, "[t]hat the traditional nation state is obsolescent in view of the technological and military conditions of the contemporary world is obvious" (1954: 313). Their perspicacious analyses zeroed in on the ways in which social and technological factors rendered the nation state ever less effective at governing. They not only anticipated present-day theses about the decay of the nation state, but in some respects arguably surpassed recent accounts. Progressive Realists, for example, focused not only on the growing difficulties faced by nation states in guaranteeing economic wellbeing and physical security, but also on the onerous ways in which they undermined noble moral aspirations. The Westphalian system constituted an ever-present source of hostility to the West's more valuable normative accomplishments: anyone who took them seriously was obliged to seek global change.

Successful reforms would have to acknowledge the existence of key political and social functions performed by the nation state, however. Despite the fact that major developmental tendencies pointed to both the desirability of "larger units of a quite different character [than the nation state], more in keeping with the technical circumstances and the moral requirements of the contemporary world," the viability of any alternative would depend on its still unproven capacity to fulfill some of the existing nation state's tasks (Morgenthau, 1954: 9). Albeit ever more out-of-date, the nation state could only be successfully jettisoned for postnational alternatives that successfully provided a functional replacement. Before turning to recall the ways in which Progressive Realists considered the nation state anachronistic, we first address those political and social changes the nation state has more or less competently met.

What is the Nation State Good For?

Progressive Realists echoed conventional scholarship in recalling how the ascent of the modern state system complemented the rise of modern capitalism (Carr, 1967 [1945]), 1–37). Nation states helped provide the indispensable preconditions of modern economic life: "a highly developed system of communications (roads, canals and postal service) for the movement of goods, information and money, and a wide internal market not limited by duties and tolls levied at every corner"(Schwarzenberger, 1941: 55). Consequently, it offered a "more formidable conglomerate of power than its predecessors in earlier periods of history" (Schwarzenberger, 1941: 54). They also highlighted its organizational superiority in the face of changing security imperatives. The exigencies of modern warfare contributed to the main organizational attributes of modern statehood: centralized bureaucracies, professionalized militaries, and central governments able to extract taxation. Whereas city-states and loosely knit empires (e.g. the Holy Roman Empire) proved unable to withstand the pressures of military innovation (and especially the early modern gunpowder revolution), identifiably modern political units, in which rulers exercised effective control over a minimum of contiguous territory, provided for secure "hard shells," i.e. effectively protected borders (Herz 1959: 39–75; 1976: 111). Spawned in part by ruthless violence, territorially based states were better suited than their predecessors to the scale and scope of modern destructive instruments.

Although initially a product of narrow European conditions, with the collapse of colonialism in the 1950s and 1960s modern statehood spread across the globe, as political communities everywhere maneuvered to take advantage of its advantages. For Progressive Realists, however, this development possessed tragic overtones, since – as we will see – contemporary states in their view were decreasingly well suited to basic functions of governance, in the twentieth-century subject to transformations no less wrenching than those of early modern Europe. Faced with high-speed air warfare and nuclear weaponry, contemporary states have ceased to possess impenetrable borders (Herz, 1959). Newly independent former colonies may have understandably celebrated the achievement of nationhood. Nonetheless, it was now a mere shadow of its former self (Morgenthau, 1958: 170–84).

Yet neither the modern state's economic nor its military advantages sufficed to explain the *particular* contours of statehood or, more specifically, the fact that modern states overwhelmingly have taken the form of *nation* states. Only when we consider why the political carriers of modern statehood since the French Revolution have typically been modern *nations* can we appreciate the innovative contours of Progressive Realist reflections.

The Nation State and Social Integration

Progressive Realists would not have been surprised by the social theorist Craig Calhoun's recent observation that "[n]o definition of national (or of its correlative terms such as nationalism and nationality) has ever gained general acceptance" (2007: 40). Nor would they have been unsettled by the findings of an enormous body of empirical literature documenting modern national identity's manifold and sometimes contradictory historical roots.[1] Like others who have pondered the nature of modern nationalism, they struggled to do justice to the multitudinous paths by which "nationhood" has been interpreted, as well as its seemingly innumerable empirical bases. Even if it is true that they never developed a full-fledged theory of nationalism, their writings spilled over with provocative reflections about the sources and prospects of nationalism, as well as the decisive role played by it in modern politics. Most important perhaps, they aptly focused on the crucial *integrative* functions exercised by national identity.

As Progressive Realists noted, shared language, religion, ethnicity, race, political history, ideological orientation, and even hostility to a foreign enemy have helped contribute to a sense of common nationhood. Yet one could still find examples which lacked some if not most such shared attributes. Heterogeneous ethnically and even linguistically diverse political communities like Switzerland and India have rested on a shared and deeply rooted national identity no less than comparatively homogeneous ones (Morgenthau, 1954: 482–5; Niebuhr, 1959: 146–81). They argued about whether subjective factors (e.g. voluntary choice or ideology) were more important to the creation of national identity than objective (or ascriptive) elements (e.g. shared language or ethnicity), or even whether conscious preferences played a greater role than subconscious emotions and proclivities (Schwarzenberger, 1941: 54–63; Niebuhr, 1959: 146–63). They recognized that the controversial idea of a national character – which Morgenthau in particular deemed useful – seemed to partake simultaneously of the subjective as well as objective, the voluntary as well as the pregiven (1954: 118–24). They all agreed, however, that national identity rested on a complex amalgam of both objective and subjective elements, as well as conscious and unconscious ones. Any analytic definition of it that dropped one side of the equation was likely to prove false, though admittedly there was substantial room for somewhat differing calculations concerning the place of any particular element.

Niebuhr best summarized the dominant view among his colleagues when he listed "common language and a sense of ethnic kinship, geographic unity and contiguity, a common historical experience, and frame of political thought, a common area of economic mutuality, and, sometimes, the fear of a common foe" as the most familiar sources of shared nationhood. Nonetheless, historical experience suggested that "*any* of these forces might be defective, but they cannot *all* be defective if the unity of the nation is to be preserved" (my emphasis). Even if a common religion traditionally had served as a prerequisite for nationhood, thriving pluralistic states like the United States demonstrated that even this condition was no longer necessary, though – Niebuhr cautiously added – "only solid communities bound by other ties of mutuality" ultimately could "afford the luxury of religious pluralism" (1959: 149). Carr analogously criticized notions of the nation as a pregiven natural or even biological grouping, a view which badly occluded the fact that "[t]he modern nation is a historical group" with contingent and historically specific roots. Nor was it a universal social phenomenon: "Today – in the most nation-conscious of all

epochs – it would still probably be fair to say that a large numerical majority of the population of the world feel no allegiance to any nation" (1967
[1945]: 39).

Simultaneously, Carr condemned the opposing analytic tendency,
according to which national identity was a product of mere voluntary
choice, an overly rationalistic view – he asserted – attractive to intellectuals yet unrepresentative of the sense of national identity found among
ordinary people. For most of them the nation was "something far more
than a voluntary association" individuals could willy-nilly quit as they
might choose a new suit or car: "it embodies in itself, though overlaid
with conventional trappings, such natural and universal elements as attach-
ments to one's native land and speech and a sense of wider kinship than
that of the family" (1942: 40; 1967 [1945]: 39). National identity tapped
into what appeared to be a deep "urge of human beings to form groups
based on common tradition, language and usage" (1942: 63). A commonplace mistake, Carr immediately added, was therefore to assume that
the existence of this urge required a system of *nation states*: alternative
political orderings might conceivably do justice to national identity as
well (1942: 60–6).

What most intrigued Progressive Realists about national identity were
the myriad ways in which it had served as a key element of integration
and social solidarity. The immediate reason that modern states had taken
the form of *nation* states was that a shared sense of nationality had consistently supplied integrative and motivational energies that no competing
political form hitherto had been equally capable of marshaling: nationally
organized political communities could tap into a deeper sense of social
belonging than their rivals. On the international scene, the resulting power
advantages were evident. The construction of national identities permitted
elites, for example, to call on common people to fight against social
peers – sometimes living just across the border – chiefly because they saw
themselves as French, for example, rather than Dutch or German. Property
owners who otherwise despised the lower classes proved willing to pay
exorbitant taxes to equip popularly based national armies because they
felt they had more in common with their own "nation in arms" than with
the hated foreign "other." Only modern nation states had achieved an
optimum of social cohesion capable of making it "such a formidable force
in the international society" (Schwarzenberger, 1941: 56; also, Morgenthau, 1946: 66–7).

Progressive Realists grasped a simple but crucial point: national identity
has repeatedly proven decisive in mixing the cement of the foundations of
modern statehood. By bringing people together to act in common, creating
incentives for them to do so, and providing a shared self-understanding of

what they were doing, as well as why it was appropriate to do so, modern nationalism has helped create distinctive social collectivities upon which viable political institutions could stand. Statehood and formal political institutions, in short, always rest on a complex array of obvious as well as less-than-obvious forms of social integration and solidarity. National identity has been crucial in modernity "because integration beyond the level of family and [small-scale] community is important" to modern politics; nationalism has played a major role in underpinning such integrative processes (Calhoun, 2007: 154). In a passage that could easily have been endorsed by Progressive Realists, Calhoun notes that

> [t]he integration nations help to achieve is of several sorts. They help to bind people together across social classes. They bridge regional and ethnic and sometimes religious differences. They link generations to each other, mobilizing traditions of cultural inheritance [and] mutual obligation. They link the living to both ancestors and future generations. They do this not simply in ideology, but in social institutions which matter to the lives of individuals, families, and communities. Nations are integrated in educational systems, health care systems, and transportation systems. (2007: 154)

Of course, as Calhoun observes, the history of modern nation-building has simultaneously been plagued by exclusion and violence. The makings of modern national identity were regularly shrouded in historical mythmaking and jingoistic ideology; its results have proven explosive and sometimes disastrous. Progressive Realists similarly refused to close their eyes to the unpleasant underbelly of modern nation-building. Yet none of the morally inexcusable horrors of modern nationalism, they believed, could plausibly persuade observers to ignore how national identity has been deeply interconnected to the complicated processes by which modern political communities have been molded into coherent social *collectivities* exercising more-or-less common wills. Even if such collectivities have committed more than their fair share of crimes, national identity has served as a constitutive element of political life and, more specifically, a necessary presupposition of many of the modern state's achievements. National identity helped secure the integrative and motivational bases upon which states provided physical security as well as new opportunities for social inclusion. Without it both modern liberal democracy and the welfare state were probably unthinkable (Rosanvallon, 2000).

For Niebuhr, national identity thus constituted a form of social tissue that had consistently proven essential to modern statehood. Although sovereign political power, or "a single organ of will and order is an absolute prerequisite" of any functioning political community, state institutions could not thrive without the underlying "forces of cohesion" that traditionally buttressed a shared sense of nationhood: "pure dominion, or the authority of government, cannot create a community if there are not some horizontal forces of community at work," among which a shared national identity was the most significant (1959: 149). Without the cohesive and integrative social presuppositions conventionally supplied by shared nationhood, government risked becoming impotent *or*, alternately, taking the form of an authoritarian Leviathan whose top-heavy coercive resources would have to be directed against an apathetic or even hostile population.

Morgenthau pursued the same argument when he decried a crude Hobbesianism asserting that the state *alone* can "maintain domestic peace ... That the state is essential, but not sufficient to keep the peace of national societies is demonstrated by the historical experience of civil wars" (1948b: 397). Working political authority always presupposed highly developed forms of social integration capable of accomplishing a demanding set of necessary tasks. Stable political systems rested on a widely shared expectation of fairness or basic justice, which encouraged participants to respect the basic rules of the political and social game even when specific outcomes seemed threatening. The employment of coercive power could then be minimized because organic forces of cohesion operated in subtle and easily overlooked ways; naive models of institutional reform sometimes ignored them because their defenders took them for granted. Social cleavages and loyalties had to be crosscutting, impressing on social actors the fundamental relativity of interests and loyalties. This "plural role of friend and opponent" reduced the potential explosiveness of group conflict: a rival in one social arena might be an ally or friend in another (1954: 471). For this reason as well, successful political communities relied only in exceptional circumstances on coercive force. In effectively integrated polities, a complicated array of social and political mores, norms, and social practices typically brought about peaceful transformations of public opinion. Formal state institutions sometimes worked to translate public opinion into legally binding political and social change. Yet state institutions always remained limited "agents of society as a whole" (1954: 414). Without a far-reaching basis in a complex set of social and community practices, laws would prove ineffective: "laws are obeyed because the community accepts them as corresponding," and not mainly because of the specter of state might (Niebuhr, 1953a: 22).

As Morgenthau followed Niebuhr in pointing out, so far only *nationally* based communities had successfully secured the requisite integrative and motivational presuppositions of modern statehood. Nonetheless, this observation led neither writer to exclude *a priori* the possibility that prospective forms of shared social life, commitment, and belonging might take a *novel* postnational form: Progressive Realists *bemoaned* the fact that the nation state and its particularistic identity remained the recipient of our ultimate political loyalties. Nonetheless, any prospective postnational or global political authority would have to rest on a developed "supranational society" or "world community" capable of accomplishing demanding integrative and motivational tasks presently performed more-or-less automatically by successful nationally based communities. Anyone serious about building postnational political entities more attuned to contemporary moral and technological needs would have to identify a functional replacement for nationally based political identity (Morgenthau, 1954: 479).

The Staying Power of National Identity

Not surprisingly, Progressive Realists struggled to make sense of the continuing valence of national identity, worried that defenders of otherwise appealing domestic and international reforms might miss its indispensable functions and understate its appeals. During the 1930s, Niebuhr pilloried his socialist comrades for underplaying the depth of national sentiment among the working classes and other prospective left-wing constituencies: their internationalist sympathies were morally praiseworthy but politically naive (1932: 142–68; 1934: 179–82). Just as global reformers were beginning to tout the makings of an international human rights regime, Morgenthau pointedly noted some two decades later, such rights might mean "something different to an American, a Russian, and an Indian" since they were "perceived by, assimilated to, and filtered through minds conditioned by different experiences" (Morgenthau, 1954: 240; also, Niebuhr, 1953a: 28–9). National character, or nationally rooted cultural and intellectual patterns evincing a surprising degree of historical constancy, still shaped political awareness.[2]

Even if social integration and social solidarity might someday draw on new springs, the lasting appeal of nationalism among those groups one might have expected to enjoy relative immunity from it had to be explained. For Niebuhr, crucial to the manner in which the nation had become the "ultimate community of significant loyalty" was its ability to exploit the limitations of humankind's moral imagination (1932: 48). To be sure, a Christian ethic of love remained rigorously universalistic: it called for moral and political reciprocity in our relations with others, and that we strive to build political and social institutions able better to instantiate Christian-inspired ideals of universal concern and moral respect. Christian ethics represented a constant spur to political and social reform, tirelessly calling on believers to construct ever more egalitarian systems of political and social justice, each providing superior approximations of the ideal of universal love.

So what then prevented the establishment of a worldwide or global political order, for example, giving direct expression to Christian-based moral universalism? Had this not been the dream of Christian as well as non-Christian thinkers for centuries? (Murphy, 1999).

In part, nationalism blocked the path. Revealingly, Niebuhr pointed out, it did so by tapping into the familiar frailties of human intelligence, imagination, and sympathy. Even if we are morally obliged to love and respect others as equals, and treat them in a perfectly disinterested manner, we find it exceedingly difficult to understand let alone sympathize with people with whom our contact is relatively circumscribed. Even when acting in a benevolent manner, our actions are typically marred by at least some measure of moral blindness and egoism. We instinctively privilege those with whom we are closest, or with whom our interests are most deeply intermeshed, and appeals to heed obligations to distant others too often fall on deaf ears. "The larger the group the more difficult it is to achieve a common mind and purpose" (1932: 48). The nation state is by no means lacking in moral attributes: it sometimes constructively funnels our moral energies, requiring of us that we identify with others and even share sacrifices and give our lives selflessly for them. Yet it encourages us to do so chiefly within the confines of a limited or *particularistic* national community, with whom we typically share organic ties (of ethnicity, for example, or language). Obligations to national consociates can – and obviously do – conflict with the broader *universalistic* obligations deriving from the Christian ethic of love.

In short, the staying power of the nation state could be partly explained by its refusal to overtax our moral imagination: while successfully superseding earlier loyalties to smaller units (e.g. kin or tribe), and providing some room for our moral energies, it did not demand extensive cooperation with distant others in any but a limited manner. For Niebuhr, the limitations of moral imagination constituted a built-in feature of the human condition deriving, in the final analysis, from our unavoidable lack of divine omniscience and disinterestedness. As a devout Christian, he considered it hubristic to hope that humans might fully overcome such limits. This, in fact, was a central reason why he believed that any quest to build a more immediately universal political and social order faced huge impediments.

Nonetheless, even in his most cautious moments Niebuhr noted that our modern "technological civilization has created an international community, so interdependent as to require, even if not powerful or astute enough to achieve, ultimate social harmony," despite the unfortunate fact that "modern man has progressed only a little beyond his fathers in extending his ethical attitudes beyond the group to which he is organic and which possesses symbols, vivid enough to excite his social sympathies" (1932: 49). The scope of our moral imagination and sympathies remained historically malleable. As modern life generated new forms of social interconnectedness, novel possibilities for extending political communities in a more richly universal direction became less farfetched. Even if the nation state seemed presently to offer a sensible institutional constellation given our moral limitations, it too remained an eminently historical creature destined to pass away.

Other Progressive Realists complemented such theological arguments with secular claims about the social and especially social-psychological functions of modern national identity. National identity represented an important *source* of social integration, helping to glue together modern political communities into coherent collectivities. Yet it also stemmed from an oftentimes pathological *reaction* to social disintegration and the widespread sense of personal insecurity in contemporary society: its most virulent and aggressive forms occurred in those societies – for example,1930s Germany – where social and political processes had destroyed even a modicum of personal security and social stability. Typically, its main carriers were the lower middle classes and working classes, "groups which are primarily the object of the power of others and are most thoroughly deprived of outlets for their own power drives or are most insecure in the possession of whatever power they may have within the national community" (Morgenthau, 1954: 95; also, Niebuhr, 1932: 18).[3] They compensated for their political and social vulnerability by projecting their power drives onto the international arena and completely identifying with national aspirations. Any attempt to counteract virulent nationalism would have to attend to the political, economic, and social roots of personal insecurity and social instability.

Whether the psychological functions performed by nationalism could someday be fully jettisoned remained unclear. Schuman was perhaps most hopeful in thinking that the presumed limitations of human moral sensibility could be attenuated by a future global order: "Human nature is very flexible and adaptable, and it is quite conceivable that under appropriate conditions the attitudes and values of traditional patriotism may be modified in the direction of international and world interests, making for harmony among states." If humankind were successfully to do so, however, it would have to "substitute for nationalism a new set of emotional responses, associated with a new basis of social integration and affording equally adequate psychic satisfaction," in order to satisfy the requisite psychological needs (Schuman, 1941b: 311). Any future-day global order could only flourish if it succeeded in building on myths and symbols able to tap into unconscious and irrational psychological traits. "The 'unconscious mind' is here to stay," and those who ignored its significant role did so at their own risk (Schuman, 1952a: 76). Defenders of a global federal polity would need to find some functional replacement for the emotionally laden symbols and narratives that had constituted a major part of modern national identity (Schuman, 1952a: 473–9).

How Nation States Destroy Morality

Even if the modern nation state had performed pivotal political and social tasks, Progressive Realists argued, it would eventually have to be replaced by a mode of political organization better suited "to the technical circumstances and the moral requirements of the contemporary world" (Morgenthau, 1954: 9). On this crucial matter, they clearly parted ways with present-day analysts like Calhoun who sympathize with what Progressive Realists would likely have considered defensive battles to shore up nationalism.[4] From their more critical perspective, the nation state to a growing extent fails to pass contemporary moral tests because it unnecessarily clashes with the universalistic moral impulses of modernity. While "the test of a morally good action is the degree to which it is capable of treating others not simply as means to the actor's ends but as ends in themselves," the nation state not only encourages moral parochialism, but also mobilizes vast power resources against a rigorously non-instrumentalist ethic (Morgenthau, 1946: 196). In the final analysis, it rests on moral tribalism (Niebuhr, 1965: 84–105; Schuman, 1941b: 300–65). From Niebuhr's Christian standpoint,

> [t]here are no limits to be set in history for the achievement of more universal brotherhood, for the development of more perfect and more inclusive mutual relations ... The vision of universal love expressed by St Paul in the words: "There is neither Jew nor Greek, there is neither bond nor free, there is neither male nor female, for ye are all one in Christ Jesus," is meant primarily for the church. But it cannot be denied that it is relevant to all social relationships. For the freedom of man makes it impossible to set any limits of race, sex, or social condition upon the brotherhood which may be achieved in history. (1943: 85)

Admittedly, this "doctrine which regards the *agape* of the Kingdom of God as a resource for infinite developments towards a more perfect brotherhood in history" hardly inferred the immediate or even ultimate inevitability of a just global order. Yet it necessarily rendered the nation state's latent collective egoism morally suspect. Skeptical of utopian visions of a perfectly harmonious social and political community, Realists thought that the existing nation state – and an international system predicated on its hegemony – unduly vitiated humanity's moral energies.

The modern nation state has become the highest object of our loyalties in whose name individuals are not only permitted but incited to commit immoral acts otherwise universally condemned. It provides a fundamental institutional support for an unacceptable dualistic morality which judges public acts less stringently than private ones, condoning egotism and horrific violence as long as they serve its provincial goals. Individual power impulses generally hemmed in at the domestic level by mores and laws are destructively transferred to the collective level: "What was egotism – and hence ignoble and immortal – there becomes patriotism and therefore noble and altruistic" (Morgenthau, 1946: 198). We teach our children to worship wartime heroes, and join together in singing their praises on national holidays. Elected officials are re-elected in part because they garner loyalty for defending national interests even at a high cost to nonnationals. The modern state's ability to manipulate instruments of mass persuasion then exacerbates the potentially dangerous moral compulsion it exerts over its members. The resulting conformism drowns out the voice of conscience (Morgenthau, 1954: 229).

In a morally disenchanted era, the nation state becomes for many people a mortal God: "for an age that believes no longer in an immortal God, the state becomes the only God there is" (Morgenthau, 1946: 197; also, Niebuhr, 1943: 212). Not surprisingly, legal, moral, and customary restraints on the nation state remain insufficient. Nationalistic ideology fills the void by claiming universal validity: we ease our conscience by falsely transcending necessary tensions between religion and universalistic morality, on the one hand, and political imperatives, on the other hand, by a complete perversion of ethical valuation in which selfish national power politics becomes an exemplar of moral action (Morgenthau, 1946: 196–200). Rather than give up altogether on universalistic morality, we irresponsibly conflate it with our own country's selfish aspirations. The relatively benign nationalism of the nineteenth century thereby gets traded in for an ominous nationalistic universalism in which cramped national aims are deceptively outfitted with the traditional paraphernalia of universal morality: "While [classical] nationalism wants one nation in one state and nothing else, the nationalistic universalism of our age claims for one nation and one state the right to impose its own valuations and standards of action upon all the other nations" (Morgenthau, 1954: 313). Nationalism increasingly becomes a secular religion "universal in its interpretation of the nature and destiny of man and in its promise of salvation for all mankind" (Morgenthau, 1954:

314). The nation state represents humankind's latest hubristic – and perhaps most dangerous – attempt to play God (Niebuhr, 1932: 96–8; 1943: 213). One immediate consequence is the irrational crusading spirit that infects foreign policy.[5]

Even if the nation state has sometimes funneled healthy moral resources by demanding the fulfillment of obligations to relatively abstract others, in the final instance it represents nothing but "a corrupt form of universalism" (Niebuhr, 1944: 160). Indeed, its role as a conduit for moral energies inadvertently masks national egotism: the genuine selflessness motivating a great deal of patriotic fervor, for example, occludes the harsh fact that it remains a servant of national parochialism (Niebuhr, 1932: 48). For Niebuhr, *any* significant collectivity – be it a social class, religious group, *or* nation state – is vulnerable to sinful pride and the inherent human tendency to dress up selfish and even immoral actions in moralistic garb. What brings such groups together, of course, is normally some constellation of common interests – in advancing one's economic status, for example, in the case of a social class, or in the case of national grouping, of protecting one's security in a dangerous political universe. Yet restrictions on the selfishness and egoism that necessarily result from the pursuit of such interests operate even less effectively at the collective than the individual level.

Niebuhr formulated the most impressive version of the Realist critique of group morality. First, the limitations of the individual's moral imagination make it difficult to realize moral ideals directly within anything but relatively small groups or collectivities: we always have a hard time figuring out how to act rightly even in relations with loved ones and friends, let alone in the context of the social class, religion, or nation of which we are members. Large collectivities are more likely to get away with terrible crimes because the requisite forces of group self-criticism and self-censure remain relatively underdeveloped (1932: 88). Narrow-minded prejudices often play a sizable role in generating group unity (1932: xx). Second, large collectivities typically depend on power and coercion in order to preserve their identity. In any but the smallest of groups, familiar forms of power and coercion compensate for the frailties and limitations of morality – in the case of the national community, for example, an enforceable system of binding law as part of some system of justice. Social collectivities, in contrast to individuals, consequently marshal hazardous power instruments, typically denied individuals, allowing them to violate mortal strictures.

Third, the limitations of moral imagination make it difficult for group members to understand why outsiders might object to their goals, or even interpret a particular set of events in an altogether opposing fashion. Men and women instinctively discount the interests and moral perspectives of those linked to social, religious, and national groups different from their own. Fourth, group solidarity is oftentimes constituted *in opposition* to outsiders: "The increasing size of the group increases the difficulties of achieving a group self-consciousness, except as it comes in conflict with other groups and is unified by perils and passions of war" (1932: 45). Group solidarity is often predicated on differentiating insiders from outsiders in ways that badly devalue the latter and occlude our common humanity. Fifth, group pride typically "achieves a certain authority over the individual and results in unconditioned demands by the group upon the individual" (1941: 208). Many familiar psychological and social processes lead individuals to conform to the outlooks of a particular class, religion, or nationality; such viewpoints often take on a life of their own, whose strictures individuals are expected to heed unthinkingly. Unfortunately, this aspect of collective identity formation blunts the force of individual conscience and encourages individuals to close their eyes to unsettling moral truths. Those who dare to stand up to the conformist pressures of their class, religion, or nation are subject to abuse and even ostracism.

Any significant human collectivity, Niebuhr believed, suffered from such perils. The critique of group morality was in part intended to highlight the stunning difficulties facing a would-be global polity: a world state might simply be crippled by the tragic human tendency to overlook the interests and perspectives of distant and seemingly unconnected people. Nonetheless, Niebuhr remained willing to entertain the prospect of a world state capable of overcoming such difficulties.[6] Even as the critique of group morality posed obvious challenges to global reform, for him it simultaneously provided a sturdy basis from which to criticize the nation state. Under existing conditions, the nation state alone possessed a monopoly on the use of legitimate force, and in contradistinction to other significant social groupings, the ready ability to unleash destructive coercive resources. Its ability to enjoin moral compulsion – and thoughtless conformism – remained unsurpassed. Like no other existing social group, nation states were able to construct outsiders as "alien" foes, and to enforce its agenda by awesome "power and to give them plausibility and credibility by the majesty and panoply of its apparatus" (Niebuhr, 1941: 209). The result was a quasi-religious reverence for and sometimes idolatrous worship of the nation state and its personal representatives: even if pride and hubris are commonplace moral ills, nation states remained particularly prone to them because they controlled instruments of persuasion and coercion denied individuals and rival social groups.

Even if a novel postnational prospective political and social order might be plagued by "the brutal character of the behavior of all collectivities," as early as 1940 Niebuhr asserted that "[w]e must undoubtedly overcome international anarchy if we are to survive as a civilization" (1932, xx; 1940: 38). One reason was that in the specific context of an interstate system now divided into ruthlessly competitive "mortal Gods," each tending to picture rivals as alien "others" with whom no common moral basis could be identified, warfare inevitably proved horrific. In Morgenthau's related conceptual framework, present-day nationalistic universalism paved the way for total wars – mobilizing all of society's resources against an alien enemy from whom nothing less than unconditional surrender could suffice – and its troublesome blurring of legal distinctions between combatants and noncombatants (1954: 41–62). International anarchy's demise *might* mean the end of at least one source of political violence and the accompanying moral evils: interstate anarchy exacerbated the dangerous egotism of (national) collectivities, aggrandizing rivalries which lead people to discount the moral status and interests of foreigners, while simultaneously encouraging forms of national cohesion that go hand in hand with moral blindness and self-righteousness. Even if political collectivities larger than the nation state would also undoubtedly have to rely on familiar forms of power and coercion, the abridgement of international anarchy might provide opportunities for moral and political improvement.

However, Morgenthau still conceded that the evils of nationalistic universalism "would not necessarily be mitigated, but might be aggravated, by the fusion of a number of nations into a supranational union." A supranational Europe, for example, might "acquire a new crusading spirit, common to all of Western Europe, to compete with the nationalistic universalism of other nations," simply reproducing the moral pathologies of existing nation states (1954: 313). Perhaps a fully *global* – and not merely multinational or regionally based – political ordering could do better. A prospective world state would only survive if it successfully provided political and institutional incentives conducive to a genuinely *universal* or cosmopolitan political identity: its members would have to identify in meaningful ways with the interests of humankind as a whole. The many ways in which international anarchy and the dominant place of the nation state helped encourage egotistical forms of identity and action would have to have been substantially attenuated. World statehood seemed to offer at least a better chance of realizing Niebuhr's aim of a "more universal brotherhood [and sisterhood], for the development of more perfect and more inclusive mutual relations," in which the arbitrary "limits of race, sex, or social condition" had finally been alleviated.

Economic Globalization vs. the Nation State

The nation state was not only morally blemished, however. Influential economic trends, Progressive Realists argued, were undermining its status as the linchpin of the global political economy.

The contemporary term "globalization" does not of course appear in their writings. Nonetheless, they anticipated some of its key elements. So Schuman described ours as a "Great Society" intertwined socially and technologically in unprecedented ways:

> Its members are completely interdependent in a thousand ways they scarcely dream of. Travel time over the planet continues to contract ... Ease and speed of travel are obviously but one of the indices of the unity of the world. Communication of messages, pictures, and voices has become almost instantaneous from each of the great centers of the globe to the others. Modern man is not content to learn from the printed page at breakfast what happened in the Antipodes the preceding evening. He expects to be able to listen later in the day to the kings and captains of other continents speaking in his living room. He also takes it for granted that he can talk by telephone to almost anywhere on the planet. As he talks, he may (or may not) reflect that the small device he speaks into and listens to contains chromium from Rhodesia, the USSR, or Turkey ... If he lives in any of the great cities of the twentieth century, he spends every hour of his day in contact with objects of use or beauty which are his only because he is a member of a Great Society and a world economy wherein people, things, and ideas, in peacetime at least, can be moved quickly and cheaply from any point to any other of his now very small world. (1941b: 248–9)

Even if his examples now seem rather quaint, Schuman successfully captured what the geographer David Harvey has more recently dubbed the "compression of space and time," a complex (and contradictory) shift in social experience underlying the core of the multiple processes now commonly associated with globalization (Harvey, 1989).[7] Globalization takes many different political, economic, and cultural forms (Held, McGrew, Goldblatt, and Perraton, 1999). Yet they all partake of three basic features. First, globalization entails *deterritorialization*, meaning that a growing array of social activities takes place irrespective of the geographical position of the relevant participants. Business people on different continents engage in electronic commerce; academics make use of video conferencing equipment to organize seminars in which participants are located at disparate geographical locations. Territory in the sense of a traditional sense of a geographically identifiable location no longer constitutes the entirety of social space (Ruggie, 1993; Scholte, 2000). Second, it entails heightened *social interconnectedness*: even those activities directly linked to a specific geographical location are ever more intensely interlinked to activities elsewhere (Tomlinson, 1999: 9). Finally, both deterritorialization and social interconnectedness are undergirded by the growing *speed* or *velocity* of social activity. The proliferation of high-speed transportation, communication, and information technologies constitutes an immediate basis for the blurring of geographical and territorial divides that prescient social analysts and literary figures have observed at least since the nineteenth century. High-speed technologies and modes of business organization play decisive roles in the globalization of production, finance, and trade, and in many other arenas of social activity (Scheuerman, 2006).

Admittedly, Progressive Realist accounts of what recent commentators commonly describe as economic globalization never achieved a sufficient level of analytic or empirical precision; those looking for answers to the vital question, for example, of whether ongoing economic shifts might better be captured by concepts such as *regionalization* or *triadization* will be disappointed.[8] Primarily concerned with explaining the role of the Great Depression in unleashing the horrors of the Second World War, their ideas sometimes seem unavoidably time-bound. Nonetheless, Progressive Realists accurately interpreted the structural dynamics of modern capitalism as having motored the internationalization of production, trade, and finance, and in creating an ever more global or world economy characterized by unprecedented levels of economic interdependence (Carr, 1942; 1967 [1945]; Schuman, 1941b: 435–58). For them, as for many contemporary analysts, the misfit between the scope and scale of a worldwide capitalist economy and the narrow institutional confines of the nation state posed tough questions about the long-term viability of the latter.

In Carr's especially rich argumentation, some facets of economic globalization had occurred well before the First World War, as a multiplicity of national economies underwent transformation into a relatively integrated liberal global economy, and political and economic power ceased to march "hand in hand to build up the national political unit and to substitute a single national economy for a conglomeration of local economies," as it had during the process of European state-building and the heydays of economic mercantilism. In the nineteenth century, an institutional disjuncture between the *national* scope and scale of major political institutions and the ever more *worldwide* capitalist economy had already emerged (1967 [1945]: 6–7).[9] At least initially, Carr noted, the misfit was successfully mediated. First, nationally based political systems accepted the sacrosanct status of property rights, which not only allowed for the creation of an international liberal market but worked to minimize potential threats to liberal policies at home. Second, economic liberalism made "possible a phenomenal increase of production and population," offering opportunities at least to the dominant (chiefly European) countries "to expand and spread their civilization material civilization all over the world." Whatever its costs to peoples elsewhere, Europe's success in exporting its population, products, and material civilization around the globe generated a "fundamental change from the static order and outlook of the eighteenth century to the dynamic order and outlook of the nineteenth" (1967 [1945]: 10–12).

However, the successful mitigation of the latent contradiction between a closely knit world economic system and "the political diversity and independence of nations" was destined to come undone. For Carr, it had rested on two core illusions. First, economic liberalism derived its legitimacy from the widespread conviction that it was impersonal and indeed "natural." In reality, it resulted from conscious political choices, both buttressed by and ultimately privileging Britain, and in which the "powerful financial machine whose seat was in the city of London" benefited disproportionately (1967 [1945]: 14). Second, it depended on an illusory separation between economic and political affairs, which conveniently favored economic liberalism and its class beneficiaries while obscuring the myriad ways in which political and economic power were always inevitably interwoven. By the onset of the twentieth century, such fictions were already coming unraveled, both as rival powers (e.g. Germany) directly challenged the global liberal system, and hitherto politically excluded social strata (i.e. the working classes) took the stage and demanded that government be employed to better their lot.

This story of the demise of nineteenth-century liberalism was a familiar one. However, Carr gave his version some twists. Liberal decay culminated in what he tellingly described as the "socialization of the nation" and simultaneous "nationalization of socialism." First, the nation state became a vehicle for popular economic aspirations requiring it "to minister to the welfare of members of the nation and to enable them to earn their living" even when such policies conflicted with laissez-faire ideology or the policies of other countries (1967 [1945]: 19). It acquired the broad social basis that its liberal (middle-class) predecessor had lacked. Second, the embrace of policies whose main function was to ameliorate the masses' living conditions functioned to fuse political and economic power in many different (and sometimes problematic) ways – e.g. Soviet communism, Nazism, the New Deal, as well as the emerging Western European welfare state.[10] This fusion consistently occurred within the narrow contours of the nation state. Despite the internationalist orientation of classical Marxism, socialism – a term Carr used loosely to refer to any of a number of conceivable mergers of political and economic power – came to be rooted unambiguously in national terrain: "National policy was henceforth founded on the support of the masses; and the counterpart was the loyalty of the masses to a nation which had become the instrument of their collective interests and ambitions" (1967 [1945]: 20). The masses identified with "their" nationally based institutions because they promised economic relief. To an ever greater extent, they also joined other social groups in jingoistically haranguing national leaders to seek economic advantages vis-à-vis foreign rivals: the augmentation of state intervention in the economy not only deepened the identification of broad social strata with the nation state, but incited its leaders to pursue economic nationalism.

Unfortunately, the result were the destructive policies thriving in the days before the Second World War and which directly contributed to its horrors: war became "an instrument for securing economic advantages for the victor and inflicting economic disabilities on the defeated," taking on brutal predatory attributes previously reserved for colonial conflagrations. When the nation state became the prime site for mass economic aspirations, "[m]odern wars are fought to a finish and the loser has no rights" (Carr, 1967 [1945]: 28). The nationalization of economic rivalry not only engendered new sources of interstate rivalry but dramatically upped the ante in new and frightening ways. This was one reason, Carr believed, why the League of Nations was unable to halt the tide towards war: "As custodians of the living standards, employment and amenities of their whole populations, modern nations are, in virtue of their nature and function, probably less capable than any other groups in modern times of reaching agreement with one another" (1967 [1945]: 29). With the nation state primarily responsible for guaranteeing the populace's economic wellbeing, political leaders garnered powerful incentives to violate and even discard international agreements blocking their attempts to do so.

To a superficial reader, Carr's anxieties about the rise of state intervention and economic nationalism might have seemed oddly reminiscent of those of a political rival and outspoken right-winger, Friedrich A. Hayek, whose *The Road to Serfdom* (1944) – published just a year before Carr's *Nationalism and After* (1945) – similarly placed much of the blame for the horrors of contemporary warfare at the doorstep of economic nationalism, which both authors accurately described as having flourished in the 1930s. While offering a catastrophic account of the demise of classical liberalism, Hayek depicted state-driven economic nationalism as a decisive check on the extension of the rule of law to the international arena (1994 [1944]: 240–60).[11]

The similarities were only skin-deep, however. In contrast to Hayek, who advocated a return to a fictional nineteenth-century liberal golden age, Carr considered the quest to do so both undesirable and impossible. The successes of nineteenth-century economic liberalism not only rested, as noted above, on a series of ideological myths, but – here Carr's socialist political preferences became evident – endemic systemic factors necessarily transformed classical competitive capitalism into a socially irrational monopolistic system in which the classical market could no longer function properly, and the needs of neither workers nor consumers were properly served (1942: 67–101). Carr broke decisively with free marketers like Hayek not only in his refusal to accept the possibility of a successful resuscitation of classical economic liberalism, but also in his tendency to see economic nationalism as stemming from classical capitalism's own inherent limitations. Economic nationalism remained undesirable and destructive in ways noted by Hayek. Yet the answer was not to discard the methods of interwar state intervention, but instead to overcome "the narrowness and inappropriateness of the geographical limits" within which they had been employed (1967 [1945]: 47). Extensive state intervention represented a sensible response to capitalism's irrationalities. State planning's destructive alliance with the nation state had to be broken by moving towards supranational – and especially continental – state-directed economic coordination. Writing during the war, Carr thought that only a postwar system of common European planning proffered an "alternative to a recrudescence of the economic nationalism of the past twenty years," which represented "the inevitable outcome in modern conditions of providing no alternative to the pursuit by national units of independent, and therefore self-defeating, economic policies" (1942: 254).

From the perspective of what Andrew Linklater has aptly described as Carr's socialist rendition of continental Keynesianism, the chief problem with contemporary capitalism was not, despite what some contemporary leftist critics of economic globalization decry, primarily its purported tendency to produce a global neoliberal economy where the rapid-fire movement of money, goods, and services overwhelms the nation state's regulatory capacities (2000: 237).[12] To be sure, Carr would have sympathized with present-day leftist critics of globalizing capitalism. Yet the Achilles' heel of their view, at least from his standpoint, was that it potentially encouraged the embrace of a defensive *nationally* based quest to rein in neoliberalism's excesses. For Carr, economic nationalism was ultimately as politically suspect as global economic liberalism: defensive endeavors to compensate for the failings of so-called free market policies by subjecting them to political controls *within the confines of the nation state* constituted a recipe for potential disaster.

Whatever the limitations of Progressive Realist analyses of economic globalization, they successfully remind us of the perils of economic nationalism especially – as Carr and also Schuman pointed out – when economic and social turmoil tends to refurbish its seeming appeal. With the world economy again in crisis, some evidence suggests that countries are in fact responding by following beggar-thy-neighbor policies that appear to provide quick economic advantages, but hardly contribute constructively to building new forms of global cooperation required by the challenges at hand. In contrast, Realists like Carr and Schuman pushed for new forms of institutionalized postnational economic policy making. Atavistic economic nationalism could not simply be blamed on the obsolescent nationalistic mindsets of misguided policy makers, but also on the existence of a Westphalian system in which the nation state remained the premier form of political organization: unless the state system was significantly altered, economic nationalism – or what Schuman described as neo-mercantilism (1941b: 348–54) – would continue to rear its unattractive head. As long as nation states remained the highest object of our loyalties, people would turn to them during economic crises for relief even at the price of embracing economic parochialism.

In contrast also to those today who seek enhanced global economic governance but hesitate to acknowledge contemporary capitalism's congenital pathologies, Progressive Realists plausibly suggested that nationalistic beggar-thy-neighbor policies, even if ultimately counterproductive from the standpoint of classical bourgeois economic thinking, unfortunately represented their likely and perhaps inevitable offshoot. For the young Niebuhr,

> [t]he real tragedy of our contemporary situation is that modern technology has made social mutuality and international reciprocity an absolute imperative, a very law of survival; while our system of economic ownership makes both intra-national justice and international reciprocity impossible. (1934: 29)

Even if modern technology helped prepare the groundwork for an interdependent world economic order, capitalism systematically undermined global mutuality and reciprocity. Like Carr, Schuman attributed resurgent protectionism, the erection of economically inefficient trade barriers, and the growth of state intervention shoring up privileged economic giants to the *core dynamics* of a capitalist political economy in which national governments were forced to join arms with privileged economic interests in order to guarantee profits and protect markets from foreign intrusions (1941b: 336–66). The paradox at hand was that contemporary capitalism had produced a deeply intermeshed global economy, while simultaneously generating dangerous disintegrative counterpressures. Economic nationalism paradoxically "coincided with the waning of the nation state as a politico-economic unit" able to deal effectively with the demands of an increasingly – or at least potentially – universal global economy. Immanent economic trends suggested the desirability of "at least great continental blocs and at most a world federation" (1941b: 365).

Especially for Carr and Schuman, the way forward was a decisive break with *both* a state system that hindered sensible government involvement in the economy *and* a fundamentally capitalist economy that contributed decisively to its pathologies. Global political – and far-reaching social – reform would have to go hand in hand (Carr, 1967 [1945]: 38–74; Schuman, 1941b; also, Niebuhr, 1934: 24–6; 1940: 153).

The Political and Military Decay of the Nation State

Even if the modern nation state had once helped provide for military security and indispensable modes of social integration, Progressive Realists argued, to a growing degree its failures to perform either function outweighed its ability to do so. Ours was a transitional period in which nation states would continue to play pivotal roles on the world scene. Yet to an increasing extent they represented hollow shells of their former political and military selves. The Progressive Realists' wide-ranging analyses revolved around the following three main observations.

First, despite nineteenth-century nationalism's close ties to admirable liberal and democratic political ideals, especially after the First World War the quest to guarantee statehood to every would-be nation became disruptive and politically disintegrative. Inspired by the Wilsonian vision of *national* self-determination, borders were redrawn along politically untenable lines, with yesterday's nationally oppressed quickly becoming tomorrow's national oppressors: "If it was right for the Czechs and Slovaks to free themselves in the name of nationalism from Austrian rule, it could not be wrong for the Slovaks and Sudeten Germans to free themselves from Czech rule in the name of the selfsame principle" (Morgenthau, 1958: 173). The fusion of self-determination with nationalism engendered instability and horrific trends according to which it came to be "regarded as an enlightened policy to remove men, women and children forcibly from their homes and transfer them from place to place in order to create homogeneous national units" (Carr, 1967 [1945]: 33). The combustible mix of nationalism with statehood paved the way for the barbarism of the Second World War. As nationalism shed its early libertarian overtones and exalted the collective over the individual, while interpreting provincial national ideals as encapsulating universal moral significance, it encouraged foreign policy irresponsibility and military adventurism.

Second, the attempt to marry nationalism to statehood unwittingly generated "the creation of an ever larger number of small independent states at a time when the survival of the small independent state as a political unit" had already become "problematical by developments of military technique" (Carr, 1942: 50). Innovations in military technique created stunning security-related inequalities between large and small states that made a mockery of the legal equality of all states (Carr, 1967 [1945]: 51–4). Despite its promise to provide political order and stability, the nation state was increasingly unable to do so. Many national units could now only realistically guarantee security by linking arms in novel ways with the Great Powers: both collective security and the pursuit of neutrality had failed to protect them during the interwar interregnum, and Carr and other Realists were skeptical that they could so after the Second World War (Carr, 1967 [1945]: 54–5; Morgenthau, 1958: 170–84).

Albeit perversely, both the Nazis and Soviets at least grasped the fact that security could only be provided by power agglomerations larger and more inclusive than the nation state (Carr, 1967 [1945]: 52–3; Morgenthau, 1958: 175; Schuman, 1941b). The trick would be to figure out how instead to do so as to preserve meaningful chances for self-determination as well as outlets for legitimate expressions of national identity. Despite his initial sympathies for appeasing Nazi Germany, Carr's wartime writings insistently criticized the Nazi-rendition of postnational politics, in which a German *Herrenvolk* ran roughshod over the rights of small countries and so-called non-Aryan people.[13] As he observed, "[t]he existence of multinational units of military and economic organization does not stand in the way of the maintenance, or indeed the further extension, of national administrative and cultural units, thus encouraging a system of overlapping and interlocking loyalties" (Carr, 1967 [1945]: 59). The Nazis had manifestly failed to build such a system; the Allies would need to succeed at doing so if they hoped realistically to bring about peace and postwar stability.

Yet it was also mistaken to presuppose that the establishment of continental military blocs could provide lasting security. Even before the bombings of Hiroshima and Nagasaki, Carr presciently argued that the rapid development of military technology, and especially recent innovations in air warfare, meant that even the largest and most powerful military units could never again hope to achieve military impregnability: not only in the economic sphere, but in the security arena "interdependence is now universal." Writing a few years after Nazi bombers had destroyed much of his own country's great cities, he argued that any future configuration of security-based continental power blocs would need to become part of some more universal international security system outfitted with a multinational police or military force able to operate across borders (1967 [1945]: 58). With military technology having rendered even the largest territorially based political units vulnerable to devastating attack, only an inclusive global security network, in which the Great Powers actively participated, had a real chance of circumventing the worst horrors of contemporary warfare. Even if such an organization could likely "not in the last resort prevent war between the Great Powers themselves," it was imaginable that the resulting "habit of cooperation and common action ... would undoubtedly tend to remove a predisposing cause of war between them" (Carr, 1967 [1945]: 60). To his credit, Carr defended and partially predicted not only the subsequent regionalization of security (for example, under the auspices of the North Atlantic Treaty Organization [NATO]), but some of his wartime proposals for a global security system – most importantly, an effective global police and military force – arguably went beyond what the United Nations has since provided (Carr, 1967 [1945]: 54–5; Morgenthau, 1958: 170–84).

Herz's *International Politics in the Atomic Age* (1959) subsequently extended this line of argumentation to the nuclear age. Nuclear weapons not only denied the vast majority of (non-nuclear) states a reasonable chance to defend themselves and thereby of the rudiments of statehood, but even for the US and USSR "atomic penetration must perpetually be reckoned with and ... therefore permeability rather than old-style independence and protection" had become the underlying condition (1959: 222). With nuclear weapons rendering the Great Powers vulnerable, the classical link between sovereignty and territoriality was coming unraveled. Although Herz conceded that he was focusing on developmental *trends*, his main point remained clear enough: nuclear warfare ultimately rendered *every* territorial political unit's borders vulnerable. Of course, previous military revolutions had undermined earlier forms of political organization; the gunpowder revolution, for example, helped pave the way for the modern territorial state. Herz doubted, however, that nuclear warfare simply represented a quantitative extension of earlier innovations: it fractured the very possibility of any territorially based political entity hoping to provide lasting security.

As Herz later conceded, a growing awareness of the terrors of nuclear weapons soon seemed to render them practically unusable as normal instruments of warfare, thereby stabilizing territorial boundaries rather than effacing them (Herz, 1976: 226–52). The Great Powers wisely hesitated to engage in military conflicts when there was any possibility of it evolving into nuclear warfare. Nonetheless, even if nuclear weaponry served some unexpected stabilizing functions, the nation state's future remained uncertain: the "unavailability of [nuclear] force" still permitted small states to defy large ones even to the point of pursuing reckless violence and at the cost of endangering world peace (1976: 234–8).

In the nuclear age Great Power security was no longer preserved exclusively by military and physical muscle, but rather by the "psychological ability to deter those who are physically able to destroy it. The prospective enemy must be induced to refrain from attacking" (Morgenthau, 1958: 178; also, Herz, 1976: 234–8). Nonetheless, Progressive Realists remained deeply conflicted about nuclear deterrence. Morgenthau questioned whether it could operate effectively if nuclear weapons were allowed to proliferate: if widely dispersed, the resulting strategic games and psychological calculations would overtax crisis decision makers and perhaps lead to cataclysmic results. Though deterrence served stabilizing functions in the context of bipolarity, in the long run it remained potentially self-defeating and even suicidal (Scheuerman, 2009: 159–64). As Richard Ned Lebow and Janice Gross Stein have recently noted in a parallel vein, "deterrence should be viewed as a powerful but very dangerous medicine" (1994: 368). Whether or not existing nation states might maintain their viability in the aftermath of the nuclear revolution remained, in the final analysis, undecided. In any event, deterrence represented a risky approach given the high stakes at hand, not the least of which remained the horrific possibility of nuclear omnicide.

Third, nuclear warfare posed morally unacceptable existential dangers to the human species. Its occurrence would represent a form of radical evil in which millions of people – and indeed probably humankind as a whole – perished "not like men but like beasts, killed in a mass," merely by somebody pressing a button thousands of miles away (Morgenthau, 1962b: 23):

> [n]uclear destruction is mass destruction, both of persons and things. It signifies the simultaneous destruction of tens of millions of people, of whole families, generations, and societies, of all things that they have inherited and created. It signifies the total destruction of whole societies by killing their members, destroying their visible achievements, and therefore reducing their survivors to barbarism. Thus nuclear destruction destroys the meaning of death by depriving it of individuality. It destroys the meaning of immorality by making both society and history impossible. (Morgenthau, 1962b: 22)

Nuclear warfare would reduce to absurd clichés appeals to traditional values like bravery, heroism, and honor: such values could have no real meaning in the aftermath of a nuclear holocaust. The common mistake was to think that "the possibility of nuclear death portended only a quantitative extension of the mass destruction of the past and not a qualitative transformation" of the horrors of warfare (1962b: 24).

Inspired by Karl Jaspers' *The Future of Mankind* (1961) and its attempt to grapple with the prospect of nuclear war, Morgenthau described nuclear weaponry as the terrifying culmination of a rapid-fire technological revolution which had fundamentally altered human existence since the nineteenth century. Of course, human beings had always made tools. Special to an era in which permanent technological revolution represented the norm, however, was its ever accelerating pace, as well as the fact that only recently had humanity tapped "artificially new sources of power as a supplement and substitution for human and animal power," rather than simply better employing the relatively static "muscles of man and beast" (1972, 116–17). Not only did high-speed scientific and technological innovation risk leaving human beings unable to master their own creations, but humanity now harnessed forms of power and force (i.e. atomic energy) whose mindboggling explosiveness might incinerate them. The results for global politics were far-reaching. No rational relationship between the means and ends of violence obtained when the specter of nuclear warfare threatened all involved parties with total destruction (1972, 139). The historically novel possibility of human extermination meant that "in no period of modern history was civilization more in need of permanent peace and, hence, of a world state" (Morgenthau, 1954: 481). The existing system of sovereign nation states was anachronistic since inter-state warfare risked preparing the way for nuclear warfare (Herz, 1959; 1976; Schuman, 1952a). In the prenuclear era, the quest to set up a global or worldwide polity represented a well-meaning but politically naive utopian aspiration. In the nuclear age, however, it constituted a historical necessity if humankind were to have any real chance of surviving. Although the precise path beyond the existing state system undoubtedly remained treacherous as well, the nuclear revolution demanded a "radical transformation of the existing international society of sovereign nations into a supranational community of individuals," and a corresponding global polity (Morgenthau, 1954: 470; also, Scheuerman, 2009: 135–65). In the existing state system, the risk of nuclear war was simply too great. Responsible political actors had to seek an alternative (Craig, 2003; Deudney, 2007: 244–64).

By the early 1960s, Morgenthau went so far as to advocate a merger of Realism with so-called utopian approaches to international politics. Given the unprecedented existential challenges at hand, international thinkers should join forces with the "great political utopians" who started with a "realistic analysis of the status quo" but then rightly moved on to underline concrete possibilities for building a new global order (1962d: 76–7).

This chapter has tried to retrieve a forgotten moment in recent international political thought, when Progressive Realists outlined a balanced yet ultimately critical view of the nation state and national identity. Their account, I believe, deserves reconsideration in part because it speaks directly to contemporary debates about the nation state's prospects.

In contrast to many present-day intellectuals and activists understandably eager to build a new global order, Progressive Realists were critical of the naive view that the nation state and national political identity represented little more than easily discarded atavistic leftovers. Both had played decisive roles in modern political and social life, and sound reasons remained why political actors might hesitate to surrender them. Notwithstanding its familiar ills, nationalism had contributed majorly to complex and easily overlooked forms of social and political integration on the basis of which some of the key institutional achievements of the modern political world had been constructed. Those hoping to transcend the Westphalian system and the nationally based instantiation of state sovereignty at its core will ultimately need to explain how a postnational replacement for national identity can be successfully secured. In short, any viable model of global reform will have to move beyond what Calhoun has described as the "thin conception of social life, commitment, and belonging" still widespread among proponents of global reform (2003: 96). Global reform can only succeed if both conscious and unconscious forms of postnational social integration can be realized.

Yet unlike defenders of the contemporary nation state, Progressive Realists simultaneously argued that we nonetheless *do* eventually need to transcend it. Under contemporary conditions, nation states to a decreasing degree are able to perform vital economic, political, and military functions; their contributions to social and political disintegration now sometimes outweigh their integrative accomplishments. Economic globalization sometimes debilitates the nation state's ability to oversee social and economic affairs, while the globalization of military and security affairs means that many and perhaps most nation states can no longer sufficiently exercise the core protective task of providing physical security. In stark contrast to those who still attribute a privileged moral status to the nation state,[14] Progressive Realists described how it cripples moral conscience and counteracts praiseworthy efforts to defend universal moral ideals. Perhaps even more effectively than its most recent critics, they creatively explored how the nation state deploys our moral energies in a one-sided and unsatisfactory way. Despite innumerable attempts to pretend otherwise, the nation state clashes with our best moral instincts.

To be sure, one might argue with many details of the arguments recounted above, each of which necessarily involves complex empirical as well as normative issues. Yet the Progressive Realists were surely right to interpret ours as a transitional historical moment in which the nation state was subject to some forms of decay.

Of course, whether or not the existing international system should be jettisoned depends on the answer to another key question: can we plausibly conceive of an appealing institutional alternative to it? If so, how might it be constructed and prove politically viable?

3 REALIST GLOBAL REFORMISM

Most Realists today treat calls for deep reforms to the international system with disdain. Cosmopolitan visions of democratic global governance along the lines advocated by Jürgen Habermas and David Held apparently represent little more than a recipe for global violence (Zolo, 1997). The idea of a world state is at best illusory and at worst the starting point for a global civil war (Waltz, 1979: 112). When they stoop to engage the burgeoning array of reform ideas put forward by normatively minded colleagues, Realists tend to revert to familiar clichés about the perils of "idealism" and "utopianism." Even the European Union, an unprecedented experiment in postnational governance, constitutes nothing new for Realists committed to the tenet that international anarchy makes up a necessary and perhaps desirable state of affairs (Mearsheimer, 1994).

So Ernie's assessment of Realism as fundamentally anti-reformist seems to gain ready confirmation. However, Realists did not always exhibit enmity to global reform. From the 1940s and well into the 1960s, Progressive Realists not only engaged extensively with proponents of radical global reform, but in fact advocated major alterations to the state system. Although still widely downplayed by both contemporary Realists and their reform-oriented (chiefly Cosmopolitan) theoretical rivals, Progressive Realists participated in a lively inter- as well as *intra*-paradigmatic debate about the virtues of global change. This chapter revisits that unfairly neglected moment in the history of twentieth-century international theory; succeeding chapters examine its legacy for present-day debates. Progressive Realists directed their impressive critical ire at what they considered to be misguided and premature reform undertakings, but hardly dramatic global transformation per se. Though differing at times on how to achieve it, they looked with sympathy on calls for postnational government. Their reform ideas, I hope to show, powerfully underlined the necessary social preconditions – what they typically described as supranational society or world community – for viable postnational political structures. Sometimes joining forces with another central European émigré, David Mitrany, they absorbed elements of his functionalist theory to explain how those preconditions might be constructed. Only in the 1960s did Realism's constructive relationship to global reform come to an end, as figures like Kissinger and Waltz abandoned the reformist concerns of a previous generation. Their reasons for doing so, however, remain implausible.

Mid-century Realism remains a rich source to a degree underappreciated even by some auspicious attempts to revisit its reformist impulses (Craig, 2003; Deudney, 2007: 244–64). Unfortunately, present-day theoretical blinders still block a proper view of its accomplishments. Yet the Progressive Realist embrace of international reform should not in fact prove surprising. The dominant figures in the debate recounted here – Carr, Herz, Morgenthau, Niebuhr, Schuman, and Schwarzenberger – were all at least initially tied to the political left. They imported the reformist impulses of mid-century socialism into international theory: their model of global reform envisioned a gradual and evolutionary process which might someday culminate in a systemic break with the international status quo.

Why should we care? The prospect of postnational reform – at both the regional (e.g. European Union) and global level – is again being creatively discussed. Even the idea of the world state seems to be gaining some traction (Craig, 2008; Deudney, 2007; Lu, 2006; Wendt, 2003). In Waltz's imposing shadows, most Realists continue to look askance at global reform. By failing to engage constructively with sophisticated reformist ideas, contemporary Realists betray the impressive contributions of their own rich and in many respects untapped tradition.

World Federalism or Bust

Readers of the left-wing US political journal *The Nation* during January 1942 were probably surprised to find its pages devoted to a spirited debate about the proper contours of a prospective postwar reconstruction of the global order by Niebuhr and Schuman, two up-and-coming international political thinkers. The Japanese, after all, had just bombed Pearl Harbor on 7 December 1941, and thus the US had only been formally at war for little more than a month when Niebuhr published a stinging review of Schuman's *Design for Power: The Struggle for the World* in the 10 January issue, with Schuman heatedly responding in an illuminating exchange in the "Letters to the Editors" section on 24 January (Schuman 1941a; Niebuhr, 1942; Niebuhr and Schuman, 1942). Despite the early stage of open US involvement, both Schuman and Niebuhr seemed remarkably self-assured in their assessments of what the war required. Far-reaching global reform, both agreed, would have to come out of it. The only real question concerned the best way to achieve it.[1]

Typically relegated to the category of obscure mid-century US Realist (Haslam, 2002: 197–8; Lebow, 2003: 14), Schuman in the 1930s and 1940s was in fact a well regarded public commentator on international affairs, a prolific writer (and professor first at the University of Chicago and then Williams College) who wrote extensively for major left and left-liberal journals. Alongside a widely used college textbook on international politics,[2] between 1929 and 1941 Schuman had managed to write an astonishing seven books dealing with US policy towards the Soviet Union, French and German foreign policy, the Weimar Republic, and the rise of fascism, a number of which appeared with major presses and were quickly reprinted (1928; 1931; 1933; 1935; 1937a; 1939a; 1941a; 1941c). His intellectual trajectory in some ways paralleled that of the already more famous theologian Niebuhr. Both were workaholic first-generation German–Americans with modest social backgrounds from the Midwest; both could be identified with what was already gaining attention as a loosely defined "Realist" approach to the study of global affairs; both were left-wingers, with Niebuhr having been active in the Socialist Party, and Schuman a self-described "Liberal" who nonetheless favored socialist economic reforms, and whose at times rather uncritical portrayal of the Soviets garnered him notoriety among independent leftists less forgiving of the crimes of Stalinism.[3] Neither was an orthodox Marxist, though both made creative use of Marxism in developing a radical critique of liberal capitalism, whose impending doom Niebuhr had predicted in the aptly entitled *Reflections on the End of An Era* (1934), and which Schuman marshaled to effective use in a widely read study of fascism, which he in turn tellingly dubbed the "social philosophy and the State-form of the bourgeoisie in the monopolistic epoch of late capitalism" (1935: 480).

Early on, both had advocated forceful action against Nazism, vociferously criticizing the failure of the Western liberal democracies to aid the anti-fascist cause. Both writers also advocated a synthesis of liberal Anglo-American political traditions with collectivist socialism. Key differences also separated them, one of which helps explain Niebuhr's fame and Schuman's relative obscurity in the postwar era. Although both were prescient – or what right-wingers later cynically decried as "premature" – anti-fascists, Schuman's antipathy to Nazism led him early in the game to call for a common front between the Western democracies and Soviet Union.

Of course, given the wartime alliances that later emerged, his position was arguably prophetic. Yet Schuman's hardheaded assessment of the need for far-reaching cooperation with the Soviets tended to go hand-in-hand with a noticeably less hardheaded view of everyday Soviet realities, an error which Niebuhr typically circumvented even during his most radical moments. While Niebuhr later was able to make a name for himself as one of America's leading anti-communist left-liberals, a former radical untainted by totalitarianism, Schuman faced hostile public attacks by the House Un-American Activities Committee and the red-baiting Senator Joseph McCarthy, attacks which he successfully escaped only at the cost of a tarnished reputation (Brinson, 2004: 77, 101–3; Oshinsky, 1983: 125–6). Although he continued teaching at Williams until 1968, Schuman would become something of a black sheep among postwar US political scientists.

Already in the inaugural edition of *International Politics: An Introduction to the Western State System* (1933), Schuman had posited that the only way eventually to circumvent the horrors of modern warfare was to replace international anarchy with a global system of worldwide sovereignty. The establishment of government – i.e. state sovereignty – constituted the sole historically proven answer to lawless violence: global government would eventually have to be created (1933: 823–54). As he proceeded to argue over the course of many decades, a loose political association or even *confederation* of states could never get the job done properly, since sovereignty there remained fundamentally in the hands of member states. Consequently, law and order was precarious because it "must of necessity rely upon good faith on the part of the local authorities ... supplemented by exhortation" (1952a: 427; also, 1932: 149; 1944; 1945; 1946b). However well meaning, the League of Nations constituted a limited instrument for achieving peace. Only a world *federal* system in which the citizenry had delegated well-defined legislative and executive powers to global institutions could secure a worldwide rule of law and lasting security.

Taking existing federal political systems (e.g. Switzerland, and the USA) as useful models, Schuman argued that they alone sufficiently mobilized the requisite coercive capacities while providing room for differentiated and decentralized decision making at the national and local levels. Most global government functions would best remain in the hands of non-federal authorities, as during much of Swiss and US history. Yet a central world government minimally would need to exercise key security functions if common lawmaking and the integrity of the political community as a whole were to be achieved. "In a federation ... the government of the union has power to make law, within such limits as the federal constitution prescribes, with the resulting legislation enforceable on individuals throughout the union through the action of both federal and state agencies of law enforcement and adjudication" (1952a: 427). For Schuman, federal states were superior to conventional unitary nation states (e.g. Italy or France). In contrast to homogenizing tendencies widespread there, federalism offered tried and tested institutional mechanisms for responsibly tackling the exigencies of political and social life on a pluralistic and heterogeneous planet.

Schuman's *Design for Power: Struggle for the World* (1941a) concluded with a stirring reiteration of his life-long advocacy of world government. The aim of the war effort could hardly be the re-establishment of the anarchical system that had plunged humanity into the terrors of a second worldwide conflagration. Given the ongoing world war and the political and social divisions that would likely outlive it, the time for full-scale worldwide federal government was not yet propitious. In the meantime, however, "[l]et America and the British Commonwealth at once proclaim a customs union now and invite all Latin Americans to join. Let America and the British democracies adopt a common currency and a common citizenship ... and establish a provisional federal government with limited but adequate powers to provide for the common defense and general welfare" (1941a: 307).[4] By doing so they might provide a positive example of a functioning supranational federal state, an institutional alternative to the emerging European "new order" dominated by "Fascist Caesars" as well as its Japanese-dominated corollary in Asia, to which they might soon invite others to join. The central issue at hand was not whether the globe would undergo a process of far-reaching political unification, but "who will build that unity, on what foundations and for what purposes" (1941a: 305). It was up to liberal democracies like the US and UK to let humankind know that they were now ready to shape its contours. Down the road, a more inclusive world government could be established, with Schuman apparently hoping for a rough convergence between the liberal democratic West and communist East: the liberal democracies could borrow creatively from the Soviets' economic experiment, while the Soviets should learn to appreciate the value of civil rights, democracy, and political toleration (1946a: xii).[5]

Modern capitalism and technology had generated an intermeshed economic and social universe, or the foundations of what Schuman dubbed "World Society" or, alternately, the global "Great Neighborhood." Yet the economic and technological facts of world society conflicted with an anachronistic state system requiring of nation states that they compete ruthlessly for power and resources. As long as peoples had lived "simply and poorly on their local lands with little business across frontiers," power politics had remained a relatively "harmless sport of kings, politicians, and patriots." In the context of an interdependent world society, however, it had become a "formula for universal ruin" (1941a: 300). Without reform, humankind could no longer benefit from the social and economic advances of world society: the existing state system posed an existential threat to modern social life's most valuable achievements, which – if properly reformed along left-wing lines – could be harnessed to serve humane purposes. *Pace* those who might scoff at his call for an Atlantic federation to be followed by world government, Schuman recalled the example of the US founding, when members of then-disparate British colonies successfully forged a new union despite deep internal divisions. As in the American Revolution, free states might again seek a more intimate federal system in order to defeat well-armed tyrants.

Niebuhr's critical response in *The Nation* is revealing for two reasons. First, he embraced Schuman's call for a novel global polity as in principle the best answer to the pathologies of modern total war. Whatever the faults of his analysis, Schuman had at least identified a desirable *long-term* goal. By the early 1940s, Niebuhr was similarly preoccupied with the question of global reform.[6] Second, Niebuhr's criticisms anticipated the central contours of his main anxieties about increasingly popular models of global reform as they were advanced by global "one-worlders" during the 1940s and early 1950s (Lent, 1955; Mangone, 1951; Wooley, 1988; Wittner, 1993). By doing battle with his fellow Realist Schuman, Niebuhr was able to formulate his provocative, albeit sometimes unwieldy, mix of fundamental moral and political sympathy for radical global reform with skepticism about its short- and perhaps even long-term viability.

First World Community Then World Government

Niebuhr's *Nation* piece praised Schuman for grasping that novel "political instruments of world organization, compatible with the necessities of economic interdependence on a world scale," alone could achieve lasting peace (Niebuhr, 1942: 43). Although identifying his own thinking closely with Realism in a related 1942 essay, he admonished its representatives for failing to grapple with the novelties of the wartime situation and thus neglecting to accept the necessity of new global institutions; in this respect, Schuman's position was superior (1967a [1942]: 208). Another 1943 essay recalled that the balance of power was unable to bring about durable peace. International anarchy was unacceptable, and only a novel global organization could circumvent future world wars (1967c [1943]: 203; also 1967b [1943]).

However, Niebuhr simultaneously accused Schuman of leaving "the important question unanswered," namely how a prospective global government "will not degenerate into tyrannical power." Alluding to burgeoning wartime calls for global reform, Niebuhr added that "every major and minor prophet in the land is talking world federation now." Unfortunately, Schuman had failed to "give us precise specifications on how this stupendous task of world organization is to be achieved," despite its normative and political desirability (1942: 44). As Niebuhr observed in another *Nation* exchange with Schuman in 1946, where the two sparred over Schuman's *Soviet Politics at Home and Abroad* (in which the author repeated his stock defense of global federalism), his writings suffered from "the bewildering habit of ascending to the most rarefied heights of constitutional idealism and then descending to the depths of *Realpolitik* without giving the poor reader a chance to adjust himself to the different levels" (Niebuhr and Schuman, 1946: 383; also, Niebuhr, 1946). How a global constitutional order could emerge out of the harsh facts of worldwide *Realpolitik* elsewhere documented so vividly by Schuman remained unexplained. The brutal realities of the existing state system hardly offered fertile soil for world government. Like too many other reformers, Schuman had succumbed to a crude rationalism: the fact that humanity *ought* to establish a new global order hardly demonstrated its attainability.

Why did Schuman's proposal open the door to worldwide tyranny? The answer was *not* because every world polity was destined to do so. Instead, Niebuhr claimed, the problem was Schuman's failure to see that a new global political system could only follow from a gradual evolutionary process. Despite growing economic and technological interdependence, no worldwide social community presently functioned like those typically found at the national level. Yet successful political organizations everywhere depended on deeply rooted "natural forces of social cohesion" and shared social tissue (Niebuhr and Schuman, 1942: 103; Niebuhr, 1967e [1953]: 216). Schuman overstated the integrative capacities of existing world society, which had not yet became a coherent community in which social ties instantiated far-reaching mutual trust and respect (Niebuhr, 1953a: 16). An international society able to "harmonize vast vitalities, abridge age-old sovereignties, arbitrate between incommensurate interests" had yet to materialize, and to claim otherwise was misleading (1942: 44). Without a vastly more integrated social community than presently found at the global level, no worthwhile global federal system could thrive. Majority rule, for example, made no sense without a far-reaching sense of shared interests and values still absent at the global level (1953a: 19–20). Successful government could never be created by constitutional fiat; state power played only a limited role in ensuring social integration. If a global government *were* set up, it would presently lack the requisite social basis and inevitably find itself forced to rely on heavy-handed authoritarian devices.

Significantly, Niebuhr refused to exclude the possibility that a prospective global society might someday perform essential integrative functions. Yet such future possibilities, he insisted, did nothing to distract from the unsettling present-day fact that economic and technological interdependence coexisted with profound moral, social, and political divisions.

Niebuhr also eviscerated Schuman's recourse to the example of the US founding. Schuman had erroneously built on an Enlightenment-era social contract model of politics that deceptively implied that out of a fictional state of nature individuals or governments could come together and create "either government or community out of whole cloth." No viable government, Niebuhr insisted, had *ever* been created in this way. At times echoing David Hume and Edmund Burke, he saw the social contract as resting on an excessively individualistic and rationalistic conception of politics that obscured the role of historically pregiven organic forces over which individuals possessed limited autonomy.[7] Even the historically idiosyncratic 1787 US founding presupposed the existence of a *prior* political and cultural community which had emerged in the colonial period and then was forged during the American Revolution. The US Constitution tellingly began with a preamble declaring its purpose to be the establishment of a "more perfect union": it built on a *previous* union, and presupposed far-reaching political, moral, and cultural commonalities predating the Philadelphia Convention (1953a: 18–19). Thriving political communities required vertical forces of cohesion, provided by the unifying power of a central state authority, as well as horizontal forces, supplied by factors of conscious as well as unconscious social integration. Horizontal sources, including forms of shared political identity deriving from many familiar sources of national identity (e.g. common ethnicity), depended at least in part on organic ties relatively immune to "conscious political manipulation or control" (1959: 260–1).

Despite the strengths of Niebuhr's critical response to Schuman, it arguably left him at something of a dead end. His exposition oscillated uneasily between an astute reminder of the necessary social preconditions of global government and a more far-reaching quasi-Burkean attack on self-consciously creative institution-building. At times, he implied that global institutions could only emerge more-or-less spontaneously out of a complex and somewhat mysterious social process, over which political actors possessed limited control. At other junctures, he left open the possibility that political actors might actively construct – if not directly, at least *in*directly – a new global order. US foreign aid to the underdeveloped world, for example, was superior to "abstract commitments to ideal and impossible world constitutions" because it contributed concretely to international community "in the making" (1955: 20).

Not surprisingly perhaps, Niebuhr's postwar writings on global reform typically offered few specifics about how political actors might help advance it.[8] Although he repeatedly insisted that the construction of an integrated world community would have to predate a developed global polity, when pressed to explain how this might be accomplished, his comments were often ambivalent.[9] As the Cold War unfolded, Niebuhr instead tended to revert to defending the newly created United Nations against what he described as idealist and "cynical realist" detractors. While challenging international anarchy, the UN had openly acknowledged the harsh realities of global power inequality and sensibly outfitted the Great Powers with special institutional privileges. Yet it also tentatively pointed the way towards a more democratic future global order: it gave weaker states some rudimentary institutional checks over the Great Powers via the General Assembly (1953a; 1967a [1942]; 1967d [1945]).

At an historical juncture when international society remained underdeveloped, this was apparently the best humankind could hope for. The resulting "semi-anarchy" was in any event a noticeable improvement over the prewar international system (1959: 31). To its credit, the UN also offered a bridge between the free and communist worlds. The General Assembly served as a forum "where every particular national interest must meet the test of its compatibility with the unity and order" of other nations (1955: 19). In opposition to those who advocated abolishing the Security Council veto, however, Niebuhr insisted that the veto merely reflected the unfortunate social and political realities of an underdeveloped global community, which no constitutional device could mechanically overcome (1959: 266).[10] For better or worse, extensive institutional alterations would have to await the maturation of global community.

Even if Niebuhr was surely justified in trying to defend the UN against its critics, he had little to say about how it someday might evolve into the global polity a war-torn humankind desperately needed. That task, he seemed to think, was best left to future generations.

In his final major contribution to international political theory, *The Structure of Nations and Empires* (1959), where the issue of the proper relationship between supranational institutions and their requisite organic bases again loomed large, Niebuhr tentatively suggested that the specter of nuclear warfare might provide an opening for those who hoped to build a more robust global order. Fear of mutual annihilation showed that both the free and communist worlds had "one thing in common: preference for life over death," even if was "still too early to predict in what form and

by what arrangements this sense of common humanity may be institutionalized" (1959: 32; also, 266). However, full-scale world statehood remained
at best a distant goal. The best chances for building effective postnational
governance were still found at the regional level, with NATO and the
emerging European Common Market providing constructive examples
(1959: 199–200, 255–57). Only there had something like a coherent postnational community already gained more than an inchoate form.[11]

A Socialist United Europe?

Niebuhr and Schuman were not alone among Progressive Realists in debating the prospects of a postnational postwar order. Across the Atlantic,
E. H. Carr was energetically developing a radical vision of a novel supranational political and social system. Carr's landmark *Twenty Years' Crisis,
1919–1939* had predicted the demise of the nation state, and the author
then followed up on his prophecy with a series of wartime studies sketch-
ing out an ambitious model of continental or regionally based social and
economic governance, to be complemented by a global security system in
which both great and small nations would pool military resources (1942;
1967 [1945]). To those who considered the latter utopian, he pointed to
the successful Allied wartime experience of combining troops from large
and small countries (1967 [1945]: 55). In response to voices skeptical of
the need for cross-border economic planning, Carr proffered a devastating
critique of both traditional liberal capitalism and conventional ideas about
national self-determination. Although it was "natural and imperative for
human beings to combine for various purposes," and this natural proclivity
opened the door to legitimate expressions of national feeling, national and
cultural identities could henceforth best be preserved within the confines
of interlocking economic and military units transcending the provincialism
of existing nation states (1967 [1945]: 59). Nor was the nation state adequately equipped to tackle the supranational demands of contemporary
social and economic affairs. Military innovations also rendered "the whole
concept of strategic frontiers" obsolescent even for relatively large and
powerful states (1967 [1945]: 58). Not even the Great Powers could escape
the harsh realities of a military universe in which airborne projectiles easily
pierced their frontiers.

Carr acknowledged that the Great Powers would still inevitably possess
disproportionate influence in any prospective postnational political order.
Yet they could successfully avoid repeating the sins of the oppressive Nazi
Herrenvolk of wartime German-ruled Europe. His proposed multinational
social and economic units would focus on guaranteeing equal economic

opportunity and full employment as well as eliminating "freedom from want" to generate social and economic equality *within* as well as *between* and *among* national units: only far-reaching economic redistribution could provide sufficiently sturdy social foundations for postnational governance. Nor was this demand politically simple-minded. The demise of the nation state was already pretty much a *fait accompli*; the question at hand was *what* kind of postnational order would replace it, and to which principles and ideals it would subscribe. Radical social reform – indeed: postnational democratic socialism via extensive state planning – could now be realistically pursued because the quest for social justice was pretty much universally shared. In contrast to those who thought that a postwar global *constitutional* order, despite deep global divisions plaguing international affairs, might be constructed on shared *political* and *legal* ideals, Carr thought it more sensible to build on the basis of an emerging universal social and economic consensus – extending from FDR's New Deal to the Soviet Union – to reduce economic inequality and jettison competitive capitalism. In his view, the Soviets represented a revolutionary force in contemporary affairs, and it was to a great extent their achievement to have placed socialist-style economic planning on the agenda everywhere. The task at hand was to meet the challenge by constructing collectivist "forms of social and economic action in which what is valid in individualist and the democratic tradition" was meaningfully preserved (1947: 113).[12] The emerging "new society" would get rid of competitive capitalism and establish both a robust welfare state and economic planning while preserving Western Europe's distinctive contributions to liberty and self-government (1951).

Much of Carr's argument echoed Schuman's. Both married a brand of socialism aspiring to preserve the lasting achievements of Western liberal democracy with a sometimes uncanny ability to overlook Soviet pathologies. Like Schuman, Carr hoped for a fruitful convergence between the systems. Both also took the emergence of the Nazi-dominated European *Grossraum* and its Japanese-dominated Asian corollary as empirical confirmation for the thesis that the nation state was *already* being jettisoned for regionalized political blocs better suited to contemporary social trends. Like many others on the mid-century left, they evinced a strong – and, in hindsight, excessive – faith in bureaucratically organized state economic planning.

Their intellectual disagreements were equally illuminating. Like Schuman, Carr fused a socialist attack on capitalism with a critique of the traditional Westphalian state system. Yet Schuman never convincingly linked the two lines of argumentation, other than simply by implying that international anarchy was somehow inconsistent with the fruits of an interdependent world society, whose reconstruction he envisioned along socialist terms. Why world government necessarily followed from his leftist critique of the global political economy remained unclear. In contrast, Carr consistently linked his defense of new continentally based social and economic units to his overall social and economic diagnosis: ongoing economic transformations gravitated "towards several competing centers of power; and the very complexity of modern life makes for division" (1967 [1945]: 45).

Closer on this matter to Niebuhr, Carr considered world government premature: "the sense of the unity of mankind, sufficient to support the common affirmation of certain universal principles and purposes, is not yet strong enough ... to sustain an organization exercising sovereign and universal authority" (1967 [1945]: 44; also, 1949). Although crucial security matters should be coordinated at the global level, and even though his wartime proposals for a global security system probably went beyond Niebuhr's, Carr deemed it counterproductive to locate the key tasks of modern government in the hands of a worldwide political organization. As a distant long-term goal, world government might be desirable. In the short term it was misleading and potentially irresponsible since humanity still lacked a mature world community. Even though such a community had already begun to develop, it lacked the coherence and integrative capacities of communities of more limited size.

Successful national communities were able for the most part to apply basic moral and legal norms of equality and reciprocity to all members. On the global scale, Carr argued, this still remained unrealistic given massive military and material inequalities between and among states. An effective global community, like its national counterpart, required a degree of not just legal but also de facto power equality (1964 [1939]: 162; 1949: 58–60). The fact that discrimination in favor of one's own country "is accepted as a normal and legitimate principle" in foreign policy spoke volumes about the world community's underdeveloped status (1949: 60). In effectively integrated national communities, at crucial junctures "the good of the whole takes precedence over the good of the part" (1964 [1939]: 162). While viable national communities were able to rely on a host of formal as well as informal mechanisms to force individuals and social groups to subordinate private to collective interests, the nascent world community was still incompetent to do so. Until greater real-life equality could be achieved at the global level, one should not expect too much from it.

Carr's paramount contribution to the Realist debate on global reform perhaps lies elsewhere, however. As noted, Niebuhr had countered Schuman's version of Realist one-worldism, but only at the cost of stumbling onto a programmatic dead-end: even if global government was an attractive ultimate goal, it remained unclear what its defenders could do to bring it about. Could global community and perhaps someday a global polity be actively created?

Carr answered in the affirmative. Regionally based political units preoccupied with social and economic undertakings, he argued, were the best place to begin creating postnational governance's necessary social tissue. Reform should focus on helping to create the underlying power (and especially material) equality indispensable to government "beyond the nation state." In a fascinating section of *Nationalism and After*, Carr also endorsed key features of Mitrany's functionalist theory of international organization.[13]

Perhaps Carr encountered Mitrany in London during the war years, while the latter was based at the Foreign Office and the former wrote for *The Times*. In any event, Carr was clearly familiar with the broad outlines of Mitrany's functionalism. A central European Jew with a left-wing background, Mitrany by the early 1940s was already energetically outlining a gradualist model for international reform, whose main tenets he sketched out in a series of short publications and then in the programmatic *A Working Peace System* (1975; 1946; also, Navari, 1995). Like Carr, Mitrany worried about the tendency in the dominant discourse of international reform to downplay the salience of national identities. He was similarly unconvinced by most proposals for a global federation: top-down models of constitutional reform depended on an excessive faith in formal-legal devices while obscuring the centrality of underlying social and economic processes. Also like Carr, Mitrany thought that a model of global reform could draw its inspiration from recent social and economic experiments. During an extended stay in the US, Mitrany had decided that Franklin Roosevelt and the New Dealers had sensibly avoided pursuing unwieldy formal constitutional changes to the US system,[14] instead opting to build creative new constellations of decision making, set up in response to down-to-earth social and economic needs, which might over time decisively revolutionize the political system's basic operations. A careful student of one of the New Deal's major accomplishments, the Tennessee Valley Authority (TVA), Mitrany praised the New Dealers for tackling the practical exigencies of economic development in the poor south with new institutional devices (i.e. a massive federally owned corporation) that effectively transformed the division of labor between the national and state governments. Yet they wisely did so without pursuing express constitutional changes probably unachievable given the rigidities of US federalism.

In his view, the institutional pragmatism of the New Deal provided a template for international reform: "by linking authority to a specific activity" international organizations could decisively "break away from the traditional link between authority and a definite territory," the fundamental presupposition not only of the modern state system but also of many proposals for "either an association or federation of nations" (1946: 6). Institutionalized cross-border cooperation on a variety of down-to-earth social and economic tasks "would help the growth of such positive and constructive common work, of common habits and interests," ultimately making national borders anachronistic "by overlaying them with a natural growth of common activities and common administrative tasks" (1946: 35).

Though he oddly neglected to mention the name of its chief architect, Carr in *Nationalism and After* similarly praised the trend towards establishing cross-border institutions oriented towards concrete social and economic functions; here was a practical method by means of which nation states might pool resources to combat a growing array of supranational social and economic challenges. Best of all, this was no pie-in-the-sky utopian dream: "a vast number of new functional organizations have been created," and given the exigencies of postwar social and economic existence, they would continue to proliferate (1967 [1945]: 48). The functionalists were right, Carr declared, to highlight the simple insight that international organizations set up for concrete purposes – he mentioned the European railway union and international commission regulating the Danube – would inevitably take institutional manifestations no less diverse than the myriad regulatory tasks they were supposed to handle. Yet the resulting "multiplicity of authorities and diversity of loyalties" might perform a favorable role in counteracting ominous trends towards excessive political centralization (1967 [1945]: 49). Functionalism offered a fruitful approach by means of which a unified socialist Europe could pursue far-reaching social and economic regulation *without* succumbing to totalitarianism. One flaw with models of global federalism was their fidelity, as Mitrany had similarly underscored, to the rigid institutional illusion of "one size fits all." The messy institutional complexity of emerging functional organizations alarmed reformers who preferred neat constitutional schemes. Instead they should have celebrated the appearance of a rich multiplicity of international organizations, set up to pursue specific technical and economic tasks, as a viable instrument for preserving pluralism and liberty:

> Organizations for different purposes can be built up on different international groupings whose scope will vary with the functions they perform; and this variety and multiplicity is one of the most important safeguards against

the accumulation of exclusive powers and exclusive loyalties under the control of the great multinational units. (Carr 1967 [1945]: 62)

Functional organization contributed to the creation of a postnational social and economic order which alone might successfully undergird stable political organization beyond the nation state. Simultaneously it checked potentially dangerous centralizing tendencies, including the pathological side-effects of a globe likely to be carved up into competing regional power blocs. A planet divided into rival multinational blocs might simply serve as a breeding ground for "a new imperialism which would be simply the old nationalism writ large and would almost certainly pave the way for more titanic and more devastating wars" (1967 [1945]: 53). Because functional organizations potentially transcended the boundaries of emerging regional blocs, they contributed to the creation of social tissue between and among them, and thus might help mix the cement for the foundations of an eventual world union.

Functionalism and the "Future of the Civilized World"

Even Carr's most sophisticated commentators have missed the importance functionalism at least briefly played in his reflections on global reform (Jones, 1998; Cox, 2000). Fortunately for postwar Realism, Hans Morgenthau probably did *not*. Despite his scathing 1948 *World Politics* review article on Carr's writings,[15] Morgenthau's model of global reform mirrored Carr's as formulated in *Nationalism and After*, one of the books discussed in his review (1948a).

Politics Among Nations: The Struggle for Power and Peace famously declared that a "world state is unattainable in our world, yet indispensable for survival" in light of the terrors of contemporary warfare (1948b: 419). Hiroshima and Nagasaki had demonstrated unequivocally that only a world state could secure lasting peace and perhaps human survival. Always more skeptical of attempts to envision federal systems like Switzerland or the United States as models for global reform, Morgenthau's theoretical position nonetheless mirrored Schuman's in one key fashion: sovereignty would have to be concentrated somehow at the global level, as it previously had at the national level, in order to secure global law and order (1954: 482–5). In agreement with Carr and Niebuhr, however, he vigorously opposed the claim that a world state could be realized anytime in the foreseeable future. Presently humanity possessed a "society of sovereign nations," in which norms and social practices (including international mores, ethics, and customs) offered a social basis for *inter*state affairs. A prospective world state, however, would require both a more intensive as well as extensive supranational society comprising all human beings and capable of buttressing global decision making in far-reaching ways (1954: 479). Contemporary proposals for a world state not only conveniently downplayed existing political and social divides (e.g. between liberal democracy and communism), but they suffered from a crude statism which exaggerated the sovereign state's ability to bring about political and social integration. Relying on John Stuart Mill's famous account of the necessary preconditions of workable government, Morgenthau announced that humanity was not yet ready to pass Mill's tests. Most people remained unwilling to accept world government, seemed unprepared to fulfill its basic purposes, and were probably unable to defend it (1954: 478). How many Russians or Americans would turn their weapons against national compatriots to enforce a prospective system of world law?

In stable nation states, Morgenthau pointed out, formal state institutions were able to translate public opinion into policy and thereby sometimes bring about peaceful social change. Unless supported by public opinion and an underlying consensus, however, even the best designed political and legal devices were doomed when confronted with the supreme test of effective government: "to change the distribution of power inside society without jeopardizing the orderly and peaceful processes upon which the welfare of society depends" (1954: 415). Within existing liberal democracies, the interplay of social and political forces was responsible for altering public opinion, with its shifting currents sometimes producing successful legislative and judicial changes. The process as a whole only worked because participants were committed to the basic rules of the game. Rough agreement at the level of general principles, as well as a shared expectation that some modicum of justice might be realized with all social groups possessing "a chance to make themselves heard," were crucial (1954: 473). Recourse to coercive state power was minimized because political actors heeded even those laws with which they disagreed. Parallels at the level of supranational or world society would someday have to emerge if a world state were to garner a sufficient social basis. Because any world state set up at the present would necessarily lack the requisite social foundations, it could only take the form of "a totalitarian monster resting on feet of clay," requiring "complete discipline and loyalty among ... millions of soldiers and policemen needed to enforce its rule over an unwilling humanity" (1954: 482).

In contradistinction to Niebuhr, however, and in analytic alliance with Carr, Morgenthau insisted that political actors could take active steps to build supranational society: world statehood represented more than a vague long-term goal about which one might longingly fantasize. While Carr had only briefly discussed functionalism, Morgenthau gave Mitrany's toolkit a major role in his alternative story of how political actors could establish the social preconditions of world statehood. As Morgenthau enthusiastically noted in a laudatory preface to the 1966 US reissue of Mitrany's *Working Peace System*, "the future of the civilized world is intimately tied to the future of the functional approach to international organization" (1966: 11). In a key section of *Politics Among Nations*, he endorsed Mitrany's functionalist model of international reform and applied its tenets to the problems of European integration, describing it with ever heightened enthusiasm in the book's many subsequent editions (1954: 497–9). To an even greater degree than Carr, Morgenthau considered functionalism a path breaking strategy for advancing the cause of social integration at the post-national level. If nation states worked together in pursuing concrete (i.e. mostly economic and technical) tasks, inventing along the way creative but eminently practical supranational institutions, the building blocks of global order could be laid. Over time such cooperation might generate new supranational forms of social practice, shared norms, and complexes of shared interests; the roots of global governance might be secured. For Morgenthau, as for Carr, the central task facing global reformers was not the transfer of national sovereignty by constitutional formulas, but instead piecemeal reform capable of transforming it by stealth.

Carr had married functional organizations to traditional socialist-style state economic planning. Always more moderate politically, and no socialist in the conventional mid-century sense of the term, Morgenthau broke the chain between functionalism and socialist planning. As he suggested in a revealing 1944 essay, grandiose visions of planning rested on an overly rationalistic vision of social life which underplayed its sheer unpredictability. In contrast to free marketers like Hayek who tossed *any* role for rational social or economic planning out the window, however, Morgenthau simultaneously gave it a crucial albeit circumscribed role: planning could work only if practitioners recognized that it provided "not the one correct solution for all the problems of social life, but a series of alternative and hypothetical patterns, one of which will supply the rational foundation for an approximate solution of a specific social problem" (1944: 184–5). Planning might prove fungible if one accepted its limitations.

Morgenthau's fame, and Carr's relative neglect during the Cold War in the United States, can surely be attributed at least in part to this difference. Morgenthau's modest conception of planning meshed well with the New Deal and postwar US left-liberal visions of a "mixed economy," whereas Carr's was much more closely linked to traditional socialist ideals.[16] Whatever Morgenthau's argument consequently gained in political appeal, however, it lost in social radicalism. Unlike Carr, Morgenthau's postwar writings consistently placed questions of cross-border economic distribution on the back burner. Supranational society, it seemed, would somehow have to be built without economic redistribution between and among nation states. While Carr quite plausibly argued that a viable world community presupposed greater de facto material equality, Morgenthau's version of Progressive Realism ultimately had little to offer impoverished peoples around the globe.[17]

Backlash Against Functionalism

Back in London, the independent-minded jurist Schwarzenberger was busily throwing a wrench into Progressive Realism's neat reform model. A forceful advocate of global federalism, Schwarzenberger doubted that Mitrany's functionalism could play the positive role ascribed to it by Carr and Morgenthau.

Schwarzenberger's contributions to the mid-century Realist debate on reform were particularly impressive. Nonetheless, they are altogether forgotten today. His critical views about existing international law and organizations always made him something of an oddball among international jurists committed to their promotion, while his enthusiasm for global reform was increasingly out of sync with postwar political scientists not only to a growing degree hostile to the traditional study of law, but also to reformist ideas like those he embraced. Nonetheless, the primarily US-based scholars whom I have been describing as Progressive Realists were intimately familiar with Schwarzenberger's writings, in part because they meshed in decisive ways with theirs. Yet he never shared their functionalist sympathies.

Unlike the somewhat loose ways in which other Progressive Realists employed categories like "community" and "society," his reflections built on a sophisticated understanding of the easily misunderstood social theory of Ferdinand Tönnies.[18] Following Tönnies, Schwarzenberger offered an admirably precise distinction between "society" and "community," with the former referring to loose social relations in which actors pursued instrumental and oftentimes selfish aims, and the latter to social ties in which relations of solidarity were deeply rooted and actors readily pursued common tasks. Examples of the former were offered by joint-stock companies and the international status quo, in which power politics predominated and only minimal ethical standards could be identified. The latter were potentially exemplified by institutions like the family, nation, or church. However, "society" and "community" were pure ideal-types. In real life, only mixtures or hybrids could be identified (1943b: 90). Even the unfortunate global status quo contained nascent community ingredients. Echoing Niebuhr, Schwarzenberger argued that the construction of a full-scale global polity presupposed the realization there of vastly more far-reaching community elements. A global federal order, an aspiration he endorsed as early as 1941, could flourish only in a well-integrated global community with which social actors readily identified and interpreted as valuable in itself and not simply as a means towards selfish ends. Since a fully developed global community remained distant, global federalism remained correspondingly far-off (1941: 401–35).

Nevertheless, Schwarzenberger never shied away from elaborating on its prospective institutional attributes.[19] Like Schuman, he believed that only global federalism could preserve the rule of law and tame interstate violence. Stop-gap institutional measures along the lines of the League of Nations (and later, he argued, the United Nations) necessarily failed to do so. Yet a prospective global state was "not necessarily identical with the idea of international standardization, a uniform world association which turns out world citizens like Ford cars" (1941: 401). Switzerland and the United States demonstrated that federalism could deal successfully with pluralism. Since national identity would and indeed should not dissipate in the future, the difficulty at hand was to find an institutional pattern that did justice to national particularities while allowing for binding shared decision making as well as the common supranational loyalties essential to it. Global federalism, Schwarzenberger frequently reiterated in the face of changing intellectual fashions, held out the best chance of solving the enigmas at hand (1941: 401–35; 1951: 767–816).

Also *contra* the more cautious Niebuhr, Schwarzenberger believed that major steps could immediately be taken towards creating a new global order. If any supranational federal system were to succeed, three conditions would have to be met. First, enough people would have to be convinced that it alone could fulfill basic functions of governance. Second, at least for the short term any federation could only be entrusted with clearly delineated activities (i.e. foreign policy and defense). Third, federation would only thrive if it rested on substantial community elements: there would have to be a sufficient modicum of shared values and preexisting institutions (1951: 805; 1957).

Where then were such preconditions already met? Not yet on the global level: a federation between liberal capitalist and communist states was both unthinkable and undesirable. Despite his occasionally dry lawyer-like tone, even during the darkest days of the Cold War Schwarzenberger did not hesitate to outline a bold proposal for an intermediate Atlantic Union, a federal union spanning the Atlantic world to include the United States, Western Europe, British Commonwealth, and perhaps some Latin and South American countries as well.[20] On both sides of the Atlantic countries shared common religious and moral values. They were also committed to democracy, the rule of law, and human rights, as well as the unfinished quest to reconcile capitalism with the welfare state and social rights. "Without unduly forcing the pace, such an Atlantic Union could immediately take over the functions of foreign policy, defense and protection of democratic institutions, the rule of law and human rights in all the member states" (1951: 807; also, 1957). Mill's tests for workable government – which Schwarzenberger considered sound (1941: 404) – could be successfully met by a union of welfare state liberal democracies.

Schwarzenberger underscored the advantages of his Atlantic Union not only vis-à-vis the Westphalian status quo but also in relation to the possibility of a European political community, already the subject of widespread academic as well as popular discussion in the early 1950s. For France and the smaller European states (for example, Netherlands and the Scandinavian countries) worried about the prospects of German resurgence, an Atlantic Union offered some advantages: German power could be checked more effectively within a larger and more inclusive Atlantic than a narrow European union. As for Germany itself, its irrepressible "driving power and dynamism" could be productively reemployed to serve supranational rather than national purposes. As members of an Atlantic Union, its citizens might finally hope to "be freed from the signs of Cain, which, as of yet, still marks ... the butchers of Auschwitz, Belsen and Ravensbrück" (1951: 808). Even a Great Power like the United States could gain from an Atlantic federation since it reduced the prospect that some allies – e.g. the members of an emerging European Community – might someday again become political and military rivals. Most important perhaps, a federated Atlantic Union held out for peoples everywhere the appealing "vista and hope of a world-wide brotherhood with ideals and standards of its own," a proud multinational community not only in possession of impressive military strength, but offering a real-life model of a free federation of peoples, committed to liberal democracy and social justice, while courageously opposed to Soviet tyranny. "In a frightened and disillusioned age," Schwarzenberger mused, "nothing is so impressive and convincing as the living example," which only his proposed union could provide to a war-weary world (1951: 814). Over time, he speculated, as its members learned to rub shoulders with each other, its governance functions might expand.

A federal Atlantic Union need not await the completion of functionalist-style social and economic integration, however. Functionalists like Mitrany had gotten things backwards. In his first major book, Schwarzenberger had criticized Carr for claiming that international economic cooperation might pave the way for political reform (1941: 378, 429). Carr had misleadingly relied on the idiosyncratic example of the world wars, when functional experiments flourished chiefly because of the existence of a common life-or-death political foe. Absent an existential political crisis, functionalism often foundered. Functionalism's friends ignored the primacy of politics: "[I]nternational analogies to the Tennessee Valley scheme only become practical possibilities if, when, and to the extent to which" nations drew closer together in familiar political and military arenas (1951: 769). Mitrany had hoped that functionalist reform might "change the substance of politics to move it from considerations of the flag, of territory, and national prestige to questions of welfare and cooperation" (Taylor, 1975: xxiii.). Schwarzen-berger found little real-life evidence that it was doing so. In a massive survey of ongoing functionalist experiments both under the auspices of the UN and in Western Europe, Schwarzenberger tallied up a sobering score sheet (1951: 565–612; 1964: 420–48). Functionalism worked well where substantial community elements *already* existed (1951: 565). However, amid tense power animosities even modest attempts to undertake joint technical and economic tasks failed, as numerous examples from the UN attested: the International Labor Organization (ILO), for example, and the UN's Food and Agriculture Organization were only able to fulfill minimal regulatory tasks when they kept their fingers away from the chess board of global power politics (1951: 597). When technical issues directly impacted Great Power rivalry, functionalist reform was stymied. Function-alism seemed to succeed only where perhaps unnecessary and conditions were ripe for global federation (for example, in Western Europe), but failed when needed.

World Community and World Statehood: An Interactive Relationship?

Other Progressive Realists similarly put a damper on functionalist-inspired reform expectations. Although cautiously noting that any discussion of "the details of a more integrated world structure, such as problems of representation and voting procedures" remained premature, Herz by the late 1950s was also promoting the eventual establishment of a global politi-cal order (1959: 302). He envisioned functionalism as contributing "a good deal to the solution of problems in a truly universalist fashion, since today, in so many fields the technical prerequisites for success exist, frequently for the first time in history" (1959: 329). When properly employed, functional organization might aid in the direction of moving towards the "universalist" social orientation that played in his conceptual framework an analytic role akin to what Niebuhr and others had called world community. Cross-border cooperation on technical and economic projects might over time affect even those activities associated with classical power politics "through a modification of attitudes resulting in an abatement of nationalist exclusions" (1959: 342). Cooperative attitudes and practices that emerged in relatively down-to-earth technical spheres could spill over and help mitigate otherwise deeply conflict-laden facets of interstate affairs.

However, Herz followed Schwarzenberger in worrying that functionalism's exponents made things too easy. They overstated what their approach could accomplish, naively believing that it was a cure-all for every imaginable political conflict; at least implicitly, the criticism was also directed at Morgenthau (and perhaps Carr), who had highlighted functionalist virtues but not its vices.[21] "It would be quite unrealistic ... to believe that the future of the world is safe because of the existence of – relatively speaking – a mere handful of men and women in New York, Geneva, and other places scattered around the word, whose services are devoted to problems of world food supplies, health standards in underdeveloped areas, and similar tasks" (1959: 326). Functional organization had already generated a class of international civil servants. Even if some of their noteworthy accomplishments recalled the Hegelian vision of a public-minded state bureaucracy, they exhibited particularism and narrow-mindedness. Cynics might plausibly "even define functionalism as a theory that defends the power positions of international bureaucracies" (1959: 327). Although struggling to distance himself from this assessment, Herz fretted that functionalism offered too little too late in a world facing the specter of nuclear warfare.

Functionalism could only aid in the construction of global political order when "based upon a broader foundation of public support and public attitude" (1959: 330). Yet this would necessarily "depend on the emergence of a universalist 'groundswell,' from which the feeling for the necessity to act in a common world interest would impose itself with compelling force upon people and people's minds" (1959: 331). Akin to Schwarzenberger, Herz worried that functionalism underplayed the primacy of politics. Functionalism might help create the building blocks of a new world order, but only a new universalist political and social awareness – and political action based on it – could put the blocks together in the right way. Unfortunately, the prospects that humankind's slowly emerging sense of "universal concern" might effectively buttress political reform seemed remote (1959: 338–57).

A complementary albeit somewhat more boisterous note of caution about functionalism was found in Schuman's most impressive book, his massive *Commonwealth of Man: An Inquiry into Power Politics and World Government* (1952a), published with a foundation grant from the world federalist movement, with which Schuman had become closely linked in the public eye.[22] The volume was obviously intended in part as a retort to Niebuhr's criticisms of Schuman's early Realist one-worldism. Along the way, however, it also countered those who downplayed functionalism's limitations. Free of the communist fellow-traveling that had plagued earlier writings,[23] Schuman flatly acceded to Niebuhr's original criticism that democratic world government was hardly on the immediate political horizon: the Cold War indeed rendered its imminent establishment impossible. Yet he still railed against Niebuhr's view that a world community necessarily *preceded* constitutional and institutional reform: historical experience suggested that "organic cohesion and unity were the slow consequence and gradual result of common [political] agreement" (1952a: 471). State building and constitutional craftsmanship constituted more than the passive offspring of gradual quasi-Burkean social evolution. They often played a decisive role in actively bringing about social integration. The relationship between world government and world community was an interactive one, in which each productively contributed to the other's success. A forceful popular movement – like the anti-nuclear one-worlders – could in fact help engender the necessary measure of social integration. A lively debate about its necessity was apparently one way to plant its political and social roots (1952a: 472–3).[24] Schuman also accused Niebuhr of overstating the requisite moral and cultural homogeneity of any future global state. To be sure, a global federal state would have to rest on some modicum of basic social consensus. Yet by the mid-twentieth century "all of contemporary mankind ... shares a greater store of common purposes, practices, and aspirations than ever before in the experience of the species" (1952a: 472). Apparently, the social cement for global governance was already being properly mixed.

If Realists were serious about the world government, they would have to join arms with so-called idealistic proponents of global institutional change. The Realists' proper role in the movement would presumably be to temper the naivety of its unschooled enthusiasts. Of course, diplomacy, collective security, and other intermediate devices might temporarily preserve the peace amid "an ever-fluctuating system of rival sovereignties, unequal in fighting capacity and dedicated to the pursuit of security and power" (1952a: 419). But in the final instance only a permanent termination of the power game among rival sovereigns – in short: world government – could spare humanity the horrors of nuclear war.

A lengthy section devoted to functionalism noted that "as a highway toward unity and peace" it was "a road well traveled and well worth traveling," but not because a "blessed destination lies at journey's ends" (1952a: 336). Schuman's global federalist "blessed destination" would ultimately need political craftsmanship and mass politics to bring it about. The real-life results of existing functionalist organization remained decidedly mixed. On a planet plagued by massive inequalities and explosive power divides even seemingly uncontroversial cross-border technical and economic matters too often proved contentious. Although functionalist-style experiments at European integration offered hopeful signs, "only future [political] decisions" could reveal what would come of them (1952a: 326–7; also, 1951). The best evidence for the limitations of functionalism in politically charged matters was the sad fate of the postwar Lilienthal – Acheson proposal to place the regulation of atomic power in supranational hands, which – as Schuman accurately noted – had been modeled partly along functionalist lines.[25] "Common interest in avoiding the suicide of the human race, it might have been supposed, would have been sufficient to foster global agreement to take the whole issue out of the arena of power politics and make it a problem of administration" (1952a: 341). Yet power politics there had destructively blocked sensible reform, as it would elsewhere, unless the fundamental rules of the state system were reshuffled. To do so, Schuman reiterated, required a forceful expression of common political will.

While Niebuhr had guffawed at his youthful appeal to the US constitutional convention, the mature Schuman stuck to his guns: the global federal vision indeed rested on the belief, shared by the US founders, that legitimate government alone derives from "an act of will and discussion and compromise and solemn compacts one with another" (1952a: 477). When push came to shove, Niebuhr was nothing more than a modern-day Anti-Federalist, while only Schuman and his one-world activist allies remained true to the noble Federalist legacy of the US founding (1952a: 468).

The Apex of Realist Reformism

In a 1964 essay originally appearing in the *New York Times Sunday Magazine*, Morgenthau effectively endorsed key Realist criticisms of functionalism. His "Future of Europe" again praised functionalism for helping to supply "the indispensable material foundations for the political unification of Europe," with the author describing unity as a desirable goal. But Morgenthau now qualified his predictable enthusiasm for functionalism and European unification. Functionalists in Europe had successfully created common economic and technological interests, protected and promoted by common institutions. These common interests, to be fully realized and to be protected from the ever present threat of disintegration, require common political institutions. The functionalists have provided the incentive for the creation of such institutions, but they have been unable to provide the institutions. (1970: 337)

Furthermore, functionalists were wrong to suggest that "the political unification of Europe will somehow take care of itself," and that qualitative changes in European politics might automatically result from "the quantitative accumulation of functional European communities." If Europeans were in fact to exploit the fruits of supranational functional organization, the "jump from national to European sovereignty must be made by an act of will," an express political decision that alone would make it possible to coordinate the divergent interests generated by functionalism and keep "recalcitrant members in check" (1970: 337).

In effect, Morgenthau conceded that functionalism was necessary but insufficient to the development of effective supranational polities. Functionalism could only flourish within the confines of common political and legal institutions it helped to generate, but whose creation ultimately transcended its developmental logic. During this juncture in his intellectual trajectory, Morgenthau in fact became noticeably more sympathetic towards precisely those calls for global government he had sometimes previously attacked. During the early 1960s, he could be heard waxing as eloquent about the perils of nuclear war and the necessity of regional and ultimately world government as the more radical Schuman. Even though he occasionally seemed ashamed by his mature idealistic indiscretions, he had joined the idiosyncratic ranks of Realist one-worldism (Scheuerman, 2009: 135–64).

Nonetheless, the Progressive Realist debate on global reform pretty much came to an end in the mid-1960s,[26] as its main figures turned their political energies to the Vietnam War, which they opposed. To be sure, the Progressive Realists had by no means developed a fully developed model for peaceful global reform. However, its core features were by then clear enough. First, Progressive Realists sympathized strongly with demands for new political units "beyond the nation state" at the regional and ultimately global levels. No single factor motored their reformist impulses: deeply rooted moral anxieties about national egoism, economic globalization, growing social interdependence resulting from technological change, as well as the rise of modern industrialized (and total) warfare, and of course the nuclear revolution, all encouraged them to insist on the nation state's unattractive and ever more anachronistic character. Even otherwise excellent accounts like Campbell Craig's which emphasize only one of these factors (e.g. nuclear weaponry) risk distorting a messier and more interesting story (2003).

Second, Progressive Realists sometimes envisioned Mitrany's functionalist model of international organization as a practical strategy for developing a mature world community. Even Schuman, after all, conceded that functionalism might strengthen the global Great Neighborhood about whose maturity he was always more hopeful than his colleagues. Moreover, such a world community would have to be able to exercise extensive integrative tasks. Otherwise, postnational government would inevitably take on authoritarian features. To be sure, Progressive Realists never developed a full-fledged theory of political and social integration, or a satisfactory account of the ways in which supranational society or world community might contribute to it. With the notable exception of Schwarzenberger, they often seemed oblivious to the ways in which their ideas touched on those of major sociological thinkers (e.g. Tönnies) directly relevant to their own concerns. Nonetheless, their reflections remain timely.[27] Like more recent writers, they at least pointed to the need for a richer sociological analysis of the underpinnings of global politics (Wendt, 1999). They hardly subscribed to a simplistic state-centered billiard-ball model of international politics, along the lines commonplace among recent Realists, in which the centrality of the international system's social bases is underplayed or badly misconstrued. Unfortunately, even otherwise sympathetic attempts to redeploy Realism for the sake of contemporary global reform miss the nuanced character of their reflections on the proper social preconditions of viable global governance. They offer far more than a well-meaning albeit anachronistic version of nuclear one-worldism (Deudney, 2007: 244–64).[28]

Third, Progressive Realists recognized that only conscious political action could eventually create continental or regional governments and then – perhaps someday – a world government. For most of them, regionalized political and economic integration represented a stepping stone to more ambitious global-level integration. They differed, of course, in their individual assessments about *when* postnational governments might best be established, as well about *how* the requisite expression of political will might best manifest itself, with (the World Federalist) Schuman tending to show the greatest optimism, and (the sometime Burkean) Niebuhr always remaining comparatively skeptical. Disagreements also remained about the proper role of postnational legal innovation: some Progressive Realists seemed to believe that supranational society or world community would have to *precede* far-reaching postnational institutional and especially constitutional reform, while others more plausibly envisioned the relationship between supranational society and institutions as dynamic and interactive. All of them rightly rejected the view that cross-border economic and technical cooperation willy-nilly would produce a new global order.

The Demise of Progressive Realism

In hindsight, perhaps the most striking feature of the intellectual history I have recounted in this chapter is its unfamiliarity. Contemporary Realists, at the very least, seem uninterested in the reformist facet of their own intellectual heritage, despite the homage regularly paid to Carr, Morgenthau, Niebuhr and others. Why did serious and constructive discussions about global reform vanish from Realist discourse especially in US political science?

The answer is a complicated one. Political factors – including the rigidities of the Cold War, and the good fortune that the nuclear war rightly feared by Progressive Realists and others never happened – played major roles. The extent to which Realists gained influence during the postwar era both in Washington policy circles and the academy also seems to have depended to some extent on their ability to jettison left-leaning reformist impulses in favor of more conservative views which sometimes mirrored Bismarckian *Realpolitik*. In short, the Cold War contributed to the hegemony of an institutionally and politically conservative Realism.

The controversial political figure of Henry Kissinger looms large in this story. Kissinger was and indeed remains a profoundly conservative thinker whose heroes were always the nineteenth-century figures Metternich and Bismarck, whom he frequently eulogized (1954; 1957; 1968; also, Hoffmann, 1978: 33–100). Although a refugee from Nazi Germany, the avant-garde intellectual and political currents of the Weimar left passed him by. Born in 1923 he was a mere youngster when Weimar collapsed and a teenager in 1938 when his family escaped to New York City. After serving in the US military, Kissinger was able to take advantage of the GI Bill to study at Harvard. His massive undergraduate thesis, *The Meaning of History: Reflections on Spengler, Toynbee and Kant* (1951), rejected Kant's philosophy of history, though not his moral theory, with Kissinger quite correctly noting that the conceptual links between the two features of Kant's philosophy were at best tenuous. Revealingly, Kissinger seems to have concluded that his critique of the foundations of Kant's philosophy of history simultaneously doomed the Enlightenment philosopher's closely related defense of a pacific federation of republics: even though readers will search in vain for a satisfactory critical discussion, Kissinger was always disdainful of Kant's cosmopolitanism. A second implication of the critique of Kant was Kissinger's apparent belief in the existence of a palpable gap between morality and individual conscience, on the one hand, and the spheres of history (and politics), on the other, with his surprisingly spiritual and overtly religious exegesis of Kant rejecting the possibility of firmly realizing morality *within* history and politics. For good reason, commentators have seen this analytic move as crucial to understanding the roots of Kissinger's morally impoverished Realism (Dicksen, 1978).[29] His doctoral dissertation, *A World Restored* (1957), then offered a flatly revisionist account of especially Count Metternich, the arch-conservative statesman who dominated the Congress of Vienna and rolled back the Napoleonic Wars as well as the tides of liberalization and democratization unleashed by the French Revolution. The main contours of Kissinger's conservative Realism – a deep nostalgia for nineteenth-century diplomacy welded to profound skepticism about modern mass democracy, socialism, and global reform[30] – were by then clear enough.

At least within US academia, greater responsibility for the demise of Progressive Realism can probably be attributed to the influence of Kenneth Waltz, who exploded into the Realist ranks in the late 1950s and 1960s, and who subsequently played a huge role in reorienting it away from some of the preoccupations of his predecessors (Craig 2003: 117–73). What Kissinger accomplished for Realism policy making, Waltz did for the social sciences: Realism abandoned its reformist impulses and became institutionally and morally complacent.

Like Niebuhr and Schuman, Waltz came from a socially modest German–American family from the Midwest (Halliday and Rosenberg, 1998). One of his teachers at Columbia University, whom he thanks in the preface to *Man, the State, and War*, was Franz L. Neumann, the refugee German – Jewish Marxist who knew Morgenthau from their Weimar days, when both had practiced labor law in the same office run by Hugo Sinzheimer (1959: iii). So the young Waltz might have been expected to build on the reformist and politically radical impulses of mid-century Realism. Instead, he rejected them.

A number of factors were decisive in leading Waltz to accept "the existence of an anarchical international structure as a fact of political life" (Craig, 2003: 129). Most obviously, he argued for a rigid positivist delineation of scientific from normative inquiry. This move – which has been widely and effectively criticized (Ashley, 1981; Craig, 2003; Oren, 2009) – extinguished existential and moral anxieties about the pathologies of the existing state system from the confines of mainstream Realism.[31] Waltz was also always more sanguine about the political and institutional impli-

cations of the nuclear revolution. While his left-leaning Realist predecessors generally believed that nuclear weapons constituted a radical novelty
in human affairs pointing towards the necessity of a new global order,
Waltz instead has repeatedly emphasized the fruitful stabilizing role of
nuclear weapons.[32]

Just as important is the revealing critical argument made – in my view,
unconvincingly – about global reform in Waltz's first book, *Man, the State,
and War,* and which he has periodically repeated. Waltz curtly declared in
the volume's final paragraph that the idea of world government as the best
remedy for world war "may be unassailable in logic," yet it remained
"unattainable in practice" (1959: 238). Given the manifest political and
social heterogeneity of global affairs, the "amount of force needed to hold"
such a society together by a prospective world state would necessarily have
to be massive. Unprecedented and indeed frightening power resources
would be required to set up and then maintain it: "were world government
attempted, we might find ourselves dying in the attempt to unite, or uniting
and living a life worse than death" (Waltz, 1959: 228). In his hugely influential *Theory of International Politics,* Waltz asserted that in "a society of
states with little coherence, attempts at world government would founder
on the inability of an emerging central authority to mobilize the resources
needed to create and maintain the unity of the system by regulating and
managing its parts" (1979: 111–12). Any world state would demand an
awe-inspiring concentration of power resources. It would inevitably
provide an open invitation to global civil war: each component political
element would have a strong incentive to wrest control from rivals. Interstate warfare would merely have been jettisoned for horrible global civil
wars pitting agonistic elements of an ostensibly united but in fact divided
world against each other.

Waltz's criticisms obviously echoed Progressive Realist anxieties about
a worldwide "totalitarian monster resting on feet of clay." They similarly
worried that premature attempts to establish a novel global order absent
a developed world community or supranational society would culminate
in a terrible statist beast; they always rejected attempts to bring it about
by military means. However, just as revealing are Waltz's gaps and silences.
As I have tried to show, his predecessors formulated innovative ideas
about how a supranational society might gradually be created. Their preoccupation with functionalism stemmed from the cautious expectation that
it might contribute to the creation of a world community: in a prospective
integrated global order, whose construction obviously represented a long-
term project, world statehood need not entail totalitarianism. No Progressive Realist naively asserted that a prospective global order would be
free of intense political or social conflict. However, they suggested that

intelligent reform measures could gradually pave the way for an underlying supranational society allowing for global conflicts to be resolved for the most part by nonviolent means.

Waltz simply ignored *this* facet of previous Realist discourse. In contrast to his predecessors, he presupposed as an unalterable *fact* that international society must always remain deeply divided and thus potentially violent. At the very least, his critical comments on world statehood failed to provide a satisfactory response to the rich and nuanced reformist arguments made by Progressive Realists about how and why the harshest facts of contemporary international affairs might be gradually but systematically modified.

The most outspoken contemporary Realist critic of world government, the Italian political philosopher Danilo Zolo, builds on the Neorealist legacy of Waltz, preferring it over the purportedly obsolete views of Morgenthau, Niebuhr, and Carr (1997: xv). Like Waltz, Zolo considers world or cosmopolitan government a recipe for political disaster. Any attempt to realize it would merely exacerbate the violent character of international politics, as supposedly demonstrated by the sad record of so-called humanitarian military intervention under the auspices of the UN. World government could only entail a brutal totalitarian nightmare given limited global political and cultural integration. Following Waltz, Zolo simply declares the possibility of a mature and effectively integrated world community to be unrealistic (1997: 153). His position, unlike theirs, is proudly indebted to Machiavelli and Hobbes: international anarchy constitutes an unchangeable fact of political life (1997: xv, 82). Zolo radicalizes the anti-normative thrust of Waltz's positivist and scientistic reworking of Realism. Insisting that the subjectivity and contingency of all moral values constitutes an essential feature of the modern condition, he discards even a minimal universalistic morality (1997: 64).

Unfortunately, Zolo's moral skepticism generates deep internal tensions, not the least of which derives from the fact that he continues to make powerful moral arguments. Outraged by the abuse of cosmopolitan norms by Great Powers like the United States, he has repeatedly chided them for employing universalistic normative language and the dream of cosmopolitan reform to veil the deadly pursuit of narrow power interests. Refurbishing familiar Realist attacks on the self-righteousness and moral hypocrisy of liberal foreign policy, Zolo has at times been an eloquent critic of so-called humanitarian military intervention undertaken with the UN's seal of approval (1997; 2002). Unfortunately, he possesses no real normative framework from which to justify his criticisms: his acceptance of the contingency and subjectivity of moral values provides at most a weak foundation. In the final analysis, Zolo throws the baby out with the bath water and offers no moral basis for opposing hypocritical and incomplete varieties of Cosmopolitanism.[33]

Progressive Realists not only participated in a surprisingly wide-ranging theoretical exchange about radical global reform, but ultimately endorsed the possibility of novel postnational political and social entities. As I have tried to show in this chapter, they provided many sound reasons for doing so. Although contemporary Realists regularly scoff at proposals for far-reaching global change, their mid-century predecessors astutely hesitated before doing so. Unlike their more conservative offspring, Realism's founding fathers rightly criticized not only naive models of international reform, but *also* static and institutionally complacent views of the global status quo akin to those now widely embraced by contemporary Realists. Despite some genuine analytic strengths, contemporary Realism looks too much like the one-sided and cynical worldview pilloried by Niebuhr and other Progressive Realists, who would have legitimately worried about its morally and institutionally self-satisfied tendencies. Those readers serious about formulating a richer variety of Realist theory could do worse than by revisiting mid-century Progressive Realism.

By ignoring the rich intellectual heritage of its own reformist past, present-day Realism make things too easy for itself. Even more important perhaps, contemporary advocates of global reform can still learn a great deal from Progressive Realism, whose legacy they have similarly neglected. Why and how they might do so is the subject of the following chapters.

4 WHAT COSMOPOLITANS CAN LEARN FROM PROGRESSIVE REALISM

Cosmopolitanism represents the most impressive movement within contemporary international thought. Cosmopolitans have developed astute theoretical ideas about global justice and the need for global economic redistribution, powerful defenses of the emerging international human rights regime, and creative models of global democracy and law. The fact that global reform has returned to the scholarly – as well as broader political – agenda is attributable in part to their energetic efforts. Despite the critical comments that follow, let me begin by acknowledging that they not only have put the right questions for debate on the table, but that their answers are generally commendable.

Unfortunately, Cosmopolitans have also made things too easy for themselves by embracing a caricatured reading of Realism. They ignore those versions of Realist theory (described in this volume as *Progressive Realism*) which offer a serious intellectual challenge, in part because such Realists endorsed versions of both *moral* and *legal-political* universalism analogous to those advocated by present-day Cosmopolitan defenders of global reform. Sizable common ground can be identified between Cosmopolitans and Progressive Realists. In part because of this shared territory, Cosmopolitans will need to heed Realist ideas particularly about global democracy. For sound reasons, and in opposition to many recent Cosmopolitans, Progressive Realists argued that any prospective global democracy would need to rest on a mature supranational society capable of generating social cohesion. They also insisted that any viable postnational polity will have need for familiar state-like institutional traits. Their neglected views help identify the Achilles' heel of the present-day preference for "global (democratic) governance without government." In part because of overlapping moral inclinations and political goals, but also because Progressive Realists thought deeper and more thoroughly about some crucial issues, Cosmopolitan proponents of global democracy can learn a great deal from Progressive Realism.

In short, only a serious intellectual give-and-take between Cosmopolitans and sophisticated mid-century Realists can end the shadow boxing now widespread within international theory. This chapter attempts to initiate such an exchange.

A Realist – Cosmopolitan Alliance?

Recent Cosmopolitanism comes in manifold theoretical and political versions, but what they all share is a deep enmity towards Realism. Ernie's categorization of Realism as inspired by the pessimistic theories of Machiavelli and Hobbes, hostile to robust models of international law and morality, institutionally conservative and overly protective of the existing Westphalian system, and as advocating flawed ideas of a parochial national interest and fatalistic security dilemma, is widespread in the Cosmopolitan literature (Archibugi, 2008: 126–31; Beitz, 1979: 11–50; Caney, 2005; Habermas, 2006: 166–8; Held, 1995: 74–5; Jones, 1999: 114–15). The view that Realism "finds moral considerations unfit" for international politics is commonplace as well (Doyle, 1997: 106).

My attempt in previous chapters to salvage the pretty much forgotten reformist impulses of mid-century Progressive Realism has hopefully succeeded in discrediting such preconceptions. To be sure, classical Realism, like any significant intellectual current, was always an unwieldy creature. Yet the *Progressive* Realists whom I have placed under the microscope hardly fit into the deceptively neat little box which Cosmopolitans label "Realism" and which they prefer to place safely out of reach. Progressive Realists drew theoretical inspiration from left-leaning intellectual and political sources. While expressly distancing themselves from the troublesome legacies of Machiavelli and Hobbes, they outlined a refreshingly demanding political ethics. They argued forcefully against one-sidedly critical assessments of international law and morality, and were in fact deeply troubled by the possibility that total war and rabid nationalism might decimate them.

Particular attention above has been paid to demolishing the myth of Realism as institutionally complacent. As we have seen, Progressive Realists in fact defended the aspiration to replace the existing Westphalian system with a novel postnational order. Their views about both the security dilemma and national interest were less institutionally smug than generally recognized. Even their seemingly nostalgic ideas about the balance of power were by no means congenitally anti-reformist. Despite their appreciation for the socially integrative functions performed by modern nationhood, they believed that the nation state was subject to decay and that its days were numbered. Although Progressive Realists remained skeptical about immediate attempts to construct a world polity, they typically deemed it an admirable long-term goal, thus devoting substantial energy to the task of figuring out how to build its presuppositions. Of course, the European Union was at most a nascent postnational polity when Realists debated its merits in the 1950s and 1960s. Nonetheless, they generally followed the process of European unification with sympathetic interest. To see the left-leaning Realist thinkers under scrutiny here as dogmatically and perhaps blindly tied to the masts of the ship of the (existing nation) state is badly misleading.

In light of this revised reading of mid-century Realism, where then can we identify analytic overlap with contemporary Cosmopolitanism?

Notwithstanding claims to the contrary, mid-century Realists did not consistently underwrite moral skepticism or relativism. Like contemporary Cosmopolitans, Morgenthau and Niebuhr, for example, both endorsed a demanding version of *moral cosmopolitanism*, along the lines described more recently by the philosopher Thomas Pogge as requiring that we "respect one another's status as ultimate units of moral concern" (Pogge, 1994: 90). Morgenthau favored a political ethics according to which moral action requires fundamental respect for other human beings as ends in themselves. Although sometimes locating its roots in the Judeo-Christian religious tradition, he remained open to the possibility that it could be justified without theological banisters, interpreting both Kant and Marx as providing noteworthy defenses of it (1946: 184). Similarly, Niebuhr advocated what he forthrightly described as "moral universalism," promoting it on unabashedly Christian grounds. He also observed that the notion of universal moral obligations to other human beings *qua* human beings, however, could be grounded in moral and political traditions other than Christianity (1944: 153–59). He often opposed the simplistic traditionalistic view that only religious believers were capable of consistent moral action: "bad religion can be worse than no religion" (cited in Bingham, 1961: 7). Both writers also observed that universalistic morality possessed what we might describe as significant real-life consequences: the universal condemnation of killing, for example, proffered evidence that the world's great moral and religious traditions all rested on a basic respect for human life.

To be sure, Progressive Realists worried that simplistic versions of moral cosmopolitanism obscured the necessity of prudence, compromise, and tragic choices. Too often it joined forces with a crude and unduly naive political ethics. In countering this danger, they turned to Weber's ethic of responsibility, which they sometimes interpreted – in contradistinction to its original architect – as consonant with a rigorous moral universalism. In foreign policy making, for example, an oversimplified moral cosmopolitanism motivated actors who irresponsibly believed that US-style democracy, for example, could be pursued everywhere, with equal fervor, despite the potential costs, and the fact that it was less likely to be productively advanced in some regions than in others: "If universal democracy is the standard of political action, Korea is as important as Mexico, China is as worthy an objective to Canada, and there is no difference between Poland and Panama" (1949: 210). Not surprisingly, they considered this a recipe for political disaster. A politically naive moral cosmopolitanism – *this* was in part the crude "moralism" they decried – was blind to concrete power relations and downplayed the fact that even major global players operated with limited political resources. Moral aims could never be achieved without discrimination. Even the soundest abstract moral principles posed difficult practical and political questions, in part because their pursuit might require acts – including political violence – that otherwise were rightly condemned. If moral cosmopolitanism were translated into a simplistic version of Kant's categorical imperative, in which the possibly counterproductive consequences of well-meaning moral action were badly neglected, it might do more harm than good. Without a proper sense of the complex political (and especially power) constellations in which moral action was always undertaken, even the most well-meaning moral cosmopolitanism could go awry.

Progressive Realists also regularly noted that the intellectual soundness of moral cosmopolitanism hardly translated directly into an actual empirical consensus about universal values or their proper interpretation. In part because nation states still filled the minds of peoples everywhere with parochial views of political morality, an otherwise seemingly straightforward common moral ideal might imply different things to a Brazilian, Canadian, or Russian (Morgenthau, 1954: 240, 244; also, Niebuhr, 1953a: 28–9). Nor did this happen in a power vacuum and thus somehow neutrally, but instead typically amid a political and social force field favorable to the privileged and powerful. At the domestic level as well, moral appeals were manipulated and instrumentalized by dominant power interests. Nonetheless, as Morgenthau observed, there one normally could identify a rough working consensus on basic values: "What justice means in

America I can say; for interests and convictions, experiences of life and institutionalized traditions, have in large measure created a consensus which tells me what justice means under the conditions of American society." Even in the domestic sphere such consensus was subject to renegotiation, with basic moral and ethical ideas under exceptional circumstances subject to radical revision.

At the global level, however, the exceptional situation was closer to the normal state of affairs: the meaning of apparently uncontested norms (e.g. abhorrence of torture) was often up for grabs, with moral appeals more likely to serve as cynical ideological masks for narrow power interests. Absent mature supranational society or a developed world community, and operating in a context of even greater inequality than extant at the domestic level, power interests found it easier to manipulate universalistic moral terms without fearing negative repercussions. Vulnerable political and social groups normally lacked even the minimal weapons available to them in the domestic arena, where the interplay of shared customs, mores, law, and sovereignty sometimes worked to check the powerful and privileged. Consequently, "supranational moral principles concrete enough to give guidance to the political actions of individual nations" remained rare (Morgenthau, 1949: 210–11). Those which apparently did function too often remained subject to the whims of hegemonic states.

Even if contemporary Cosmopolitans have sometimes succumbed to the perils diagnosed by Progressive Realism, the latter's arguments hardly pose a fundamental theoretical challenge to a nuanced moral cosmopolitanism that acknowledges the complexities and paradoxes of practical action, which even today stem partly from disparities in social and national experience where "the same moral and political concepts take on different meanings in different environments" (Morgenthau, 1954: 238). They do, however, take aim at *naive* versions of moral cosmopolitanism, along the lines probably endorsed by one recent defender of global democracy who declares that "it will not be necessary to employ" morally deplorable or "evil means" (i.e. political violence) in order to achieve a novel democratic postnational order (Archibugi, 2008: 287). Progressive Realists would legitimately have pointed out that this position risks ignoring the familiar paradoxes of political action: morally good intentions and acts can produce counterproductive and morally deplorable consequences, while otherwise immoral acts may sometimes be necessary if normatively admirable goals are to be secured.

Progressive Realists also subscribed to what recent Cosmopolitans have described as *legal (and political or institutional) cosmopolitanism*, defined by Pogge as a "commitment to a concrete political ideal of a global order under which all persons have equivalent legal duties – are fellow citizens of a universal republic" (1994: 90). They typically envisioned the establishment of a unified global political order – a world state or global federation – as a desirable long-term goal, picturing its construction as essential to peace and security in a dangerous world. When contemporary Cosmopolitans defend a parallel goal by pointing out that in the existing international system "governments therefore have very powerful incentives and very broad opportunities to develop their military might, [and that] this is bound to lead to the proliferation of nuclear, biological, chemical, and conventional weapons of mass destruction," they are unwittingly reproducing a stock Progressive Realist argument in defense of global reform (Pogge, 1994: 103). In fact, Progressive Realism's brand of political cosmopolitanism was arguably more ambitious than that of present-day Cosmopolitans who apparently shy away from state-building at the postnational level, believing that a robust human rights legal regime can succeed absent ambitious forms of postnational government (Benhabib, 2006).

Like more recent Cosmopolitans, Progressive Realists evidently hoped that a future global order would take a basically liberal – democratic form and thus rest on a system of universal rights, though they generally said little about its likely institutional attributes in light of its temporally far-off character. Positing that far-reaching social change was inextricably linked to the establishment of new and ambitious forms of postnational decision making, some (i.e. Carr, Herz, and Schuman) also sympathized with demands for egalitarian social and economic global reforms. They thereby anticipated a major strand in contemporary Cosmopolitan thinking which similarly links postnational political reform to the quest for social justice and global economic redistribution. Like many recent Cosmopolitans, Progressive Realists married global political reform to identifiably social democratic – and sometimes more radical – policy preferences.[1]

Now one might perhaps challenge my attribution of legal and political cosmopolitanism to Progressive Realism by noting, as the political theorist Simon Caney has recently done, that its representatives frequently made disparaging comments about international human rights and human rights-oriented foreign policies, along the lines of a public lecture given (and later published) by Morgenthau in 1979 (Caney, 2005: 93–5; Morgenthau, 1979). For those Cosmopolitans who interpret the growing respect paid even by powerful nation states to regionally based as well as international universal rights declarations as a major step towards an identifiably cosmopolitan legal system, Realism's apparent hostility to human rights law understandably raises red flags.

Yet the interpretative perils here are manifold. First, Progressive Realists had relatively little to say about the admirable expansion of human rights law, chiefly because it occurred well after most of them had passed the most productive junctures in their careers. Second, what they in fact said was by no means unequivocally critical. Although Carr, for example, doubted that social and economic rights could be interpreted as mere extensions of liberal civil and political liberties, he described the 1948 Declaration of Human Rights as a problematic and paradoxical yet nonetheless "great turning point in history," an important attempt to update the idea of the rights of man in accordance with contemporary social conditions (2003b [1949]: 11). Always best attuned among the Progressive Realists to ongoing trends in international law, Schwarzenberger considered it "urgent to lay down generally valid standards making at least articulate the gap between present-day reality and the minimum requirements of civilized world community" (1964: 464). He pictured efforts at building regionalized human rights legal regimes – e.g. the European Convention on Human Rights – as worthwhile undertakings more likely to succeed than parallel initiatives at the global level because of West Europe's comparatively high level of political and social integration. On the international plain, where rights were supposed to be binding on a panoply of heterogeneous as well as antagonistic political and social units, the prospect of achieving consistently enforceable human rights was less certain. Even in the less-than-ideal political conditions of the Cold War, however, human rights declarations performed some vital law-inspiring and law-promoting functions, with national courts already basing their rulings on the 1948 Declaration and other international agreements despite their vague and legally ambivalent character (1964: 464–6).

Third, as a matter of political practice, Progressive Realists openly defended human rights-oriented foreign policy, with Morgenthau – just to mention one famous example – vociferously defending attempts in the 1970s to make the liberalization of US policies towards the Soviets conditional on their acceptance of the right of Russian Jews to emigrate.[2] Fourth, and most important, Progressive Realists in fact admired the goal of a worldwide liberal democratic government, and thus were by no means opposed to the eventual establishment of binding universal rights. They did not, in short, share the fundamentalist hostility advanced by some recent Realists (and others), who see in international human rights nothing but an ideological veil for Western – and especially – US imperialism (Zolo, 1997; 2002). When read in this light, Morgenthau's 1979 critical comments, for example, can be interpreted as motored chiefly by anxieties about what we might describe as the necessarily *ambivalent* character of premature efforts to advance human rights in a divided international system. In a state system characterized by power rivalry and deep inequalities, a principled defense of human rights by national governments could not consistently mesh with the pursuit of the national interest. Reasonable interpretations of the national interest might conflict with a strict human rights-oriented foreign policy; policy makers would be forced to make unfortunate compromises and tragic choices. Even if moral cosmopolitanism demands that political actors vigorously pursue human rights, the best that could reasonably be expected of nationally based political leaders would be that they *minimize* unfortunate but unavoidable moral compromises. How could one plausibly expect of present-day political leaders that they give up power and privilege for humanitarian aims which might prove costly to those who elected them? Easily misunderstood, Morgenthau was not attacking the admirable quest for a strengthened human rights regime, but instead the view that nationally based leaders could readily and indeed consistently do so in an international system that placed structural restraints on such efforts.

In contrast to a naive political cosmopolitanism which celebrates the emerging international human rights regime while ignoring its ambiguities, Progressive Realists correctly noted that under contemporary global conditions the interpretation and enforcement of human rights was plagued by selectivity and partiality even more so than domestic law. In the case of conflicting interpretations, powerful states and their allies sometimes effectively determined the meaning of the relevant legal clauses, whereas longstanding mechanisms at the national level at least reduced the advantages enjoyed by the politically and socially privileged. Even when nation states claimed that their foreign policies could be placed under the mantle of human rights, they often did so in self-interested and narrowly egoistical ways: the United States, for example, has generally advanced an interpretation of human rights reflecting its own idiosyncratic anti-statist national political traditions.[3]

Yet such Progressive Realist reservations hardly constitute a principled attack on the quest to strengthen the enforcement of human rights. On the contrary, they implicitly highlighted the limitations of human rights in the context of a Westphalian system, Progressive Realists tirelessly repeated, which humankind should work towards transcending. Such failures, they believed, highlighted the virtues of a more mature postnational polity in which basic rights could finally gain sufficiently impartial application and enforcement.

Realist Contributions to Cosmopolitan Democracy

The gap between Cosmopolitanism and at least one significant variant of Realism is overstated: Progressive Realists and Cosmopolitans agree on many important matters. So where are the differences, and how might they prove intellectually useful as we pursue global reform?

Cosmopolitans have recently advocated the establishment of extensive democratic decision-making beyond the national level. Progressive Realists would likely have greeted this development with sympathy. Many of them similarly acknowledged the virtues of constructing a new system of global political authority; their anxieties about nuclear war made them as determined as contemporary writers in their advocacy of reform. Developing their ideas in the context of a lively discussion in which politically active global federalists, major politicians, and famous intellectuals like Bertrand Russell and Karl Jaspers debated the pros and cons of international reform, Progressive Realists were familiar with normative defenses of global federalism and the world state, at least some of which anticipated contemporary Cosmopolitan proposals. Like present-day Cosmopolitans, they astutely described the serious challenges posed by globalization to democratic legitimacy (Herz, 1978). Two pivotal arguments from the mid-century debate remain relevant here. The first (1) concerns the necessary social presuppositions of effective global political authority, as well as the closely related issue of how institutional change might be put into motion. The second (2) refers to the proper status of state sovereignty in a new global order. Finally, we briefly consider the case of the European Union and the possibility that its developmental trajectory counters Progressive Realism's theoretical amendments to Cosmopolitanism (3).

Cosmopolitan Democracy and Supranational Society

In the concluding section of *Democracy and the Global Order: From the Modern State to Cosmopolitan Government*, David Held asserts that a functioning global democracy will "not require political and cultural integration in the form of a consensus on a wide range of beliefs, values, and norms." A worldwide or cosmopolitan democracy might achieve a high level of integration and efficacy merely by citizens "participating in public deliberation and negotiation," and this chiefly presupposes a basic " 'commitment' to democracy, for without this there can be no sustained public deliberation, democracy cannot function as a decision-making mechanism, and divergent political aspirations and identities are unlikely to reach an accommodation" (1995: 282).[4] Because Held apparently believes that this commitment is nearly universal today, he offers a relatively sanguine account of cosmopolitan democracy's prospects. Although it would be a mistake to try instantly to construct full-fledged global democracy, political actors can and should undertake far-reaching institutional alterations to the status quo.[5] Humankind, it seems, is pretty much ready and willing to embrace global democracy, and "in the wake of, for instance, a severe crisis of the global financial system, or of the environment, or of war," far-sighted reformers might expeditiously undertake institutional change (1995: 281).

Trying to counter communitarian-inspired models of political community and identity, Held outlines what Craig Calhoun has dubbed a "thin conception of social life, commitment, and belonging" (2003: 96). As Calhoun points out, this thin conception is commonplace among Cosmopolitans. Habermas, for example, has pointedly criticized the thesis that viable postnational democracy requires cultural homogeneity or pre-political ties of solidarity and trust. He occasionally endorses a strong version of the thesis that nothing more than "public, discursively structured processes of opinion- and will-formation" are necessary for "maintaining the integrity of a functionally differentiated society." Deliberation can "guarantee a sort of emergency backup system" providing the minimal social and cultural preconditions necessary to democracy at the postnational as well as national levels (Habermas, 2001: 73, 76).[6]

This thin conception contrasts sharply with the ideas of defenders of the nation state like David Miller, who aggressively criticize Cosmopolitan reform proposals by insisting on a significantly thicker model of social integration and motivation, arguing that a viable political community presupposes a far-reaching sense of trust, fair play, and a more-or-less spontaneous willingness to cooperate voluntarily among compatriots. In successful political communities, citizens typically follow the rules even when they could get away with not doing so, in part because they expect that others will heed them as well. A desirable liberal democracy can rely only to a circumscribed degree on state coercion. So it inevitably must count on citizens, for example, to pay their taxes even when no government official is looming over their shoulders. In Miller's view, a mere "commitment to democracy" is insufficient to the integrative tasks at hand. Democratic discourse along the lines Habermas apparently considers capable of serving an "emergency backup" for political integration can thrive only if embedded in deeply rooted pre-deliberative social ties. The necessary communal ties are generated most effectively by a robust shared national identity, which many existing nation states – to varying degrees, depending on historical particularities – have in fact relied on to secure the preconditions of political freedom and social justice. In light of the ways in which political life is directly parasitical on nationalism, the call for far-reaching cosmopolitan reform represents a naive and probably irresponsible panacea (1995: 90–7).[7]

Like such critics, Progressive Realists would have expressed concern about the thin account of social existence and membership found among contemporary global democrats. They also would have raised tough questions about "how social solidarity and public discourse might develop enough" within postnational social and political relations so as to generate a sufficiently robust basis for global governance (Calhoun, 2003: 96). Without succumbing to rigid and sometimes essentialist ideas of community or nationhood, or overstated expectations about democratic participation and citizenship, they at least *hinted* at the possibility of an alternative and somewhat thicker account of social integration.

Progressive Realists forcefully criticized postwar globalists for privileging top-down institutional and constitutional change and for advancing overblown expectations concerning the integrative capacities of political institutions. Popular models of global reform too often relied on a crude Hobbesianism positing that the state *alone* can "maintain domestic peace. ... That the state is essential, but not sufficient to keep the peace of national societies is demonstrated by the historical experience of civil wars" (Morgenthau, 1954: 476). Progressive Realists thought that productive reform would have to start from the "bottom up," meaning that its advocates should focus on figuring out how the underlying social bases of postnational institutions could be forged and gradually strengthened over time. The allure of Mitrany's functionalism stemmed from its promise to provide an answer: nation states could work together on concrete economic and technical tasks, over time building workable supranational practices. To be sure, there were possibilities here as well for legal and institutional creativity, but only as part of a broader set of initiatives helping to create a rich postnational social life. In contrast, a premature push for constitutional reform at the global level put the cart before the horse and might prove counterproductive.

The crucial theoretical category here was supranational society or, alternately, world community, whose realization Progressive Realists considered indispensable to global political and social integration. Only with its fruition, they argued, might a postnational polity prove workable: "laws are obeyed because the community accepts them as corresponding," and not primarily because of the state's monopoly over the use of force (Niebuhr, 1953a: 22). Reminiscent at times of the English School of international thought, they grappled seriously with the theoretical and practical challenges of what scholars now frequently describe as "global community" or "global society" (Little, 2003; Shaw, 1994).[8] Like sophisticated variants of Constructivism, they rightly underscored the centrality of the social underpinnings of global political order (Wendt, 1999). In fact, they had many provocative – though by no means altogether consistent – things to say about supranational or world community, and how best to bring it about. Some key features of their somewhat discordant reflections deserve reconsideration here.

Most important, Progressive Realists pointed to the necessity of some shared expectation of fairness or basic justice, which they thought best able to motivate social groups to abide by basic political rules even when their particular consequences seemed unattractive. Political and social integration could only be realized "when all groups can rely upon the chance of taking at one time or another some forward steps toward the attainment of justice," even if under most circumstances powerful groups would likely get their way (Morgenthau, 1954: 473). If weak and vulnerable groups were to have a reasonable chance at gaining a measure of justice, de facto power (and especially material) inequalities would have to be reduced (Carr, 1964 [1939]: 162–9]. The weak would minimally have to be strong enough to force concessions from the powerful; some measure of basic social and political equality would have to be achieved.

Shared expectations of justice or fairness might of course rest on some express belief in common political or moral propositions. However, conscious normative commitments were only the tip of the iceberg. Perhaps even more significant than verbal assent to a clearly articulated set of shared values was an implicit social awareness of what they entailed, why they were worth upholding, and at least some willingness to defend them. Only then could the motivational presuppositions of shared political life be fulfilled, and the basic norms of the political and social game garner regular compliance. For Progressive Realists, as for some astute present-day analysts, social integration was at least as much a matter of "doing" as "being": concrete social practices which generated meaningful cooperation and relations of trust could prove even more vital than shared values or notions of collective destiny. Even without the latter, the former might flourish; in turn, "doing" might gradually contribute to a salient sense of mutual "being" (Howorth, 2000).

To the extent that a common sense of justice or fairness might take the form of expressly shared political ideals, it was misleading to describe it as pre-political. Yet since many times in history it had been realized on the basis of social experiences only distantly related to the operations of the political system, along the lines of the organic ties described by Niebuhr (e.g. common religion, ethnicity, or language), it was also wrong to overlook its potential non-political roots. Progressive Realists underscored the pivotal role of a pluralistic social order in which one could identify a rich variety of crosscutting social cleavages and loyalties, which they thought most likely to mitigate intense conflict. Under the proper conditions, social pluralism potentially civilized conflict: social actors could learn that a rival in one social arena might be an ally or even a friend in another (Morgenthau, 1954: 471). Such experiences imbued them with an appreciation not for the virtues of social cooperation, but also the advantages of peaceful conflict resolution. Trust and even mutual respect could develop between and among social agents. An amorphous yet politically indispensable "we-feeling" might materialize. Over time, compliance with the political order's rules and norms could become habitual.

In global politics, however, nationality still generally trumped competing cleavages: people "compare their own nation with other nations and realize how much more they have in common with each other than with members of the other nation" (Morgenthau, 1954: 471). Until the overriding importance of national identity was defied by competing cleavages it remained premature to speak of mature supranational society or world community.

Progressive Realists frequently observed that a sense of shared nationality, language, religion, political history, ethnicity, and even hostility to a foreign enemy had played decisive historical roles in creating a sufficiently robust domestic society and thus the presuppositions of nationally based political entities. Unfortunately, they did not say enough about possible functional replacements for such ties at the global level. Although their reflections, for example, sometimes overlapped with those of another refugee from central Europe, Karl Deutsch, whose path breaking work on political and social integration still provides fertile ground, their account sometimes pales in comparison to his.[9] Nonetheless, Progressive Realists can still help us escape from the straitjacket of present-day normative political theory, which typically focuses on questions of shared values or "being," or what is now fashionably described as "political identity," while missing some of the more subtle sociological and even psychological presuppositions of viable political community. As they astutely grasped, a satisfactory theoretical and empirical reckoning with the dynamics of political and social integration will need to draw on many scholarly disciplines and take a rich variety of complex factors into consideration. It will have to pay attention to complex social practices and forms of everyday cooperation as well as shared ideas and values.

However, even their analytic vagueness arguably constitutes a hidden forte. Nowhere did Progressive Realists systematically exclude the possibility that new forms of shared belonging, social life, or commitment might take postnational forms. They would probably have rejected contemporary communitarian arguments that global democracy must founder because it obfuscates the need for a thick sense of shared life based on the commonalities of particularistic nationality or perhaps even a far-reaching as well as widely shared vision of the good life. Morgenthau's account, as noted, placed special weight on the development of social *pluralism* and its accompanying array of intersecting group cleavages. *Pace* the usual communitarian anxieties about heterogeneity and social conflict, he instead envisioned pluralism and conflict as potentially facilitating social integration. In striking contradistinction to Miller, for example, Morgenthau and others were alarmed by the fact that the nation state remained the object of our highest political loyalties.

Even if Niebuhr periodically noted that selfhood was constituted by deeply rooted and sometimes pregiven social and communal ties, and his emphasis on the socially embedded context of selfhood occasionally recalled elements of contemporary comunitarianism, he consistently refused to draw anti-cosmopolitan conclusions. His nuanced philosophical position approximated what political theorist Toni Erskine (2008) has recently dubbed "embedded cosmopolitanism": while endorsing demanding ideas consistent with both moral and political (or institutional) cosmopolitanism, he simultaneously envisioned the self as fundamentally embedded in dense networks of social and communal particularity. To be sure, Schwarzenberger – and perhaps others as well – employed a rather idealized conception of community. Yet he always rightly insisted that it represented a conceptual ideal-type, and thus never fully achievable or perhaps even desirable in social life. Revealingly, he believed that a federation of Western democracies – based on a rich diversity of peoples with different languages, national self-understandings, religious backgrounds, and a multiplicity of ethnicities and races – instantiated sufficient community elements and thus could serve as a stepping stone to global federation.

Unlike recent republican and participatory democratic critics of global democracy who worry that it conflicts with the preconditions of meaningful citizenship and effective self-government, they also defended sober models of representative liberal democracy and rejected the view that it demanded intense small-scale or even face-to-face participation.[10] Progressive Realists never precluded the possibility that global political authority could be made consonant with liberal democratic aspirations, even if they correctly pointed out that familiar decision-making mechanisms – for example, majority rule – indeed seemed highly problematic at the global level given its stunning political and social heterogeneity (Morgenthau, 1954: 480). To their credit, they hesitated to presuppose *a priori* the sheer impossibility of developing new social and political mechanisms by means of which individual citizens might participate meaningfully even in astonishingly large and populous political systems.[11]

Nonetheless, Progressive Realists would still have worried that Held's thin idea of mere democratic commitment is likely to prove insufficient to a robust cosmopolitan democracy. To be sure, democratic deliberation and participation make indispensable contributions to any shared sense of political belonging and commitment. Yet political life relies on additional social foundations about which global democrats have had far too little to say.[12] A mere "commitment to democracy" does not a world community or supranational society make. Writing at mid century, Progressive Realists legitimately doubted that such a supranational society had already sufficiently emerged to buttress global democracy. Although they never denied the possibility of a global public opinion "that transcends national boundaries and ... unites members of different nations in a consensus," they questioned whether it was already advanced enough to support global democracy (Morgenthau, 1954: 236). At the global level, not much of a politically efficacious shared sense of fairness or justice could be identified, and national identities still trumped the cross-cutting cleavages that would have to operate there, as on the domestic sphere, if supranational political institutions were to prove durable.

Cosmopolitan reform advocates today might credibly point out that in the last half century huge steps have been taken towards creating a deeply rooted supranational society. Global public opinion and civil society have gained in political significance; a host of shared norms, institutions, and complexes of interest (e.g. the UN, EU, International Monetary Fund [IMF], World Trade Organization [WTO]) have built on and simultaneously deepened humankind's sense of a shared fate and indeed membership in a global community. Cross-cutting social cleavages can now be identified at the global level. Some legitimate grounds for skepticism remain, however. In part this stems from the fact, accurately predicted by Progressive Realists, that globalization produces at least as many *new* sources of social conflict and enmity as it mitigated old ones. Globalization sometimes works to aggrandize national identity, for example, even as it concurrently undermines the nation state's political and economic independence. There is simply no good reason to presuppose that globalization's contradictory social, economic, and cultural dynamics inexorably lead the way towards more sensible forms of global governance. However desirable and rational such reforms might be, political actors – and in particular rich and powerful nation states systematically privileged by the global status quo – will continue to oppose normatively attractive demands for reform and especially the call for global democracy.

The refusal of many members of the global community – and not simply Great Powers like the United States – to support even modest reforms to the Security Council, or to fund the UN adequately or support its peace-keeping operations, should at least put a damper on overblown reform expectations. We continue to subscribe to the universal rights of man (and woman), but when refugees arrive at our doorstep, we slam the door. We shrug our shoulders when reminded that tens of thousands of foreign children die daily of curable illness, while keeping our eyes glued to televised news broadcasts blaring out reports about the fate of a handful of national compatriots killed in a plane crash, or subject to criminal attacks abroad. National identity still tends to trump competing cross-border social cleavages (of social class, for example). Mindboggling political and social inequalities bedevil the global political economy to a degree inconsonant with a functioning supranational society. Meaningful cross-border social and political integration cannot be stabilized as long as some of us face starvation while others worry chiefly about buying a second Range Rover or where best to acquire a vacation home.

Cosmopolitan theorist Daniele Archibugi claims that those who bemoan the lack of a global demos miss the crucial point that "institutions create the demos" (2008: 143). Progressive Realists also saw institution-building, when done at the right time and in the right way, as conducive to global reform. Institutions have an important role to play in supporting any political community. Confirming the worst fears of Progressive Realists, Archibugi claims too much for them: he implies that constitution-making and institutional reform can effectively create their own social and political presuppositions. Taking the US founding as evidence, Archibugi downplays some historical facts which Niebuhr, Morgenthau, and others delighted in recalling against an earlier generation of naive globalists: the US Constitution was ratified only after a bloody revolution and the failures of the Articles of Confederation had helped transform the former colonists into a unified people. It presupposed a *previously* created political community resting on extensive political, moral, and cultural commonalities (Niebuhr, 1953a: 18–19). Archibugi's naive constitutional fetishism potentially opens the door to a paternalistic reformism in which purportedly far-sighted actors are outfitted with the task of *creating* global democracy, notwithstanding the admitted lack of a world demos.

Global democracy remains an admirable long-term aspiration. Yet Progressive Realists were right to warn that without the requisite social foundations far-reaching postnational constitutional reform could prove premature and even counterproductive.

In Defense of Sovereignty

Progressive Realists accused postwar globalists of ignoring the decisive role to be played by a mature supranational society in buttressing any prospective cosmopolitan polity. However, they *also* approved of the "true message of Hobbes' philosophy" that the state is insufficient yet also "indispensable for the maintenance of domestic peace" (Morgenthau, 1954: 476). In short, they waged a two-front battle against those advocating new forms of postnational polities while obscuring their requisite social bases, on the one hand, and against anti-statists who belittled the indispensable role of state institutions, on the other hand. A global political order would have to be able to mobilize preponderant power against law-breakers: its ability to do so eventually presupposed locating the legitimate monopoly of organized force in global state hands. Even if existing inter-national law and human rights agreements were often respected by the Great Powers, they remained vulnerable to egregious violations because the international system still delivered "the enforcement of the law to the vicissitudes of the distribution of power between the violator of the law and the victim of the violation" (Morgenthau, 1954: 270). So Hobbes was right to link the regular enforcement of law to the creation of sovereign state institutions capable of forcefully employing institutional muscle to enforce norms against the powerful and privileged as well as the weak and vulnerable. Hobbes was wrong, however, to tie his defense of sovereignty to an Absolutist vision of politics and law. "Sovereignty is not freedom from legal restraints": the effective mobilization of preponderant power resources against lawbreakers – the *core* element of the idea of sovereignty – hardly demands that state institutions be envisioned as operating beyond or outside the law, or that they literally possess supremacy in the sense that *no* constitutional or legal restraints on them can be identified (Mor-genthau, 1954: 291). On the contrary, state sovereignty is most effectively exercised when operating *according* to law: the medium of law permits state institutions to "get things done" more expeditiously than otherwise possible (Fuller, 1964; Preuss, 2002).

Too often, critics of state sovereignty have distorted its lasting insights. Many well-meaning mid-century global reformers, Progressive Realists pointed out, advocated seemingly attractive models of differentiated or divisible sovereignty. In the process they obscured the truth that a function-ing global political and legal order will need possession of supreme author-ity and thus core features of state sovereignty. Viable federal states like Switzerland or the United States, Morgenthau insisted against those who interpreted them as offering potential models for a new post-sovereign global order,[13] established binding political and legal mechanisms for the mobilization of power against both domestic and foreign challengers: it was simply wrong to see them as evidence for the possibility of effective political authority operating without a monopoly on organized coercion, even if their exceedingly complex constitutional dynamics veiled its mech-anisms (Morgenthau, 1954: 303–8, 473–7, 482–5). There as elsewhere, at crucial political junctures recourse to the state's legitimate monopoly on force remained essential to legal enforcement. *Contra* those who falsely conflated the institutional complexities of modern federalism with its abrogation or even demise, Progressive Realists rightly grasped that sovereignty could potentially take a relatively rich diversity of institutional forms.

Admittedly, their discussion of state sovereignty now seems overly traditionalistic. Progressive Realists sometimes incorrectly interpreted the idea of sovereignty as requiring that it be located in a *single* institutional site *within* the state apparatus (Morgenthau, 1954: 305–6). Modern democratic states typically lack such a site; nor does state sovereignty demand it. By uncritically building on the Weberian notion of state sovereignty as entailing a *monopoly* on legitimate force, they downplayed that even viable states generally only possess a substantial or preponderant degree of "authoritative binding rule making backed up by some organized force" (Mann, 1993: 55). Empirically decisive for modern statehood has been possession of a capacity to enforce rules most of the time, and in any event when necessary in order to maintain the community's fundamental political and legal integrity. Supranational society can and should contribute to political cohesion so as to reduce the necessity of employing police and military force. Effective state power in fact *depends* on what the political sociologist Michael Mann dubs "power through society," whereby state institutions funnel social activities for the sake of guaranteeing the enforcement of common rules and procedures (Mann, 1993: 59).

The troublesome conflation of power, force, and violence that one of Morgenthau's closest friends, Hannah Arendt, astutely attributed to Weber's political thinking probably plagued their reflections as well (Arendt, 1970). According to Arendt, power rests on seemingly spontaneous and even unexpected forms of interaction or "action in concert" between and among individuals and groups. Power is a common or shared *activity* which initiates change and potentially engenders something novel and even unprecedented. Yet this conception of power still depends implicitly on core elements of state sovereignty. If power is to bring about a stable change in policy, for example, state institutions will need to guarantee that its results take a binding (i.e. universally enforceable) legal form. If the relations of basic equality and reciprocity upon which power-generating political action implicitly are to flourish, they require state (and legal) devices able to guard them, for example, from potentially hostile political and social forces. Power can only regularly emerge when basic rights are more-or-less consistently enforced, and the politically and socially vulnerable have some chance to act freely. If state institutions are to successfully buttress the possibility of power-generating action, they will have to be able to guarantee the integrity of basic decision making norms, procedures, and rights against political or social interests and competing institutions which may seek to violate them, or might simply prefer to ignore unpalatable policy outcomes. In other words, they will need to effectively mobilize preponderant or superior power to preserve basic decision making rules and their sometimes controversial results.

So Progressive Realists were right to hold onto the concept of state sovereignty, even if their rather old-fashioned ideas sometimes unnecessarily confused matters. Without it, no prospective postnational polity will likely prove able to guarantee the equal or consistent enforcement of the law, let alone the systematic implementation of general policies sometimes opposed by the powerful and privileged. Revealingly, even some hitherto enthusiastic defenders of the fashionable idea of "global governance without government" have begun to concede the basic soundness of this position (Weiss, 2008: 215–33).[14] Unfortunately, many Cosmopolitan political reformers continue to reject it.[15]

The international lawyer Richard Falk writes off sovereignty as at best an ambivalent conceptual product of a now bygone modernist Eurocentric epoch (1995). Accordingly, the quest for the world state is congenitally misconceived. Falk notes that given present-day political divides world government "would require considerable coercion and hierarchical ordering arrangements." Seeing no viable path beyond nationalism and other similarly divisive traits of global society, he rejects world statehood even as a long-term goal (1987: 15). Presumably, global society cannot be fundamentally altered so as someday to provide the requisite building blocks. Falk proceeds to construct an ambitious and in many respects appealing model of global (democratic) law and governance, which he then implausibly and indeed inexplicably deems achievable *absent* corresponding modes of global statehood.

Archibugi and Held similarly repudiate the intuition that their in many ways admirable vision of cosmopolitan democracy points to the necessity of a global state. Asserting that his model alone might successfully circumvent the eerie specter of a world state outfitted with a centralized monopoly on violence, Archibugi contrasts it favorably to that of competing ideas of a global federal republic. Final coercive power would be distributed "among several actors and subjected to the judicial control of existing and suitably reformed international institutions" (Archibugi, 2008: 129; also, Held, 1995: 23–31). This is doable because cosmopolitan democracy demands entrusting only a minimal set of regulatory tasks to global institutions. State sovereignty, the conceptual backbone of the modern state, is accordingly criticized and duly discarded (2008: 89). Even a cursory glance at Archibugi's *anything but* minimal list, however, raises tough questions. Global institutions would be given authority to regulate the use of force, strengthen the self-determination of peoples, secure cultural diversity, monitor the internal affairs of states to ensure fidelity to democracy and human rights, and encourage the "participatory management of global problems" (2008: 88–9). His proposal calls for a massive augmentation of global decision making authority but no corresponding increase in global-level state enforcement capacities. What happens when a reformed UN, for example, tries to enforce the legal prohibition on torture against the United States or other Great Powers which happen to violate it? Or when redistributive social and economic measures are to be pursued even in opposition to rich countries? How the dispersion of coercive authority along with a world court (minus an effective global executive) could get the job done remains unexplained.

A similar anti-statism plagues contemporary critical theory's otherwise illuminating contributions to Cosmopolitanism.[16] As always, Jürgen Habermas has offered one of the strongest defenses of the relevant ideas.

In his recent writings on globalization, Habermas defends a tripartite model of global governance, where decision making at the national level would be supplemented by new forms of what he dubs *supranational* (e.g. global or worldwide) and *transnational* (regional or continental) authority (2006). At the supranational level, he seeks a single world organization, for all essential purposes a reformed United Nations, equipped more effectively than at the present with the capacity to protect basic human rights and consistently prevent war. Only a drastically reformed UN, Habermas plausibly insists, is capable of counteracting the debilitating partiality with which international law is presently enforced and thereby clearing the way for a cosmopolitan legal order where the citizens of Burundi and Indonesia, for example, might enjoy the same rights as Germans or Americans. An empowered and refurbished UN need not take the form of a global federal republic or superstate, however. At the transnational level, economic, energy, environmental, and financial policies, or what Habermas dubs "global domestic politics," would be negotiated mainly by those global political actors (e.g. regional organizations like the EU, or Great Powers like the USA or China) singularly muscular enough to implement policies across large territories and thus help counteract the pathologies of global-izing capitalism. Only major global players of this type, Habermas believes, are adequately equipped to realize far-reaching experiments in cross-border regulation beyond the neoliberal economic integration now advanced by existing multilateral organizations like the WTO or IMF. Although some of the relevant actors might possess state-like characteristics, others apparently would not. Nor would effective coordination between and among regional blocs and/or the Great Powers require subservience to a world state. Finally, at the *national* level, states would hold onto some core elements of sovereignty as classically conceived, though the right to wage war and the protection of basic human rights would now be primarily located at the supranational level. Both transnational and supranational governance would stay in decisive respects dependent on the nation state: "States remain the most important actors and the final arbiters on the global stage" (2006: 176).

Defending a substantial expansion of postnational decision making, Habermas similarly resists the conclusion that doing so demands the institutionalization of state or state-like structures there. Supposedly, we can achieve dramatically improved global security, the systematic protection of human rights, and even ambitious forms of politically progressive transnational social policy *without* having to build postnational states. Those who posit that democratization beyond the nation state has need for a global federal republic remain prisoners of anachronistic early modern conceptions of state sovereignty. In this account, the historically contingent but obsolescent view that democratic constitutionalism relies on state sovereignty keeps us from seizing the possibility of achieved multi-layered democratic global *governance* without global *government*.

Unfortunately, Habermas' model raises the same questions left unanswered by Archibugi's. How might uncooperative governments (e.g. China or Russia) be rendered as accountable to international law as minor powers unless the UN gained independent military and political muscle to force its will upon them? Even if it lacked a *monopoly* on the legitimate use of force, it would still require impressive and probably preponderant political and military muscle if, as in the inevitable case of conflict, it attempted to enforce cosmopolitan norms in opposition to the Great Powers. In short, the impartial application of global law rightly sought by Habermas inevitably engenders the specter, if not of a hyper-centralized global Leviathan, then at least the possibility of a supranational political order in which the UN operates, if only in the final instance, as a binding arbiter. Generality and consistency in the law presuppose some capacity to enforce legal norms without undue dependence on potential violators: state sovereignty remains essential to law's generality. If individual nation states (or perhaps, as Habermas occasionally suggests, regionally based political units) remain final arbiters on a global stage plagued by stunning power and especially military inequalities, it seems improbable that such dependence could be easily reduced, let alone made fair and calculable. Despite his claims to the contrary, a robust cosmopolitan political order underlines the virtues of eventual global statehood (Scheuerman, 2008).

Habermas is surely right to be concerned about obsolete interpretations of state sovereignty which envision it as a more-or-less impermeable, supra-legal entity, a concrete substantial subject that somehow stands beyond and outside the deliberative and participatory practices of democratic politics. This insight leads him and other cosmopolitan-minded critical theorists to jettison outdated ideas of state sovereignty for a robust conception of *popular* sovereignty, according to which it is reinterpreted as meaning that "those who are affected by binding legal decisions have to be included as free and equal members in the procedures of producing these decisions' (Brunkhorst, 2004: 99; also, Maus, 2006). In this view, it is the *people* who should be seen first and foremost as outfitted with sovereignty, now creatively reinterpreted along the lines of a demanding normative model of democracy in which strict egalitarian procedures guarantee that those impacted by binding decisions freely and equally participate in their making.

Although this analytic move seems sensible, it risks ignoring democracy's dependence on state institutions. Even if we plausibly reinterpret sovereignty as a robust model of democracy, we still face the question of what role state institutions should play in helping to realize it. Democratic equality and liberty are best guaranteed by fair and reasonable legal procedures which can realistically be expected to have a determinative impact on action. Influence of this type can only be achieved by forms of institutionalization with which we rightly associate significant elements of statehood. Democratic deliberation and participation only make sense if we can reasonably hope that our voices will result in some course of action binding on others: we require state institutions outfitted with administrative power and coercive instruments, and thus at least something approaching what traditionally has been described as a monopoly on organized force, to preserve equal participatory rights in the fact of potential violations, for example, and enforce majority decisions even against powerful actors who may have a vested interest in resisting them (Schmalz-Bruns, 2007).

Robust democratization beyond the nation state, where egalitarian procedures of decision making are effectively protected and the results of the political process systematically enforced, points to the ultimate necessity of working state institutions. Decentralized systems of legal enforcement, as we know from the mixed record of international law, suffer from relatively substantial doses of irregularity and inconsistency. They also founder in the face of opposition from powerful social groups or, as in the context of loose confederations, recalcitrant member states. Unless contemporary Cosmopolitans can identify *a priori* reasons for presupposing that a prospective postnational political order would somehow be less conflict-ridden than what modern history suggests as the likely norm, it seems premature to presuppose that it could do without recourse to conventional features of modern statehood. Postnational governance would never be plagued by violent secessionist movements, regions or social groups who refused to make minimal financial contributions to the common good, or armed extremist groups which systematically violated the rights of racial, religious, or ethnic minorities? It would not need to act expeditiously and forcefully squelch locally based political tyranny or injustice?

Progressive Realists were right to insist that a normatively attractive as well as viable cosmopolitan polity will have to rest on core components of modern statehood. This, of course, was a major reason why they conceived of it as representing a distant – though still normatively meaningful – goal: powerful states in particular are unlikely to rush to hand over core attributes of sovereignty to novel supranational institutions over which they will possess limited authority. Another crucial reason for their advocacy of world government was that they believed, like Pogge and other contemporary Cosmopolitans, that the terrible destructiveness of contemporary weaponry called for its reduction and perhaps elimination, which in the nuclear age was "much less dangerous than continuing the *status quo*." Such a reduction indeed seems improbable if it remains directly dependent on "the voluntary co-operation of each and every national government" (1994: 103). Nonetheless, they would almost certainly have criticized Pogge's rendition of the Cosmopolitan critique of state sovereignty, according to which the centralized regulation of weapons of mass destruction is consonant with a vertical dispersion of sovereignty and therefore requires no movement towards a world state. To be sure, power at the global level as elsewhere rests on many sources, military or otherwise. Yet it remains difficult to fathom the possibility of global institutions exercising an effective monopoly over legitimate force – and this is ultimately what Pogge wants – without them in fact gaining a preponderant power status in relation to their national institutional rivals.

As should be clear even from our brief discussion, the theoretical and practical issues raised by the concept of state sovereignty remain exceedingly complex. Unfortunately, Pogge reproduces some frequent Cosmopolitan misunderstandings about it. He mistakenly associates state sovereignty with a normatively troublesome as well as empirically implausible idea of *legally absolute* authority, whose anachronistic character is purportedly demonstrated by successful federal states which allegedly *already* disperse sovereignty (1994: 98–103; also, 1988). Sovereignty, it seems, is little more than an anachronistic Hobbesian leftover that has already been overtaken by real-life institutional practice. The argument downplays the key point that successful federal states possess clear legal and political, as well as underlying social and cultural, devices for mobilizing preponderant power resources to resolve dire conflicts: state sovereignty is consonant with a variety of institutional models and far-reaching differentiation as long as effective devices for marshalling superior power resources remain operative. On the global arena Pogge proposes that "persons should be citizens of, and govern themselves through a number of political units of various sizes, without any one political unit being dominant and thus occupying the traditional role of the state" (1994: 99). Here as well, however, the question of how potentially explosive conflicts between and among competing political units could be effectively resolved absent an overarching – and universally binding – system of general law, supported by global-level institutions exercising fundamental state or at least state-like functions, is never sufficiently explained.

The EU: A Stateless Polity?

By any account, the European Union represents the most impressive ongoing attempt to construct a postnational polity. According to a growing number of commentators, however, its experience undermines the view that robust postnational political systems must take on elements of state sovereignty. For defenders of what Glyn Morgan aptly calls the "postsovereignty thesis," the glaring fact that the EU exercises key functions of governance *without* having built a European state highlights the possibility of unprecedented post-statist political forms (2005: 11–32). In the eyes of the German political theorist Hauke Brunkhorst, for example, the EU already exercises "the classic characteristics of sovereignty, albeit without a state" (2005: 131). European law functions at least as reliably as national law, and the EU is already more deeply integrated in some ways than even the US (2002: 530).[17] In Brunkhorst's provocative account, the EU best anticipates the possibility of a historically novel democratic *confederation*, a highly decentralized polity lacking a shared monopoly over violence. Its historical predecessors, he claims, are the United States under the Articles of Confederation [1776–88], the German *Bund* [1815–66], and Switzerland. In contrast, however, it is not simply a *confederation of states* but also a *confederation of citizens* (2008: 493–501).[18] In any event, it is neither realistic nor desirable to pursue European statehood, notwithstanding the dreams of many intellectuals and politicians who helped get the EU off the ground in the first place. The admirable quest to deepen EU democracy can rest satisfied with its emerging character as a decentralized confederation: viable European democracy does not need European statehood.

This argument obviously raises a cardinal challenge to the Progressive Realist ideas discussed above. Yet Progressive Realism can ward it off.

Recall first that Progressive Realists in fact predicted the possibility that cross-border social and economic cooperation within Europe might clear the way for substantial arenas of shared policy making and ultimately economic and political unification. A number of them considered functionalism a useful way to construct its social foundations. Significantly, some preliminary evidence strongly suggests that functionalism – and its influential offspring, neo-functionalism – played a by no means minor part in European political and social integration during the 1950s and 1960s (Pentland, 1973: 64–146). On this point at least, Morgenthau and others were prophetic. In any event, Progressive Realists never denied that when a shared postnational society or community had emerged, ambitious policy-making between and among nation states might succeed. The EU now possesses a relatively far-reaching common political and social identity (Outhwaite, 2008). Progressive Realism can help explain how this happened.

So the real point of contention is that Progressive Realists would be skeptical of the view, endorsed by exponents of the postsovereignty thesis, that the EU might somehow fully mature without ultimately moving towards European statehood. To be sure, this disagreement raises countless empirical as well as normative questions. However, there are sound reasons for defending the Progressive Realist position.

First, even ardent defenders of the postsovereignty thesis typically end up admitting that the EU does *not* in fact presently fulfill all the functions of the existing democratic nation state. For example, Brunkhorst revealingly concedes that key tasks of so-called positive economic integration remain at the national level. Social policy is still primarily the prerogative of national governments, while a great deal of EU regulation has been preoccupied with matters of (limited) negative economic integration. The EU remains in key respects a paradigmatic case of primarily *neoliberal* supranational governance (2003: 530–43). Yet this means that it probably has yet to face sufficient trials of what Morgenthau called the supreme test of any effective government, namely the proven ability "to change the distribution of power in society without jeopardizing the orderly and peaceful processes upon which the welfare of society depends" (1954: 415).

Core attributes of sovereign statehood have oftentimes played a decisive role in allowing political communities to pass this test because "without the chance to resort to force," it is difficult for "governments to implement policies in cases where powerful political constituencies put up resistance to particular rules and regulations" (Funk, 2003: 1059). Although Hobbesian and other excessively statist theories occlude the paramount role played by non-state mechanisms in mitigating conflict, we should avoid forgetting the familiar fact that the state's control over legitimate force has repeatedly helped guarantee both the fairness of democratic procedures and the effective enforcement of sometimes controversial social policies generated by them. Wherever we face collective action problems we need "some kind of authoritative regime that can organize common solutions to common problems and spread out the costs fairly," and then make sure that common solutions are rigorously enforced (Craig, 2008: 135). Particularly within large and pluralistic political communities, government remains necessary if an authoritative regime is to operate efficiently. In social policy, as perhaps in few other political arenas, polities are likely to face resistance from powerful social groups, as the oftentimes bloody history of the rise of the welfare state dramatically documents. Not surprisingly, explosive battles about social and economic policy have played a significant role in the history of modern state making, with the augmentation not only of the central state's taxing powers but also its capacity to redistribute economic resources, however modestly, working to augment both its effectiveness and legitimacy. It remains difficult to see how controversial social and economic policies could ever be systematically advanced without some possibility of recourse to a common system of effective enforcement. If redistributive measures are to be regularized and ultimately legitimized in the EU, and not simply undertaken as temporary ad hoc measures pushed through by insufficiently accountable political elites, there are good grounds for suspecting that the EU will need to develop shared enforcement mechanisms along the lines best institutionalized by modern states.

Second, some evidence suggests that Europeans are *in fact* moving towards a more robust form of statehood. Even though the empirical story here is complicated, individual EU states "no longer have total sovereignty over decision making and implementation of policies in matters of internal security" (Occhipinti, 2003: 2). Anxieties about transnational criminal networks, drug trafficking, terrorism, and immigration have resulted in ever more deeply shared and increasingly complex forms of common European policing and security policies (e.g. the European search warrant), with one German expert describing the movement towards supranationalized policing in Europe as "one of the strongest expanding fields of activity" in the EU (Jachtenfuchs, 2006: 85). Political elites are responding, albeit oftentimes opportunistically and irresponsibly, to popular anxiety about globalizing crime, terrorism, and illegal immigration, all of which indeed cry out for novel forms of postnational state action. As they try to deal with popular fears, they find themselves – at times inadvertently and even unwillingly – enhancing the state capacities of those institutions which alone provide a modicum of security and protection. In our globalizing age, those institutions are now located increasingly at the postnational level. Not surprisingly perhaps, we are witnessing a normatively ambivalent but probably irrepressible expansion of postnational state-like capacities (Shaw, 2000).

To pretend that this is not happening, or to suggest that we can have all the benefits of modern statehood without constructing state or state-like institutions, obscures not only the tough questions faced by Europeans, but also the dangers. Taming the Leviathan at the level of the nation state has proven difficult enough. Can we do so in the EU? Has the process of

European social integration advanced sufficiently so that Europeans need not worry about the specter of political authoritarianism?

Revealingly, Cosmopolitan defenders of the postsovereignty thesis celebrated the massive peace demonstrations of 2003 opposing the US-led invasion of Iraq, seeing in them the harbinger "of a social movement that could mobilize the power used to enforce a new, citizen-based European constitution" (Brunkhorst, 2004: 103; also Habermas, 2006: 39–56). In their view, the 15 February marches served as concrete evidence for the possibility of a mobilized European public able to shape decisively the course of political affairs. In hindsight, however, the impact of the protests on the subsequent course of events was rather minimal: the US not only blustered on with its invasion, but also successfully played off European governments against each other in order to ensure their complicity. Of course, one can only speculate about the likely course of events if the EU had been in possession of a more developed common foreign and military policy. Nonetheless, it remains striking that what undoubtedly was one of the most impressive shows of European-wide popular protest in history resulted in no common European policies able to stem US aggression, while in the US itself, a war that was only half-heartedly supported by a plurality of the population for a limited period was launched and disastrously impacted the lives of millions of people worldwide. If the EU is to operate as an effective "counterbalance" to the US, it will probably have to garner some traditional attributes of statehood: a coherent European defense policy along the lines sought by Brunkhorst and Habermas demands of the EU not only that it shed its postsovereign form, but that it also develop a capacity for independent military action. Otherwise Europeans are likely to remain excessively dependent on American military power, an uncomfortable fact which those who tout the possibility of fusing democracy with postsovereignty ignore (Morgan, 2005: 133–57). Without statehood, Europeans in some important arenas simply will not enjoy as much public and private freedom as those on the other side of the Atlantic. They can sign petitions and demonstrate until they turn blue in the face, but without a common system of state-like institutional devices by which those energies can be forcefully funneled, the US, and perhaps China and Russia will continue, *pace* defenders of the postsovereignty thesis, to determine disproportionately the planet's future.

In part because the idea of a European police or military force able to enforce EU laws against individual member states still worries and indeed repels so many today, any discussion of a prospective European federal state inevitably seems naive and unrealistic. Yet the noble old vision of a federal Europe arguably remains better able to provide constructive guidelines and a clear normative orientation than naive models of a non-statist EU that has miraculously freed itself from the prospect of serious political conflict requiring resolution – as in the past – by a democratically legitimate as well as an effectively equipped system of common enforcement via binding law. To be sure, a serious push for European statehood might easily clash with attempts to strengthen state capacities at the global level. At least for the near future, however, the two processes may prove complementary. As Thomas Weiss points out, the harsh realities of US military hegemony create massive impediments to "bullish notions about multilateral peace operations": US military predominance means that UN security operations remain unduly dependent on American political whims (2009: 131). Refurbishing UN peace-keeping operations arguably requires strengthening them in Europe as well.

Do Cosmopolitans and (Progressive) Realists have to be enemies? This chapter has tried to explain why the real source of their longstanding hostility is based partly in mutual misunderstandings. Indeed, they could be allies, and maybe even friends. Like friends everywhere, they not only share a great deal in common but could learn from each other.

In this spirit, I have outlined some lessons contemporary Cosmopolitans can take from a renewed engagement with mid-century Realists. Progressive Realism provides vital correctives to otherwise appealing Cosmopolitan reform ideals. Admittedly, the news on that front remains sobering. The admirable goal of a global democratic order presupposes a functioning supranational or world society, which we probably still lack. Anyone serious about global democracy will need to think hard about the ultimate necessity of a global or world state, which hardly seems to be on the immediate political horizons. Despite widespread assertions to the contrary, the case of the European Union hardly disproves the admittedly old-fashioned view that democratic governance eventually requires government. Yet even the idea of a European federal state seems unappealing to many today.

For those understandably impatient for overdue global reform, this conclusion will surely seem unsatisfactory. Yet it remains better to look the hard tasks of reform directly in the eyes than pretend that cosmopolitan democracy can be constructed without also building its fundamental prerequisites. A house without a sturdy foundation is unlikely to remain standing for long. As Morgenthau warned global reformers half a century ago, suggesting that one might build such a house would be "tantamount to the advice to close one's eyes and dream that one can eat one's cake and have it, too" (1954: 308).

5 WHAT OTHER GLOBAL REFORMERS CAN LEARN FROM PROGRESSIVE REALISM

Cosmopolitans are by no means alone in seeking changes to the global status quo. Today they are joined by representatives of Liberal Transgovernmentalism, the English School, Republican advocates of global government like the US international theorist Daniel Deudney, and Alexander Wendt, a leading exponent of Constructivist international relations theory and the world state.[1] Where their views are sound, we can identify illuminating overlap with Progressive Realism. Yet on crucial matters Progressive Realism offers a superior starting point for tackling the challenges of global reform.

Liberal Transgovernmentalism's New World Order

Proponents of global reform are likely to be initially gladdened by the forceful thesis being advanced by Anne-Marie Slaughter, a former Princeton University Dean and now Director of Policy Planning at the US State Department: even though world government as traditionally conceived is both infeasible and undesirable, its main functions are *already* being performed by a multiplicity of ambitious varieties of transgovernmental cooperation, or what Slaughter dubs *transgovernmental networks*, defined in her account broadly as "regular and purposive relations among like government units working across borders" (2004b: 14). As she has documented exhaustively for well over a decade, these networks bring together mostly nationally based administrators, judges, and legislators to tackle the myriad policy challenges generated by globalization, while taking a rich diversity of both informal and more formalized organizational attributes (1995; 1997; 2000, 2004a). Transgovernmental networks – for example, the Basel-based system of financial regulation set up by the G-10 countries – induce national officials to share information, harmonize existing norms and rules, and better secure compliance. They are both horizontal in structure – that is, they link nationally based regulators to their peers abroad – and sometimes vertical, i.e. they rest on the involvement of national officials in identifiably supranational organizations to which some governance functions have been delegated. Confronted by a multitude of complex globalization-related tasks, lawyers and judges are also participating in unprecedented types of cross-national cooperation. Because so many facets of national law spill over into arenas hitherto considered foreign, they find themselves regularly meeting and coordinating their actions with colleagues abroad, while increasingly relying on legal precedents and arguments from outside their own national jurisdictions (1999–2000).

For Slaughter, whose analysis leans towards the optimistic and even upbeat, transgovernmentalism is not only potentially supportive of many attractive normative aspirations, but its multilayered, complex, and decentralized attributes mesh well with the dynamic and increasingly high-speed demands of the complicated policy arenas with which it must deal. Unlike the unrealistic and purportedly authoritarian visions of top-heavy world statehood endorsed by mid-century global reformers, the flexible "new world order"[2] of liberal network governance is potentially egalitarian and latently liberal democratic. Perhaps best of all, transgovernmental networks acknowledge that nation states remain the primary vehicles for both effective state action and democratic legitimacy. Although they should be expected to pay heed to global as well as national interests, transgovernmental networks are still primarily problem-solving extensions of the nation state, albeit nation states increasingly dependent on far-reaching foreign cooperation for even relatively rudimentary public policy (2004b: 233). Despite the evident overlap with Cosmopolitan models of "global governance without government," Slaughter criticizes them for downplaying the pivotal role played by national officials. Rival models are also taken to task for occluding the extent to which transnational networks have successfully *refurbished* nation states, allowing them to thrive in a globalizing universe which otherwise might have debilitated them. In part because of such trends, the nation state is on no account withering away.

Though well underway, global reform nonetheless remains incomplete. Building on its existing but oftentimes overlooked successes, transnational network governance needs to be "self-consciously constituted and strengthened" (2004b: 167). Slaughter describes a number of sensible things national governments could better do to tap its potential. In particular, more could be accomplished by way of helping networks share useful information and policy experience by identifying, for example, "best practices" which national governments might be encouraged to pursue. Countries should be invited to join the relevant networks perhaps only if they promise to abide by such practices. In general, reformers should look to the present-day European Union, about which Slaughter tends to wax enthusiastic and from which she thinks many vital constructive institutional lessons can be gleaned. In the face of a number of powerful criticisms highlighting the technocratic overtones of network governance, where core policy matters are dealt with primarily by bureaucrats and judges (Alvarez, 2001; Howse, 2007; Kratochwil, 2010), Slaughter has taken some steps towards explaining why and how reform measures could make it normatively more satisfactory. The nationally based voters to which networks should be accountable should have better opportunities to monitor their activities; Slaughter is particularly keen on using new information technologies (i.e. the Internet) to allow them to figure out what transnational regulators and judges are up to. Most important perhaps, transnational networks need to be structured in accordance with a potentially demanding norm of "global deliberative equality" (2004b: 245–7).

Where then do familiar international organizations – for example, the United Nations – fit into the picture? In refreshing contrast to the recent Bush Administration, whose hostility to basic human rights she eloquently criticized on a number of occasions,[3] Slaughter is certainly appreciative of the constructive role to be played by existing international institutions. Repeatedly asserting that transnational network governance should be seen as *complementing* bodies like the UN, she has endorsed some potentially far-reaching and (at least in the US) controversial reforms, including the expansion of the Security Council and abolition of its members' veto (Ikenberry and Slaughter, 2006). Nonetheless, Slaughter clearly thinks that transnational network governance is where the "real action" for reformers is found; critics have accurately identified a certain tendency in her writings to downplay the potential of more conventional forms of public international law and organization in part by exaggerating their inflexibility, excessive legalism, and rigidity (Alston, 1997). Not surprisingly, she simultaneously overstates the organizational and normative virtues of emerging forms of network organization, while underplaying the ways in which they reproduce relatively traditional forms of inequality and privilege. The United States will remain a dominant global player not only or even chiefly because of its exceptional capacity for participating in global networks, as she has recently suggested, but instead because it possesses impressive military, political, and economic power advantages (Slaughter,

2009). Slaughter seems insufficiently attuned to analytic frameworks providing a more balanced assessment of our emerging "network society" (Castells, 1996).

From the perspective of Progressive Realism, Slaughter's model still has much to be said on its behalf. Although she operates with the usual misleading clichés about Realism (1995: 507), she shares with Progressive Realism a methodological commitment to integrating the study of international law into a broader theory of international relations. Like its mid-century representatives, she endorses basic economic and social reform, worrying – as many of them did – about spiraling social and economic injustice within the US (2007).[4] Even more important, her descriptive account of transnational networks can be readily interpreted as consonant with their sympathy for functionalist-style nuts-and-bolts international cooperation. By describing transnational networks as trial-and-error style experiments capable of generating social trust while responding effectively to down-to-earth policy needs, Slaughter builds on the best of the functionalist legacy.

Unfortunately, the productive intellectual overlap with Progressive Realism ends there. Unlike her Realist predecessors, she endorses – without any sustained defense – the usual prejudices against world government (2004b, 8; 2007, 100–1). For Progressive Realism, functionalism was a practical means towards an ambitious normative and institutional end (i.e. global government). In her reformulation, the (functionalist) means becomes the end, with a cautiously reformed version of elite-dominated transnational network governance – inspired by the existing EU – serving as a brave "new world order" which global reformers have been struggling unknowingly for years to build. For many good reasons, they are likely to be disappointed with the results. Progressive Realism's sensible appreciation for the limits of functionalist international reform simply vanishes from Slaughter's version of the story.

Although in crucial respects a defender of the nation state, Slaughter's theory nonetheless suffers from a latent anti-statism not unlike that plaguing related Cosmopolitan reform ideas. As noted, she overstates the flaws of conventional models of international and global organization, whereas the mere fact that network governance breaks with traditional modes of hierarchical bureaucratic organization is misleadingly taken as prima facie evidence for its normatively attractive – and latently liberal democratic – potential. As her critics have repeatedly pointed out, however, the networks she appreciatively describes (e.g. the Basel-based banking regulatory system) often involve representatives from a narrow and rather homogeneous range of nation states, with at least some evidence suggesting that their secretive and relatively informal decision making mechanisms favor the powerful and privileged. Such "clubs" of policy-making insiders are only congruent with democratic ideals given the empirically implausible pre-supposition that "network 'insiders' are simply publicly interested regulators who implement revealed popular preferences" (Howse, 2007: 234). Whether ambitious attempts to extend such networks into new policy arenas, or the inclusion of heterogeneous representatives from hitherto excluded states, could operate efficaciously without more traditional forms of compliance and enforcement (i.e. state-like mechanisms working to make sure that the strong as well as the weak are required to play by the same set of rules) remains unproven.

Revealingly, Slaughter has relatively little to say about networks emerging between and among elected parliamentarians and legislators, forthrightly conceding that they remain noticeably less developed than those linking (unelected) bureaucrats and judges. Although she advocates greater transnational legislative cooperation, her account ultimately seems conflicted about the capacity of elected officials to participate effectively in transnational networks, let alone properly oversee the activities of unelected officials (2002: 104–30). Notwithstanding the crucial fact that transnational networks are now expected to represent global as well as national interests, she provides no real institutional mechanisms whereby nascent global publics could make sure that they do so. In her account, the chief device for securing the accountability of transnational networks remains located at the national level: national publics are expected to supervise networks of bureaucrats and judges about whose existence they are not only likely to be in the dark, but even if they became aware of them and their activities, would likely seem distant and perhaps impermeable. At best, the relationship between national publics and transnational policy-making seems unnecessarily – and perhaps fatally, at least from the perspective of a robust conception of democratic legitimacy – indirect. Since Slaughter admits that many of those activities now speak directly to identifiably global matters, why not pursue a more immediately global political system to provide for proper accountability? Why not consider the possibility of institutional devices better capable of allowing emerging global publics to supervise transnational networks, and not count primarily on nationally based political interests to get the job done? And if we are serious about securing universal compliance, why not at least consider the prospect of world statehood as a potentially legitimate long-term goal?[5]

Despite her polemical and indeed dismissive comments about world government, Slaughter in fact needs it if democratic network governance is to live up to its ambitious policy and normative potential. As noted, she now argues that network governance must meet a demanding test of "global deliberative equality," according to which "all human beings belong at the table" and have a right to be treated equally in deliberations about our shared fate (2004b: 245–6). For reasons outlined previously in this volume, Progressive Realists might plausibly have suggested that strict fidelity to this norm will require that global governance someday take on state-like characteristics: only states outfitted with a monopoly on legitimate violence can regularly preserve equal participatory (and deliberative) rights in large pluralistic political communities and guarantee that policy outcomes are enforced even in the face of powerful opposition. For better or worse, democracy and statehood represent two sides of the same coin. Notwithstanding her impressive theoretical efforts, Slaughter's reform vision fails in part because it neglects this old but invaluable lesson.[6] To be sure, Slaughter has "identified an important trend [i.e. transnational networks] but significantly overstates its actual or even potential impact" (Alston, 1997: 441). Those of us serious about global reform can legitimately demand more than what she offers.

English School Global Reformism

As first formulated by writers like Hedley Bull and Martin Wight, the English School envisioned the possibility of a third theoretical alternative to Realist and "universalist" (read: Cosmopolitan) visions of international politics. Realists were accused of succumbing to a simple-minded Hobbesianism that inaccurately conceived of interstate relations as an amoral state of nature. Realists accurately capture the rough-and-tumble of power politics, first-generation English School writers conceded, but they miss the existence of a common normative and social framework without which the modern international system could not function. If interstate relations were consistently Hobbesian, how could a modicum of peace and order ever be preserved?

International politics was instead best analyzed as resting on a corresponding international or "anarchical society" in which politicians and diplomats follow a complex array of social conventions, norms, and rules. Realists were chastised for obfuscating the significance of international society, famously defined by Bull as operating

> when a group of states, conscious of certain common interests and common values, form a society in the sense that they conceive themselves to be bound by a common set of rules in their relations with one another, and share in the working of common institutions. (1977: 13)

Only because of international society could sovereign states "cooperate in the workings of institutions such as the forms of procedures of international law, the machinery of diplomacy and general international organization, and the customs and conventions of war" in the first place (Bull, 1977: 13).

The English School notion of international society might at first glance seem conducive to Cosmopolitanism. Given its existence, why not establish a corresponding international political order or even world state? Generally highlighting the unattractive contours of ambitious proposals to extend transnational legislation and adjudication, the English School's original exponents resisted reformism's allure. International society was interpreted as decidedly *thin* in character; its goals were limited and conservative. Presupposing state sovereignty, it contributed modestly to the reduction of interstate violence, political stability, and respect for *pacta sunt servanda* (i.e. respecting treaties) (Bull, 1977: 19). Sovereign states remained suitable vessels for moral, political, and cultural difference, and existing international society constituted no "mid-point along the path to a universal community of mankind" (Dunne, 1998: 11). Universalism's mistake was to overstate the depth of shared norms and values at the international level as well as the manifold fashions in which the state system serves as a sensible, though by no means ideal, complement to cultural and political pluralism.

To be sure, English School writers have typically oscillated between this thin (or pluralist) and a thicker (i.e. solidarist) interpretation of international society. Its pluralist wing emphasizes the existence of deep and probably irrevocable moral, political, and cultural diversity on the international scene. In contrast, proponents of solidarism admit the possibility of a richer and more robust international society and with it also extensive postnational governance. Significantly, some recent English School writers now concede that international society might possess the resources requisite to supporting "new standards of international legitimacy built upon world-order values" such as universal human rights (Dunne, 1998: 11).[7] Blurring the frontier with Cosmopolitanism, English School solidarists have turned their attention to the enterprise of global reform.

What does this all have to do with Progressive Realism? Most immediately, the revisionist interpretation of mid-century Realism outlined above confirms Richard Little's (2003) contention that the English School caricatured a number of its major figures. Progressive Realists neither endorsed a crudely Hobbesian view of international affairs nor ignored the decisive role of international society.[8] When Bull accused Carr of jettisoning "the idea of international society itself" by overstating the ways in which it was crudely instrumentalized by the Great Powers, for example, he exaggerated the degree to which Progressive Realism's preoccupation with power inequalities encouraged its advocates to downplay its analytic status altogether (1969: 638). The differences in their thinking were prob- ably more quantitative than qualitative: Bull himself recognized that politi- cal and economic injustice threatened international society. Progressive Realists also offered a parallel critique of hyper-statist models of global reform, similarly debunking them for ignoring its social presuppositions. Ideas about international – and potentially: supranational society – were always part of their theoretical framework. Unlike present-day Cosmopoli- tans who embrace the mirage of postnational democratization absent post- national state building, both Progressive Realism and the English School underscored the civilizing functions of modern statehood. In contrast to some recent Cosmopolitans, Bull was troubled by the perils of what he presciently described as an emerging neo-medieval global order, in which sovereign nation states were demoted in favor of a confusing and violence prone system of overlapping public and private authorities (1977: 264–76).[9]

So substantial shared territory between Progressive Realism and the English School can be found. The commonalities are most striking among recent expositors of the English School who have tapped its analytic framework for reformist purposes. Barry Buzan, for example, remains critical of contemporary Cosmopolitanism, and hesitant to defend anything approaching a world state. However, he reworks English School ideas about international society – and especially the notion of a *world* society incompletely developed by its main theorists – to defend novel forms of global governance. Especially at the regional or sub-global level, he plau- sibly argues, a deeply textured solidaristic international society has already materialized in some places, allowing for extensive experiments in post- national governance like the EU (2004: 148). Some even take a step further, along the lines of Andrew Linklater and Hidemi Suganami (2006) who marry core ideas about international society to a developmental per- spective which leads them to discard the English School's traditional suspicion of Cosmopolitanism. In part by outlining an ambitious global historical sociology of harm, they properly describe international society as dynamic and evolutionary. A normatively superior global political order constitutes more than mere wishful utopian thinking: crucial developments "have led the modern society of states to expand its interest in [preventing] harm to include the mistreatment of citizens by national governments," and the result is a vastly more developed global society than that described by the English School's original representatives (Linklater and Suganami, 2006: 176). Like Progressive Realism, this admirable reworking of the English School partly joins forces with Cosmopolitanism, while emphasiz- ing the centrality of a complex process by means of which the demanding social and normative presuppositions of a global political order might gradually be constructed.

Despite this overlap, Progressive Realism remains superior even to subtle renditions of English School global reformism in four interrelated ways.

The first difference has already been alluded to: Progressive Realists were generally more attuned to the risks to international society posed by inequality, Amid massive inequality, shared social and normative practices are likely to prove fragile and easily circumvented. Carr, Schuman, and others would have been skeptical of Buzan's claim that a relatively stable global society can be built on the basis of a liberal or free market economy "organized around a host of rules about trade, property rights, legal process, investment banking, corporate law and suchlike" (Buzan, 2004: 151). A liberal global economy generates stunning inequalities and injustices which necessarily tear at the fabric of international society. A normatively attractive as well as workable global community ultimately presupposes the realization of substantial political and economic equalities. Little evidence suggests, however, that neoliberal economics on the world scale can produce them.[10]

Second, even sophisticated English School theorists tend to conceive of international society in a decidedly elite-oriented fashion. It tends to get reduced to a set of normatively imbued elite-level social practices, "a game that diplomats and state leaders reproduce through their action," a series of shared understandings and practices concerning international politics generated by state officials and diplomats (Wheeler, 2000: 21–2). In contrast, Progressive Realists suggested a more multifaceted idea of international (and someday supranational) society, in which the question of why and how *non-elites* might come to comply with and participate in supranational political structures figured just as prominently as elite-level behavior. Their competing approach rested on the implicit assessment that the achievement of supranational society at the level of ordinary political actors was both more difficult and ultimately more vital. It was more difficult to bring about because diplomacy still parasitically depended on the "common framework of moral precepts" which had decisively shaped the classical European-dominated state system as well as the normative outlook of the socially homogeneous groups which traditionally staffed the diplomatic corps (Morgenthau, 1954: 228). For Morgenthau, the threat to the classical state system's relatively high degree of moral consensus primarily came from modern democracy and mass-based nationalism. Correspondingly, his analysis emphasized the need to strengthen social (and normative) ties at the mass or popular level.

Yet his grounds for doing so were more than an analytic leftover from a nostalgic view of classical diplomacy and the "relatively small, cohesive, and homogeneous group" which once filled its ranks (1954: 221).[11]

He and other Progressive Realists recognized that anyone serious about global *democratization* would have to explain how ordinary citizens at the global, as at the national, level could be motivated to play by and defend the basic rules of the political and social game. Without dramatic social and cultural shifts in popular consciousness and practice, no global democracy could thrive. In contrast, the English School's focus on foreign policy elites seems poorly suited to dealing with the analytic and political tasks at hand: democratic politics, unlike traditional diplomacy, is at least *supposed* to be "of the people, by the people, and for the people." The English School approach can surely help make sense of changing views among political leaders and diplomats concerning humanitarian intervention,[12] for example, but it seems limited as a basis for building global democracy.

Third, even those English School theorists who have astutely corrected for such weaknesses reproduce another. Bull's famous definition of international society pointed to the centrality of a *conscious* awareness of *common* values and interests, a *self-understanding* especially among state officials that they were bound by shared rules and institutions (1977: 13). In a similar vein, even as sophisticated a thinker as Buzan tends to analyze recent shifts in international society as entailing a deepening and extension of consciously held shared norms and values (2004: 139–60). Although taking note of the role to be played by an inchoate "we-feeling" in postnational society, his view, like Bull's, places special weight on commonalities in basic moral and political values. In part because he doubts that value homogeneity can be established globally, and because he perhaps unfairly associates Cosmopolitanism with the quest for such homogeneity, he rejects many of Cosmopolitanism's constitutive normative and institutional aspirations.[13]

Progressive Realists also saw shared values as central to supranational social and political integration. Yet they were better attuned to the myriad sociological and psychological attributes of integration which sometimes are only indirectly related to consciously articulated beliefs. So Niebuhr made much of the organic ties on which political communities rest, turning to thinkers like Hume and Burke to explicate how successful polities presuppose latent social and communal ties whose contours are typically misinterpreted by rationalistic models of society. Unfortunately, he also occasionally reproduced, as noted in Chapter 3, some of the problematic implications of such theories. Yet he was still right to worry about views of political and social integration that devalue the key place of psychological and sociological mechanisms about which political and social actors themselves may possess only limited self-awareness. Even if socially meaningful human activities *always* possess some normative significance, their links to consciously expressed norms and ideals can prove surprisingly distant.

Fourth, the English School was never able to "give a proper account of how a system can move towards society, or society towards community" (Linklater and Suganami, 2006: 265). Its main figures deployed the concept of international society for the most part in a historically static way, neglecting to say much about causal mechanisms that might augment or transform it. Like Bull, they also worried about the dangers of fusing scholarship and political advocacy.[14] One unfortunate result was a tendency to avoid prescribing a possible course of action for those committed to deepening international society, notwithstanding their own anxieties about its fragility. To be sure, Buzan and other recent thinkers have tried to correct for this failing as well. However, their interpretation of recent changes to the social underpinnings of the state system still seems relatively ad hoc (Buzan, 2004: 240–8). Progressive Realists were also hostile to naive reformists who crudely conflated "ought" with "is." However, they devoted a great deal of energy to the question of *how* supranational society could be deepened, and with it the basis for postnational government established. One result was a refreshingly free-wheeling debate about how best to initiate global reform. Admittedly, not everything they had to say on the matter represents the final word. Yet they did score some important points; their commitment to rigorous scholarly inquiry never got in the way of well-informed political advocacy. Even if some elements of Progressive Realism now seem obsolescent, its quest to sketch out a hard-headed path to viable global reform should continue to inspire us.

Neorepublican One-Worldism

Daniel Deudney has recently provided a refreshingly creative reinterpretation of republican political thought as a basis for a correspondingly innovative defense of global reform. Building on the legacy of the US framers and especially the *Federalist Papers*, which Deudney interprets as the intellectual high point of modern republicanism, he echoes Progressive Realism by arguing that contemporary realities of "intense interdependence and particularly intense violent interdependence" demonstrate the necessity of postnational governance and eventually world government (2007: 274). Against Neorealists like Waltz, Deudney shares mid-century Realist anxieties about the limitations and perils of nuclear deterrence. Given the accelerated pace of globalization, and especially recent technological innovations that have revolutionized the spatial and temporal contours of military affairs, deep transformations to the traditional state system are imperative. In Deudney's account, the globalization of security is already well underway: since the Second World War, a richly interconnected network of free liberal democratic states, whose political and social dynamics contradict conservative Realist ideas about an international state of nature, has matured under US tutelage. The US' leading role can be attributed in part to the greatness of its nineteenth-century republican legacy (2007: 183).

Nonetheless, Deudney rightly considers the international status quo unsatisfactory. He therefore proposes a novel variety of world government whose fundaments can be located in what he calls "republican security theory." Republican security theory not only allegedly offers a superior alternative to competing perspectives, but what remains valuable in them can sometimes be traced to republicanism. So the Realist preoccupation with the balance of power, for example, can be fruitfully reinterpreted as a somewhat distorted reworking of the older republican view that "mutual restraints" or, in more familiar language, "checks and balances" are essential to security and liberty.

Unfortunately, potentially illuminating overlap with Progressive Realism is obscured by Deudney's tendency to accept some conventional scholarly clichés about it. He characterizes Realists like Morgenthau and Herz as anachronistic "classical nuclear one worlders" whose advocacy of a world or *omnistate* reached "something of a conceptual impasse" (Deudney, 2007: 251). Their fundamental mistake, he argues, was to hold onto a traditionalistic hierarchical idea of state sovereignty. They necessarily pictured the demise of international anarchy as pointing towards what Deudney considers a normatively unattractive and politically unrealistic centralized world government (2007: 252).

Although he is to be praised for taking reform-minded Realists seriously, Deudney misplaces key pieces of the puzzle.[15] First, he ignores the degree to which their reformist aspirations derived from economic, moral, and political as well as security-related concerns. Second, at least some mid-century Realists (i.e. Schwarzenberger and perhaps Schuman) anticipated a model of global governance along relatively decentralized federal republican lines, and not as a hyper-centralized world state, which Progressive Realists uniformly feared. They all worried about excessive political centralization; they repeatedly suggested ways to circumvent it. Third, Deudney fails to pay heed to the argument that a normatively attractive as well as viable global government will have to rest on a corresponding supranational society: the supposedly repressive hierarchical facets of modern statehood could be effectively restrained, Progressive Realists hoped, by a mature world society able to reduce state coercion to acceptable proportions, gradually built via reform (Deudney, 2007: 258). In contrast to both Progressive Realism and the English School, Deudney has surprisingly little to say about the social preconditions of statehood, postnational or otherwise. Perhaps predictably, he provides comparatively meager practical advice about how we might actively advance reform.

Deudney's most significant thesis for our purposes is that an emerging world government could do without the key attributes of so-called hierarchical state sovereignty, a notion in his view rendered obsolete by republican theory and security practices. H. G. Wells turns out to be the pivotal unsung recent figure in the republican tradition since he recognized that "without interstate competition and war to stimulate the erection of a centralized hierarchical state," world government could dispense with key fundaments of modern statehood (2007: 238; also, Partington, 2003).[16] "[B]arring extensive colonization of outer space or alien visitation" world government would not, *pace* Progressive Realists like Morgenthau, need to possess a monopoly on legitimate violence, or in fact look much like most modern polities at all, where state institutions outfitted with centralized power resources exercise sovereignty *over* society (2007: 276). Inspired by scholarship showing how power and especially military competition in early modern Europe determined the contours of modern statehood, Deudney believes that the demise of interstate anarchy might also mean the end of state sovereignty. Absent international anarchy, why would a prospective global state need a massive military apparatus, for example?[17]

Deudney mounts no empirical defense for this provocative claim, in part obviously because no world government has ever existed. Nonetheless, the initially appealing view that a workable postnational government "could be completely lacking in the hierarchical admixtures that free polities have been compelled to adopt to navigate the treacherous realm of external anarchy" does a disservice to the role played by modern statehood in policy arenas *unrelated* to international anarchy (Deudney, 2007: 263). Governments sometimes redistribute wealth from the rich to the poor, or at least from developed regions to less developed ones, and are periodically forced to mobilize state power against privileged groups. In any prospective global polity, a prohibition on genocide or torture would similarly have to be strictly enforced – if necessary, by means of hierarchical political institutions – able to unleash political muscle and potentially force against powerful member states. Minimal hierarchical and indeed coercive "statist" functions will surely have to be exercised by any prospective (democratic) global order.

Preliminary empirical evidence also speaks against Deudney's antistatism. Even postwar liberal democracies like Japan and West Germany, placed more or less directly under the US nuclear umbrella, and partly protected from the exigencies of international anarchy and discouraged from developing a full-fledged military and security apparatus, quickly re-established massive state bureaucracies capable of impressive deployments of power resources. The familiar reason is that internal as well as external political and social conditions require recourse to the organizational advantages of modern statehood. We need a state administrative apparatus capable of enforcing general rules not only in order to grapple with international anarchy, but also to guarantee the more-or-less successful operation of a host of necessary social functions. The modern educational system, whose history has been closely tied to modern state building, is probably inconceivable without state intervention. Contemporary capitalism cannot function in even a minimally tolerable way absent the regulatory and welfare states. Not surprisingly perhaps, and in contrast to prominent Progressive Realists, Deudney has little to say about the significance to international politics of modern capitalism and especially our globalizing political economy, which cannot be stabilized without massive state activity at the national (and increasingly postnational) levels. What he does say lacks the appropriately skeptical tone found, for example, in Carr, Schuman or the young Niebuhr: his at first glance seemingly *critical* theory of international politics seems quiescent when it concerns the economic bases of global politics.

Perhaps because his empirical case for a republican rendition of the fashionable notion of "global governance without government" turns out to be fragile, Deudney devotes massive energy to a historical retrieval of what he considers to be the neglected insights of modern republicanism. Unfortunately, this move fails to shore up his views.

Deudney joins forces with prominent contemporary political philosophers in providing a revisionist reading of republicanism, defined as entailing a commitment to "a plural political order marked by political freedom, popular sovereignty, and limited government" (2007: 13).[18] Republicanism becomes a variant of liberal democracy: unlike an earlier generation of thinkers who salvaged it (for example, J. G. A. Pocock), Deudney is unfazed about alleged declines in civic and martial virtues, public-mindedness, or political participation. Nor does Deudney worry about the ways in which capitalism privileges consumerism and a privatistic social orientation and thereby undermines active citizenship. Nonetheless, this move at least allows him to consider the possibility of meaningful self-government in large, diverse, and populous polities where citizens are unlikely to identify directly with a robust view of the common good, for example, and where direct face-to-face participation cannot have the sort of impact it possesses in small and homogeneous states. It also permits him to circumvent the nostalgia for the male citizen-warrior plaguing at least some renditions of the so-called republican revival.

Yet it comes at a high price, as Deudney then proceeds to interpret the US framers, and especially the *Federalist Papers* (1961), as the apex of republican political wisdom. Despite his ecumenical theoretical interests, this facet of his argument seems surprisingly provincial: Deudney offers an excessively celebratory interpretation of the ideas of writers like James Madison and Alexander Hamilton. As he tends to downplay, the framers were in fact skeptical not only of unhampered majority rule but of democracy in an identifiably modern sense. So their commitment to popular sovereignty was far more cautious and problematic than he admits.[19] The unfortunate result is that Deudney not only reduces republicanism to liberal democracy, but then translates the former into a *thinly democratic* – and anti-statist – liberalism. By means of the arcane intricacies of the US constitutional system, and a stunningly complicated system of checks and balances, the framers sought to circumscribe or at least attenuate the exercise of power by the people as a whole. Not surprisingly, liberal democracies of more recent – and, yes, sometimes institutionally superior – vintage have rightly abandoned many of the more controversial facets of the US system (Levinson, 2006).

In contrast to a large scholarly literature legitimately skeptical of the US rendition of liberal democracy, Deudney sees its excessive countermajoritarian vices as composing its greatest virtue: US republicanism represents a non-statist and non-hierarchical "mutual restraint arrangement" (2007: 277), by means of which popular sovereignty (but not *state* sovereignty) is exercised by "at least roughly symmetrical reciprocal relations of restraint among all the members" (2007: 47). To put the point (only somewhat) more crudely: republican government is "governance without government," where liberty and security are preserved by a complex dispersion of institutional authority and power resources, and competing political authorities can cooperate while always possessing sufficient instruments to block attempts by rivals to gain hegemonic status. Appropriately, he chooses the word "negarchy" to describe what for all essential purposes is a rather eulogistic interpretation of nineteenth-century US liberalism: Deudney admires the system chiefly because of the manifold ways in which it checks political power. Best of all, Deudney asserts, the antebellum US (1789–1861), demonstrated the empirical viability of a purely republican mutual restraint arrangement as a model for a prospective world government. More than a loose confederation, but also less than a conventional federal state, nineteenth-century America achieved a historically unprecedented system of republican governance dispensing with core features of coercive and hierarchical state sovereignty, along the lines commonplace among its European political rivals. In the antebellum US, there was no Weberian monopoly on violence: military force was dispersed among and between a weak central government, state militias, and an armed citizenry.

Even if we ignore the conceptually controversial move by means of which the normatively demanding and multifaceted idea of popular sovereignty is effectively reduced to an updated version of the old (and by no means intrinsically democratic) idea of checks and balances, other problems still plague his exposition. Recall how Morgenthau and Niebuhr, for example, emphasized the key role played by the US constitutional system's preexisting social foundations: because Deudney's approach neglects this crucial matter, he has too little to say about the social presuppositions of the Philadelphian system he defends. Recall as well their criticisms of mid-century efforts to model global reform on the United States and Switzerland for downplaying their respective historical idiosyncrasies. Not surprisingly, Deudney conveniently underplays those facets of US history which challenge his programmatic agenda. Many historians and social scientists will be surprised to learn that the United States before the Civil War (1861–65) was fundamentally non-statist. As Native Americans and the Mexicans tragically figured out, for example, the US federal state, despite its widely noted weaknesses, could rapidly mobilize substantial military muscle. The federal government was strong enough to help maintain a massive system of chattel slavery despite the rise of abolitionism, and it contributed at least indirectly to a spectacular process of economic development. Like other recent critics of the idea of state sovereignty, Deudney takes the idea of a monopoly over legitimate force too literally to mean that decentralized decision making (as found in the antebellum US) provides evidence of its anachronistic character. Yet relatively decentralized republican systems like Switzerland or the early United States flourished because they typically were able to mobilize a preponderance of power resources: they possessed key elements of state sovereignty.

Alternately, we might tentatively accept Deudney's claim that the antebellum US constituted a republican system of "governance without government." Even so, it hardly represents an unalloyed success story since it was torn asunder by a horrific civil war. Deudney discusses this historical fact at some length (2007: 171–6). Yet his interpretation is unsatisfactory. On the one hand, he sees nothing in the experience of the US Civil War to suggest that his favored model of a loose states-union was somehow congenitally flawed. In his account, it was instead the rapid *expansion* of the federal union across the continent that dangerously redistributed power between and among its competing parts and ultimately triggered the system's violent breakdown (2007: 173). On the other hand, he admits that the federal union's flawed character as a "half free/half slave" political entity made "a day of reckoning probably inevitable" (2007: 173–4). In other words, the original US republic was probably doomed from the outset.

This concession, however, supposedly represents no threat to his interpretation of the US as a successful non-statist republican mutual restraint arrangement. Why not? Apparently, we can neatly separate the so-called Philadelphian republican security model from the horrors of slavery: no essential link exists between the two. Interestingly, Deudney never offers a sustained defense of this position, in part perhaps because many core aspects of the system about which he waxes enthusiastic were directly linked to slavery, or at least to political and institutional compromises necessitated by it. The defense of states' rights, just to mention the most obvious example, was immediately tied to the preservation of slavery. John Calhoun, whom Deudney describes as "the theorist who offers the best starting point for conceptualizing the principles and architecture of purely negarchical world government," was the most impressive political thinker associated with the slaveholders' cause (2007: 263).

To be sure, Deudney admits that following the civil war, and then in the face of massive global pressures in the twentieth century, the United States eventually took on conventional statist characteristics (2007: 176). In other words, the US was stripped of those exceptional traits which once set it apart from the rest of the planet. Yet he simultaneously interprets US-dominated liberal internationalism as building on the grand legacy of the framers' republicanism (2007: 181–9). Perhaps this explains why he wastes little time raising the necessary critical questions about the deeply ambivalent and by no means consistently beneficial role of the US in foreign affairs in the last century.[20] Deudney wants to have his cake and eat it as well: he cannot consistently interpret antebellum republicanism as a historically bygone and unfairly neglected political treasure *and* simultaneously see it as crucial for understanding the US' global ascent.

More important for our purposes, Deudney's defense of a historically unprecedented non-statist form of world government delivers less than it initially promised. Despite its admirable intellectual ambition, the argument depends on a one-sided interpretation of state sovereignty, an idiosyncratic rereading of modern republican theory and the US framers, and somewhat tendentious view of US history. For those serious about pursuing global reform and perhaps even some sort of world government, Progressive Realism offers a more fruitful starting point. Progressive Realists recognized that global governance would necessitate the ultimate establishment of traditional elements of *statehood*. They also were rightly skeptical of the view that a loose states-union could provide lasting peace. Even a relatively decentralized republican mutual restraint arrangement will need to concentrate and centralize power resources – including force – in order to maintain its integrity.

Constructivism and the World State

The most important theoretical representative of international relations Constructivism, Alexander Wendt, has also offered a provocative reformulation of the globalist dream of world government. Although Wendt's one-worldism rests on the now familiar collection of misleading preconceptions about mid-century Realism, it occupies some important common territory. Like Progressive Realism, he rejects the view of international anarchy as representing a historically unchanging state of nature, accurately interpreting it as constituted by a complicated array of norms, mores, and shared practices. He goes even further than Progressive Realists, both in underscoring how anarchy is determined by historically alterable ideas which emerge in the context of social practice, and in integrating insights from social theory and social psychology in order to make sense of its underlying dynamics (1992). This argument in fact serves as one inspiration for his definition of Constructivism as committed to the thesis that "structures of human association are determined primarily by shared ideas" (1999: 1). He also acknowledges that power relations shape ideas and norms, even if Progressive Realists might legitimately have worried that he fails to do complete justice to the enigmas resulting from the ways in which ideas and power tend to be mutually constitutive.[21]

Like Progressive Realism, and in contrast to Deudney, Wendt refuses to write off the organizational accomplishments of modern statehood. To his credit, he insists that global governance ultimately demands global statehood. Only a world state can effectively guarantee that the powerful as well as the weak respect global political and legal procedures: it alone has a real chance of taming "unauthorized violence by rogue Great Powers" (2003: 506). *Pace* Neorealists like Waltz, he doubts that a world state requires an ominously hyper-centralized bureaucratic and military apparatus: "[a]s long as a structure exists that can command and enforce a collective response to threats, a world state could be compatible with the existence of national armies, to which enforcement operations might be subcontracted (along the lines of NATO perhaps)" (2003: 506; also, 2009: 193–245). The collectivization of organized violence, in short, can be institutionalized in many different ways. Echoing Progressive Realism, he sympathizes with the view that technological factors (for example, nuclear weaponry) highlight the organizational advantages of global government. Yet he also notes that it could only be successfully built if "the boundaries of state identity ... expand to include all people," that is, if a global political identity and sense of solidarity, or what Progressive Realists dubbed global or supranational society, could come into existence (2003: 510). Like Progressive Realism, global change is envisioned as taking a gradualist evolutionary path. While admitting that proponents of the world state still need to answer tough normative and institutional questions, he considers them in principle answerable. Although the sheer scale of world government might widen the gap between individual citizens and central government, for example, existing large-scale liberal democracies already face similar dilemmas (2003: 526).

Wendt's view is also reminiscent of Progressive Realism's conception of politics as fundamentally agonistic and conflict-laden. Building directly on Hegel's social philosophy, he sees the ongoing and unfinished *struggle* for mutual or *reciprocal recognition* between and among individuals and states as ultimately driving the construction of global government. Also like Hegel, he links a demanding empirical as well as normative argument about recognition to a teleological view of history: not only does a proper analysis of the social dynamics of struggles for recognition demonstrate the inevitability of the world state, but it "will emerge whether or not anyone intends to bring it about" (2003: 529).

Wendt's argument is a rich and nuanced one. Unfortunately, it rests on a number of problematic features. Although Wendt offers the most impressive contemporary defense of world statehood, the Progressive Realist view remains in some crucial ways superior.

Wendt starts with a series of theses about mutual – or what Hegel called reciprocal – recognition. First, the argument is at least implicitly normative: a desirable state of affairs between and among individuals (and ultimately political communities) is reached only when an exacting normative vision of egalitarian social interaction is realized, in which we are "recognized" by others as equals. Even a thin version of recognition, Wendt notes, requires that others be acknowledged as independent legal subjects. Thicker versions imply that we respect others not only as legal equals, but also for those traits which make them special or unique (2002: 511). What ultimately appears crucial to Wendt's redeployment of Hegel is the intuition that reciprocal recognition is impossible amid social relations in which the possibility of violence looms large. In part because violence potentially means the destruction of the "other," but also because the specter of violence poisons social interaction, a political order in which violence has yet to be sufficiently pacified conflicts with the normative requirements of reciprocal recognition.

This is ultimately why Wendt considers any system short of a world state inconsonant with reciprocal recognition. Only in a world government will "[i]ndividuals and states alike ... have lost the negative freedom to engage in unilateral violence," which over time has become ever more terrifyingly destructive (2003: 525). International anarchy, even when hemmed in by the familiar institutions of state-less global governance, leaves individuals and states imperiled by the most powerful states (and, potentially, non-state actors such as terrorists). Reciprocal recognition entails legal as well as moral duties: "Recognition that is not enforceable is in the end not really recognition at all," since it then depends on goodwill or charity, both of which are potentially paternalistic. So if individuals and political communities are to be rendered as secure as possible against violence, and recognition is to be firmly institutionalized via enforceable rights and obligations, we eventually need a world state.

Wendt then couples this implicitly normative argument with an ambitious historical claim, according to which social relations which insufficiently embody reciprocal or mutual recognition – in his language, "asymmetric recognition" – are necessarily unstable (2003: 512–13). With Hegel, or at least with one plausible interpretation of Hegel, he describes history as taking the form of a series of struggles for recognition, in which individuals and states fight to gain respect from those who typically prefer to deny it. In the short run, of course, injustice often appears "legitimate in the eyes of subordinate actors" (2003: 514). Yet in the long run progress results: slavery, for example, gets jettisoned for legal equality, as normatively more satisfactory modes of recognition ultimately gain an institutional footing. Progress is inevitable not in the sense that backsliding is inconceivable, but because over time only mutually satisfactory forms of recognition prove socially resilient. Asymmetric or unequal recognition inevitably faces deep challenges: "If people are denied something of fundamental importance to themselves their acceptance of a regime is likely to be half-hearted," for example (2003: 513). Political and social systems resting on one-sided and unfair recognition eventually founder.

When reinterpreted in terms of the underlying logic of the struggle for recognition, history thus reveals a hidden plan unbeknownst to most of us: unaware of its necessary telos, people for untold millennia have in fact been advancing the cause of world statehood. History is not altogether lacking in human intentionality: "[s]truggles for recognition are intentional" (2003: 529). Yet, paradoxically, social actors need not – and typically do not – aim to establish world government. Nonetheless, even seemingly mundane battles for respect and equal rights point the way towards its eventual creation. Struggles for recognition also transform political identity, over time generating a shared common identity in which far-reaching mutuality and reciprocity can finally be realized (2003: 527). Prior to the creation of a world state, international systems are always transitory: they fail to satisfy our yearnings for respect and recognition. Reminiscent as well of Hegel, Wendt depicts world state formation as passing progressively through five world-historical stages, each of which allows for more advanced and morally satisfactory modes of recognition than its predecessors, with only a world state maximally able to protect us from violence while paving the way for rich and multisided individual as well as collective subjectivity (2003: 516–28).

Like the Progressive Realists, Wendt is implicitly disdainful of naively rationalistic accounts of global reform. His view, as noted, underlines the unavoidability of an arduous series of intense political struggles. Unfortunately, it reproduces a different sort of rationalism of an equally problematic character.

For Hegel, history could best be understood as the progressive unfolding of human and ultimately divine rationality (or what he famously called *Geist*). Despite its horrors and inanities, it constituted a stage on which reason followed a necessary as well as immanent developmental logic, manifesting itself over time in ever more advanced institutional forms and eventually the so-called rational modern state (interpreted by Hegel in a bureaucratic-authoritarian fashion) and a regulated market economy. The weakness of this interpretation, as countless critics have observed, is that it downplayed the irrationality of history as well as the contingency of political and moral action. The young Marx correctly observed that it whitewashed the inhumanity of modern capitalism. Others who broke more decisively with Hegelian teleology observed that it obscured the unpredictable and accidental nature of political and moral action, misleadingly and perhaps quiescently implying that at least *in the long run* rational political and social forms unerringly triumph. On some unsympathetic readings, Hegel's philosophy collapsed moral and political action into a mere accessory of The March of History, able perhaps to accelerate (or decelerate) otherwise inexorable historical processes, but unable to shape human affairs decisively.

Wendt's argument occasionally reproduces these faults. In response to those who worry that his teleological theory distorts the place of human agency, he points to the "possibility for a more globally oriented intentionality in the form of actors who believe in the inevitability of a world state, and try to speed it up" (2003: 529).[22] It remains unclear that the role of political or social movements, or creative political interventions (functionalist reform, for example, or changes to the UN Security Council), consists of more than stepping on the accelerator on a basically predetermined highway towards world statehood. He also seems insufficiently troubled by the prospect that political actors might make bad choices and simply derail global change. When explaining why Great Powers are destined to obey history's underlying one-worldist laws, he optimistically seems to expect them to do so rather than jealously guard what remains of national sovereignty (2003: 524). Nationalism, he analogously argues, is only an apparent or a perhaps short-term threat to world government: as part of the struggle for recognition, it too eventually contributes to its realization (2003: 526–7).

Following a century plagued by terrible political disasters, this account fails to deal adequately with the existential threats posed by stupid and irresponsible political actors. In the long run, only the construction of a world state – and also arguably democracy and social justice, both of which are neglected in Wendt's account – indeed fully meet the normative tests of reciprocal recognition. In the short run, however, political leaders may simply commit horrible acts, or manage to blow us all up.

In part because of such anxieties, Progressive Realists offered comparatively hands-on advice to political actors about how we might prevent nuclear war, tame an increasingly transnational capitalist economy, and actively lay the groundwork for postnational statehood. Even if they similarly believed that innovations in weapons technology demonstrated the advantages of world government, they lacked Wendt's apparent faith that "History" was taking us in the right direction. Welding moral universalism to a Weberian ethic of responsibility, Progressive Realists defended a rigorous political ethics. Not simply an "acceleration" of an impersonal historical process, but instead tough and even tragic choices, as well as creative moral and political action, were called for. In Wendt's contrasting account, the overall status of moral argumentation remains murky. Although relying on demanding normative ideas about recognition, for example, he strangely claims that the question of the normative desirability of the world state is somehow irrelevant to his theory (2003: 529). Following Hegel in opposing a crude juxtaposition of the "ought" to the "is" (i.e. normative to empirical matters), Wendt sometimes risks collapsing the former into the latter.

One source of the argument's occasional Panglossian overtones is its implicitly one-dimensional political sociology. The key social agents in Wendt's philosophy of history are *individuals* and *states* (2003: 494, 507–16). Other relevant social groups – social classes, for example – are excluded from his idealized narrative. Like Neorealism, but in contrast to the mid-century Realism of Carr, Schuman, and others, he offers an oddly circumscribed view of the global system in which capitalism makes no appearance, and rival nation states apparently operate outside of any economic context. The "materialist" factors discussed by Wendt are chiefly technological. His purportedly critical international theory, like Deudney's, remains peculiarly silent on matters of political economy.

At the very least, this lacuna seems methodologically problematic since it excludes *a priori* the possibility that political economy complicates the underlying logic of history. The sociologist Christopher Chase-Dunn, for example, argues that modern capitalism and the interstate system represent two sides of the same coin: the Westphalian system is essential to the reproduction of capitalist relations of production. Even if a world state now represents a normative necessity, capitalism impedes its construction (1990). Admittedly, one might plausibly challenge this claim on empirical grounds, arguing instead that (capitalist) economic globalization requires postnational governance (Held, McGrew, Goldblatt, Perraton, 1999). The point for now is merely that Wendt's reductionist reading of the complex history of struggles for recognition distorts the importance of such controversies. Even more troubling, it prevents a sufficiently serious consideration of a possibility which terrified Herz, Morgenthau and other Progressive Realists: some of the structural tendencies at work in contemporary society may be deeply irrational and potentially suicidal.

To Wendt's enormous credit, he has reignited serious theoretical debate about world government. In the final analysis, he provides a more powerful vision of global reform than Liberal Transgovernmentalism, the English School or neorepublicans like Deudney. Much of his defense of global government overlaps with the best of Progressive Realism. In some telling respects (i.e. its problematic philosophy of history), however, it takes the wrong steps in the wrong direction.

The previous two chapters have undertaken to demonstrate the continuing relevance of mid-century Realism to contemporary ideas about global reform. In significant ways, Progressive Realism offers a more reliable theoretical basis for successfully advancing the cause of global change. Yet at least one tenet of Progressive Realism still needs a proper exposition and rigorous defense. Most readers – and even those like Ernie and Connie sympathetic to Cosmopolitanism – still surely remain skeptical of the idea of the world state even as a long-term institutional goal. In the chapter to follow, I hope to dispel at least some of that skepticism.

6 WHO'S AFRAID OF THE WORLD STATE?

International political theory today comes in many different shapes and sizes. Yet almost all of its practitioners agree that a world state is both infeasible and undesirable. In this chapter, I modestly buttress an immodest point: commonplace criticisms of world statehood are less persuasive than generally thought. Given the limited space available it is unrealistic to undertake a full-fledged defense of world government. However, I can begin to challenge some widespread misconceptions.

When thinkers decry world government as utopian, they generally mean two different things. For some, world government might in principle be attractive, yet it represents at best a distant goal destined to be established – if at all – by future generations. Its utopianism derives exclusively from its temporally far-off character. For others, world government represents both a counterproductive and irresponsible "bad" utopia. The world state, in this competing view, conflicts with essential verities about moral and political life. When Progressive Realists dubbed world government utopian, it was for the most part the first meaning they had in mind. They doubted that world government, when properly conceived, necessarily represented an unattractive goal. In their spirit below I counter key arguments frequently leveled against it. Even if world statehood represents at most a long-term aspiration unlikely to be achieved in our lifetimes or even those of our children or grandchildren, this fact by no means renders it an empty delusion unable to guide political action. Many of us readily admit that ambitious ideals of justice, equality, and democracy which we endorse are unrealizable in the foreseeable future. Nonetheless, we continue to argue about and defend them, as we simultaneously keep our eyes open for footpaths on which we might pursue steps towards their practical realization. Why simply reject systematic reflections about the world state while philosophers, political theorists, and others devote so much time to other equally ambitious and (presently) unrealistic ideas? (Tamir, 2000: 250–1). One possible response, namely that democracy, equality, and justice have already been partially realized in existing practices and institutions, also obtains for the idea of the world state: no one today seriously disputes that new and far-reaching forms of global governance (e.g. the UN, IMF, WTO) have emerged during the last century. According to some scholars the rudiments not just of global governance but perhaps *government* can *already* be identified (Shaw, 2000). In short, we need to consider the possibility that world statehood represents a worthwhile political goal, albeit one which undeniably raises difficult questions.

By now Ernie, Connie, as well perhaps as some readers have begun to reconsider their previous misperceptions about mid-century Realism. Now it is time to take the next step and relinquish unfairly dismissive views of world government.[1]

Why Defenders of the Global State Need to Stay Sober

Given the world state's temporal distance from present generations, most Progressive Realists were sensibly hesitant to proffer institutional blueprints. What role, for example, conventional majoritarian decision making instruments might play alongside countermajoritarian institutions (for example, an independent judiciary) was best left to future generations. Nonetheless, we cannot discuss the world state unless we have a rough outline of its main features. Fortunately, Progressive Realism provides a preliminary template. If I am not mistaken, it suffices to ward off some common criticisms.

First, Progressive Realists believed that any functioning global polity would need to rest on a *supranational society* or *world community* capable of successfully achieving extensive integrative operations. As argued in previous chapters, even if their reflections on the social preconditions of global politics were incomplete, they offer fertile ground for thinking about how a prospective worldwide polity might gradually emerge and someday flourish.[2] Although one might legitimately squabble with some features of their account, they were justified in arguing that political communities necessarily depend on complex underlying cohesive mechanisms which regularly motivate citizens to participate, respect the basic rules of the game, and defend them when necessary. Any full-fledged defense of world government will have to provide some account of how such mechanisms might operate on the global scale. Chiefly because supranational society had not yet matured, Progressive Realists insisted, it was still premature to establish a world state. This point probably still remains valid today.

Second, even as they simultaneously underscored government's social presuppositions, Progressive Realists held onto the now unfashionable idea of *state sovereignty*. As I argued above, they were right to do so.[3] Even if "global governance without government" can perform myriad useful functions, it cannot satisfactorily guarantee that laws and rights will be consistently and fairly enforced, or that policies conflicting with the interests of privileged individuals, social groups, or political entities can be effectively pursued. In order for global institutions to pass some fundamental normative tests, they will eventually need to take on crucial elements of formal *government*. Only a system of binding law, backed up by the not inconsiderable power of the state, can properly ensure a modicum of political and legal reciprocity and equality. To be sure, existing forms of global governance can still be improved *short* of full-scale global government. In the long run, however, significantly bettering both the legitimacy and efficacy of global institutions (for example, the EU or UN) will require that they gain state-like attributes.

Nor does this position entail a soft spot for obsolete notions of "absolute" sovereignty, or a literalistic interpretation of statehood as resting on a perfect monopoly over legitimate force. In real-life terms, many states have generally done quite well with somewhat less, just as they have managed with less than a complete centralization of police and military power. In the United States, for example, decisions to deploy the National Guard by the federal government require assent by the relevant state governors. Nonetheless, no one could plausibly deny that the US government possesses effective capacities to mobilize preponderant power resources and thus core components of statehood. State sovereignty is consistent with a relatively diverse array of institutional constellations.

But does not the contemporary liberal idea of the "democratic peace" show that pacific relations can be secured between democratic states even without overarching postnational political structures? (Doyle, 1983). Progressive Realists would likely have endorsed some recent Realist critiques of this view. They would have worried that it downplays nationalistic and militaristic tendencies found within some existing liberal democracies (Morgenthau, 1970). They always questioned the more naive elements of Enlightenment liberalism – for example, the idea that interstate commerce breeds peace – upon which the thesis probably indirectly depends. They would have recalled that liberal democratic societies have periodically waged horrific wars against colonial peoples and non-democratic states. Even if one concedes the empirical point that democratic states typically avoid war with their political kin, not simply security but a host of additional social and economic imperatives underline the virtues of postnational political coordination. Progressive Realists would have agreed that ultimately "[m]ore robust international political and economical organizations are needed to counter power politics" and deal successfully with globalization's many faces (Marchetti, 2008: 138). Even if empirically sound in some ways, the idea of a democratic peace fails to show how an emerging system of global law could be consistently enforced in opposition to powerful states, let alone how increasingly far-reaching interstate decision making might possess enough democratic legitimacy (Höffe, 1999: 282–95).

Third, Progressive Realists presupposed that any desirable global polity would have to institutionalize *core liberal democratic political ideals* (e.g. equal votes, representative government, and so on). Even as they worried about the parochialism of Western political leaders, the notion of a government accountable via free elections and the rule of law as somehow intrinsically "Eurocentric" and thereby unduly monistic, was alien to them. Peoples everywhere ultimately deserved the fruits of the liberal democratic revolution even if, of course, its main features could be achieved in diverse ways. In part because they noted that such ideals were not universally shared at the present, and that attempts to force them on others oftentimes proved counterproductive, they pictured world statehood as a long-term aim. They consistently attacked the idea that world government might be established by conquest (Morgenthau, 1954: 481–2).

Even if liberal democratic norms have now arguably become more widespread than when Morgenthau, Niebuhr, and others were writing, it surely remains the case that they remain poorly rooted in many parts of the globe. This is one reason, as noted, why Progressive Realists considered institutional blueprints for global liberal democracy premature. Yet their silence on this matter may also have been implicitly predicated on a second sound intuition: given its special challenges, and especially the stunningly pluralistic character of any foreseeable global polity, worldwide liberal democracy will need to rely on at least some institutional devices different from those employed by its nationally based cousin. Just as liberal democracy in large and populous states employs institutional devices different from those found in smaller republics, so too will world statehood demand institutional creativity.[4]

Fourth, Progressive Realists highlighted the manifold advantages of *federalism* for a prospective global polity. As Schuman and Schwarzenberger argued most clearly, federalism possessed the best chance to combine successfully political and legal autonomy in the hands of sub-global political units with new global rulemaking and enforcement. Global federalism provided for differentiated decision making, with global mechanisms complementing local, national, and perhaps regionalized devices, best suited to the arduous charges of global heterogeneity. Its laws would have to be directly binding in some spheres on both member states and individuals. As a more recent advocate of global federalism similarly notes, "federalism proposes a democratic rather than diplomatic union of states, according to which all political representatives are directly elected to a law-making assembly by the people, and political decisions taken by the federal government apply directly to citizens rather than states" (Marchetti, 2008: 154). In contrast to looser forms of confederation, a federal state would have to be capable of readily mobilizing power resources against its constituent parts. In order to do so, it will need to be able to tap effectively into independent sources of revenue, while also maintaining enforcement capacities sufficient to the duties with which it had been constitutionally designated. So a global polity will surely require some sort of supranational police and military force, even if federal-level institutions might hypothetically rely on national police and military capacities just as existing nation states periodically call upon local or state-level police. In any event, when push comes to shove, federal institutions will have to be able to unleash preponderant power – if necessary, in opposition to powerful social groups or member states – in order to ensure the binding character of their decisions.

Fifth, even if Progressive Realists never used the term, they sometimes pointed towards what is now commonly described as *subsidiarity*: unless the scope and scale of the issue at hand or its potential impact requires otherwise, policy matters are ideally left to those directly affected by them. Issues best tackled at the local, national, and regional levels should be dealt with there. Federal authorities should only act when others cannot reasonably confront the enigmas at hand; a prospective world state would have legitimate authority to deal only with those matters which cannot be competently and effectively legislated elsewhere. In this spirit, Morgenthau called for a "limited world government" whose exclusive task would be to police nuclear weapons and break the stranglehold of national sovereignty over them (1960: 173).

The principle of subsidiarity hardly provides ready answers to many tough political and institutional questions. Even under the best of circumstances, global-level federal and national institutions will sometimes be at odds, as sometimes happens in existing federal systems. However, subsidiarity seems essential if we are to ward off the excessive centralization (as well as bureaucratization) of decision making at the global level, which Progressive Realists rightly sought to circumvent.

Admittedly, this preliminary model of a liberal democratic federal world state – resting on supranational society and committed to the principle of subsidiarity – remains underdeveloped. Yet even the bare outlines of the Progressive Realist vision provide a starting point for warding off commonplace criticisms of world government.

World Government Means Nowhere to Hide

Hannah Arendt once asserted that world government "could easily become the most frightful tyranny ever, since from its global police force there would be no escape –until it finally fell apart (1972: 230; also Walzer, 2004: 185). In this view, a global polity is a recipe for disaster since by definition it denies the possibility of alternative political communities to which we might need to flee. Its price is simply too high: world political unity would be achieved at the cost of destroying that minimum of political pluralism necessary to provide us with a reasonable chance of escaping tyranny.

Given the horrors of a century in which millions have been forced to flee from their homes for political reasons, the argument initially seems incontrovertible. Yet it rests at least implicitly on three flawed assumptions. First, it risks idealizing the extent to which under present conditions individuals or groups can successfully escape oppressive governments: would-be refugees cannot simply get up and go where they wish. The existing system of national sovereignty gives states many familiar incentives for opposing open borders. Second, it excludes *a priori* the possibility that a substantial dose of political pluralism might be institutionalized *within* the confines of a differentiated federal polity, in which national communities maintained substantial independent decision making powers. A global polity might in fact alleviate some of the dangers presently faced, for example, by religious or ethnic minorities: movement across borders would presumably be somewhat easier than under contemporary conditions, where the fusion of sovereign statehood and national identity often impedes their free movement. Third, the claim prioritizes political pluralism vis-à-vis democratic self-rule. A world state would only be worth having if its liberal democratic credentials were sound. Of course, any prospective global political majority will surely make some dumb and indeed unjust decisions. But then the proper response would be political mobilization and civil disobedience or –in a worst case scenario – perhaps revolution. Yet there is no principled reason why the right to escape from a global polity should be privileged over the right to establish and live under a universal democratic polity (Horn, 1996: 250–1; Marchetti, 2008: 159–60).

World State Means World (or at least Civil) War

As two prominent German political scientists have recently claimed, since it is difficult to imagine all states voluntarily joining a global federation, one "must thus assume that reluctant states would have to be constrained by the use of military force" (Rittberger and Zangl, 2000: 213). War would result. Alternately, even if a world state were somehow set up, extensive cultural, social, and political heterogeneity would mean that not foreign but instead horrific civil wars would occur. Since a world polity could only thrive given an unprecedented centralization of coercive state capacities it would be prone to global civil war: its hostile constituent parts would each have strong incentives to try to seize control of the powerful central state apparatus (Waltz, 1979: 111–12).

This view eliminates by definitional fiat the possibility of a peaceful and gradual evolutionary transformation, along the lines advocated by Progressive Realists. Under *contemporary* conditions, a world state could indeed only be established violently, and if somehow miraculously set up would immediately be plagued by civil war. But there is no argument even attempted by such critics explaining why the long-term possibility of a robust supranational society adequate to the task of supporting world government has to be dismissed out of hand. At the very least, the rich history of large and diverse federal systems (e.g. India) offers examples of stunningly diverse, populous, and more-or-less politically and socially integrated liberal democracies. To endorse the claim – made recently by the international lawyer Eric Posner as well (2009: 8–9) – that global pluralism dooms movement towards a robust global society and corresponding global state seems both conceptually dogmatic and ahistorical.

Not surprisingly, such critics revert to a more subtle version of the argument: the attempt to realize a cosmopolitan polity would lead to a disastrous intensification of political conflict. Undertaken in the name of a cosmopolitan vision of a unified humanity, the battle for world government necessarily unleashes horribly violent political and martial energies. Its opponents will inevitably be targeted as "enemies of humankind," and violent bloodshed on an unprecedented scale must result. Self-righteously armed with a naive faith that they alone speak for a universal humanity,

one-worlders will quickly abandon conventional moral and legal restrictions on warfare (Schmitt, 1996 [1932]: 36, 51–4).

Even if we ignore the fact that most global federalists today seem like
a peace-loving bunch, and that Progressive Realists unequivocally rejected
a violent path to world government, at its core this is really an argument
about the dangers of a naive moral cosmopolitanism. As we saw above,
Progressive Realists openly acknowledged such dangers.[5] However, they
thought that they could be contained by building on a stringent ethic of
responsibility demanding of political actors that they recognized that even
morally well-meaning actions sometimes produce counterproductive consequences. The real target of this criticism is a simplistic cosmopolitanism
which closes its eyes to the complexities and perils of political action in a
violent world. Any attempt at global reform obviously needs to take such
complexities seriously. Moreover, it is hardly empirically self-evident that
wars waged under the banner of universal humanity have consistently
proven more bloodthirsty than those justified by non-universalistic appeals.
The Nazis abandoned the barest rudiments of moral cosmopolitanism, for
example, yet their style of warfare cannot be described as having been less
barbaric than that of their rivals.

World State Means the End of Politics

According to Carl Schmitt, political life always "presupposes the real
existence of an enemy and therefore coexistence with another political
entity" (1932 [1976]: 53). A world state would mean the demise of politics
since we would no longer find ourselves in a universe where distinct organized collectivities faced off against each other in an agonistic and potentially violent fashion. "[A] completely pacified globe," and thus a world
state where state sovereignty was collectivized, "would be a world without
the distinction of friend and enemy and hence a world without politics"
(1932 [1976] 35). Echoes of this argument can be found not only among
Schmitt's disciples, but also among communitarians and nationalists who
otherwise reject his idiosyncratic ideas about politics (Mouffe, 2000;
Walzer, 1986: 239–40).

One sensible response to this position would be simply to reject the
thesis that politics requires potentially violent antagonistic groupings or
collectivities, a hostile "other" with whom nothing of political note can be
shared. As the political theorist Arash Abizadeh argues, defenders of the
view that a global polity means the demise of politics sometimes accurately
describe political identity as presupposing complex processes of differentiation, dialogue, and struggles for recognition. Nonetheless, they fail
sufficiently to prove the case that such processes necessarily culminate in

what Schmitt bluntly described as a hostile "existential other" against whom "the real possibility of killing" looms large (1976 [1932]: 33). Such arguments reify unattractive but historically contingent features of identity-formation under the aegis of the Westphalian system, where state sovereignty and national identity joined forces so as to transform political outsiders into life-or-death alien threats against whom force was periodically unleashed (Abizadeh, 2005: 45–60).

Progressive Realists opted for a more modest yet similarly effective counterargument. Not unlike Schmitt, they endorsed an agonistic model of politics: intense conflict constitutes an indispensable feature of the human condition. Morgenthau, for example, was not only intimately familiar with Schmitt's views on politics, but in fact claimed with some plausibility to have influenced their more palatable components. He similarly grounded his agonistic model of politics in philosophical anthropology. Nonetheless, he spurned Schmitt's conclusion that a plausible vision of politics implied the impossibility of a global community in which intense conflicts no longer readily took violent forms. Not coincidentally, he also abandoned Schmitt's peculiar thesis that a world without the prospect of potentially violent rival collectivities was somehow lacking in moral value or seriousness (Scheuerman, 1999: 225–52). In his alternative account, politics could thrive in a setting where "the real possibility of killing" had been substantially reduced. Intense political conflict might flourish within the boundaries of well-constituted political communities. It exemplified not only theoretical rigidity but in the nuclear age also normative callousness to accept as historical necessity the irrepressibility of interstate violence. Notwithstanding Schmitt's quest to exclude *a priori* the vista of an intensely politicized yet simultaneously pacified universe, history in fact provided countless examples of how political conflict could be fruitfully civilized by

> social pressure which is capable of containing the evil tendencies of human nature within socially tolerable bounds; conditions of life, manifesting themselves in a social equilibrium which tends to minimize the psychological causes of social conflict, such as insecurity, fear, and aggressiveness; and finally, the moral climate which allows man to expect at least an approximation to justice here and now, and thus eliminates the incentive to seek justice through strife. (Morgenthau, 1945b: 437)

World Government Means No Real Political Identity

Without endorsing troublesome Schmittian ideas about a necessary linkage between politics and violent conflicts among rival collectivities, one might still legitimately worry that the dream of world statehood obscures the need for deeply rooted *particularized* political identities, typically of a national but perhaps taking other forms as well, without which underlying relations of trust, solidarity, or an inchoate yet decisive "we-feeling" necessary to political life cannot exist. Today this argument comes in many different communitarian, nationalist, and republican bottles (Lu, 2006; Tan, 2004). What they all endorse is deep skepticism that a cosmopolitan polity could ever cohere with the preconditions of meaningful political identity. At best, a world state would rest on a thin or bland common identity inadequate to the tasks of modern government: even under the best of circumstances, citizens of a heterogeneous global polity could never share as much, for example, as the national consociates of Greece or China. At worst, a world state would open the door to the decimation of desirable existing practices by subverting local and national identities on which liberal democracy and the welfare state alone can flourish (Miller, 1995).

Needless to say, this is a noteworthy criticism, earlier versions of which quite reasonably preoccupied mid-century Realists. For reasons described at length in previous chapters, however, they at least wanted to hold open the possibility that postnational polities might replace existing – and primarily national – roots of political and social integration with new ones. Rather than again reciting those claims, let me suggest another possible rejoinder.

Even if we accept a nationalist or at least particularist conception of political identity, why must a global federal polity based on subsidiarity impoverish it? As even Raymond Aron, a writer sympathetic to nationalistic views of identity allowed, the most obvious answer would be a federation in which specific "communities of culture" were preserved, with individual political units merely renouncing "those powers needed by the superior unit in order to insure the protection and welfare of all" (1966: 752).[6] As a matter of historical fact, pluralistic federal systems like Canada and India have done reasonably well in terms of protecting discrete cultural and linguistic communities while simultaneously allowing for the shared political culture requisite to effective governance at the federal level. Those, like the political philosopher Michael Walzer, who instead endorse a Wilsonian model of national self-determination, badly downplay the ways in which it has consistently failed to protect small and fragile national communities (1986: 227–40).[7] With disastrous results, precisely the completion of the Wilsonian model advocated by Walzer was attempted in interwar Europe: as Carr and Morgenthau accurately chronicled, the Wilsonian ideal of one nation/one state destabilized existing states and paved the way for the cataclysms of a Second World War. Such experiences understandably suggested to them that particularized political identities might in fact gain superior protection under the auspices of larger postnational units.[8] In an alternative global system in which statehood was decoupled from nationality, security between and among national groupings better preserved, and the state deprived of incentives presently motoring cultural and national homogenization, particularistic national communities could thrive.

World Government Means Homogenization

Yet this last defense of world statehood still remains vulnerable to the anxiety

> a world government faced with the coordination of vast resources, a myriad of communication and trade facilities, and other giant economic challenges which must be met by general solutions will certainly be subject to the same tendencies to stereotype its society by constantly widening the sphere of world jurisdiction at the expense of local predilections. (Mangone, 1951: 67)

Like existing nation states, a federal global government outfitted with tangible regulatory tasks will require an extensive shared political culture and common "way of life." The modern state is an intrinsically homogenizing force which stereotypes or normalizes society into general patterns according to modern legal and administrative imperatives. Note that this argument transcends the relatively commonplace assertion that a global liberal democracy requires a *minimal* commitment to core procedures and rights. Instead, it supposedly needs a far-reaching shared global identity: world or cosmopolitan government means political and constitutional monism (Cohen, 2008). This criticism also aptly zeroes in on the troublesome disciplinary attributes of modern statehood, suggesting that they would inappropriately undermine pluralism and particularized political identities.

It seems both naive and disingenuous to downplay the force of this claim. Nonetheless, four points need to be made. First, such critics have to concede that such tendencies are already at work at the national level, where the state's homogenizing tendencies squelch occasionally – but by no means necessarily – admirable particularized identities. A global state might simply mean "more of the same"; it is unclear why it would entail a qualitative increase. Second, different political and social systems already counter normalizing tendencies more or less effectively. So we should probably not picture them as unchanging historical constants. Federal systems, for example, check tendencies towards cultural and national assimilation more effectively than centralized nation states. Subsidiarity helps do so as well. Global federalists, to be sure, will need to think hard about new institutional devices able to circumvent the specter of a homogeneous and perhaps bland political monoculture. Yet given the rich institutional history of modern democracy, it seems short-sighted to discard the possibility of developing them.

Third, even if world government requires a sufficiently robust cosmopolitan political culture and shared global identity, it is hard to see why it could not coexist fruitfully with familiar national or local loyalties (Tan, 2004). Hybrid political identities are already part and parcel of political modernity. A Scotsman in Glasgow can be proud of both his local heritage and his UK citizenship. A religious Jew may send her children to Israel for the summer while staying home to celebrate the Fourth of July in Brooklyn; in Texas, Latinos celebrate the same holiday with Spanish songs and rituals imported from Mexico. Quebecers insist on strong linguistic and cultural rights even while cheering on the Canadian national hockey team when it plays its US arch-rival. To exclude the prospect that new and sufficiently robust hybrid political identities might emerge seems strangely ahistorical.

To be sure, as in any other viable political and social order, a world state will inevitably place some limitations on difference: cultural and national practices incongruent with basic liberal democratic norms will raise tough political and legal questions there as they presently do in large and diverse nation states, federal or otherwise. Yet the dogmatic assertion that cosmopolitan identity entails homogenization seems blind both to the lived experiences of many of us on an increasingly globalized planet and to the possibility of constructing new global-level political and social supports for pluralism.

Fourth, the argument perhaps recalls one sound reason why any global polity should perhaps only centralize decision making concerning a limited range of policy matters (e.g. security and human rights). By narrowly fixing the scope of issues on which a prospective world state directly acts, its homogenizing tendencies might be circumscribed. For those worried about the homogenizing and imperialistic implications of a global political culture, limited world government may be the best way to go.

World Statehood Means Despotism

Perhaps the most common criticism of global government is that it would inexorably generate a despotic concentration of coercive power if it were to preserve law and order on an unavoidably heterogeneous and divided global order. Typically appealing to Immanuel Kant, figures as diverse as the political philosopher John Rawls and Neorealist Waltz have endorsed this thesis (Rawls, 1999: 36; Waltz, 1979: 111–12; 2008: 3–18). Despite the fact that Kant's own version of it probably rests uneasily with some core feature of his political philosophy, his good name has provided a convenient fig leaf for lesser thinkers who fail to defend it adequately (Horn, 1996).[9] No world government could take a limited let alone legally and constitutionally legitimate variety: it demands a massive despotic state apparatus, perhaps even a "totalitarian monster" along the lines nervously described by Morgenthau.

When examined more closely, proponents of this critique seem to have two different worries in mind. First, and least convincingly, they posit that government on a global scale would have to marshal an awesome range of power and especially coercive instruments; no such government could ever secure basic liberal or democratic ideals, let alone be restrained by conventional legal or constitutional devices. Unfortunately, this version of the thesis dogmatically and ahistorically vetoes the possibility that social mechanisms – in other words, supranational society – might someday civilize cross-border political and social tensions sufficiently so as to undergird a decent global polity. For that matter, why accept what amounts to a revival of the early US Anti-Federalist critique of large compound federal republics at the global but not, for example, also at the regional or continental levels? (Marchetti, 2008: 160). Not coincidentally, such critics neglect the US Federalist theorist James Madison's famous insight that large and diverse federal systems generally do a better job than small and homogeneous polities at circumventing political domination by narrow and parochial factions. If so, might not a world state prove even more success-ful than existing nation states at counteracting tyranny? (Cabrera, 2004: 99). Such critics also obfuscate the harsh reality that for many hundreds of millions of people today, the global status quo *already* seems tyrannical and perhaps despotic: rich and powerful states, undemocratic transnational organizations (e.g. the WTO, IMF), and powerful capitalist firms mostly based in the rich countries determine to an alarming degree not only whether or not they and their offspring will flourish, but whether they will even survive (Tamir, 2000: 263).

Though I criticized Daniel Deudney in Chapter 5 for positing that global governance could relinquish the basic accoutrements of modern statehood, his ideas contained a valuable core insight: interstate competition helps undergird the expansion of the state apparatus and especially its police and military functions. Rival states participate in costly arms races, their mili-tary elites gain ascendance over civilian peers, and they regularly augment potentially repressive security apparatuses. At least potentially, the demise or at least mitigation of such tensions under the auspices of a global polity might reduce the scale and scope of the security apparatus, particularly if it could rest on a thriving and well integrated supranational society. In short, this criticism overlooks familiar ways in which the existing Westphalian system augments despotic "big governments": some of the structural forces supporting the modern garrison state derive from existing – and historically alterable – political conditions.

Second, and more persuasively, critics argue that a world state could never satisactorily respect fundamental constitutional and legal ideas, let alone efficaciously employ state power via proper legal and constitutional channels (Maus, 2006). Political and social complexity at the global level would render global government not only unworkable, but its actions would ineluctably violate normatively sound notions of the rule of law and constitutionalism. A global government forced to engage in extensive social and economic regulation, for example, would have to sacrifice any notion of the rule of law as demanding of states that they act according to general, clear, stable, and prospective norms. This criticism gains some force from a disturbing tendency in recent scholarship to inflate ideas about the rule of law and constitutionalism so as to render them descriptively useful while obliterating their normative substance (Somek, 2011).

Three responses are called for here. First, those who defend this version of the despotism thesis typically accede that such trends are *already* manifest at the national level. Here again, a dramatic disjuncture between national and global politics is asserted but in fact never demonstrated. Of course, we should worry about excessive legal arbitrariness and challenges to constitutional government. Yet it remains unclear that their likelihood is increased at the global over the national scale. Ungovernability derives from poorly conceived policies and bad legal design: this remains a danger at *any* level of government. Second, critics also downplay the centrality of both federalism and subsidiarity to legitimate world government. Many central decision-making mechanisms would necessarily remain at the national level; it would likely prove both politically unrealistic and administratively ineffective to outfit global federal authorities with complex legislative tasks for which they are poorly suited. If global political actors instead stupidly tried to do so, global citizens should do what their national peers do: throw the bums out.

Third, and most important, the criticism counts out any chance of initiating novel mechanisms for governance which might do justice to global complexity while also upholding sound legal and constitutional ideals. In this vein, elsewhere I have tentatively proposed a model of global *reflexive law*, in which centralized decision makers would primarily be responsible for coming up with a set of clear *procedures* by means of which more specialized legislative bodies would then derive specific *norms* or *rules* attuned to local, regional, or national conditions. Lawmaking would be reconceived so that central (or federal) actors typically need not be responsible for promulgating substantive policies or universally binding rules. Instead, their main job would be to create clearly formulated – as well as fair and equal – procedures for legislation to be generated elsewhere. Not only might such a model sufficiently conform to a robust interpretation of the rule of law, but it might also prove suitable to the imperatives of complex global decision-making (Scheuerman, 2004: 210–24; 2008: 105–21).

The general point here is that both the idea of the rule of law and constitutionalism are potentially realizable in novel ways, even if we obviously need to avoid unnecessary normative compromises which endanger their existing achievements. Only a cramped view of modern legal and constitutional traditions suggests that their institutional possibilities have already been fully exhausted by modern nation states.

Global Government Means the End of Democracy

According to some critics, "the enormous scale of a single global government would render representation and other aspects of democracy hopelessly problematic" (Cabrera, 2004). The scope and scale of world government make its operations distant and alien from ordinary citizens; no participatory or representative mechanisms could ever successfully compensate. For Robert Dahl, the foremost exponent of this view, "the opportunities available to the ordinary citizen to participate effectively in the decisions of a world government would diminish to the vanishing point" (1999: 22). If many citizens in existing systems already feel alienated from the machinery of lawmaking, they would do so to an unacceptable degree in a worldwide global polity where every citizen's voice was now only one among *billions*.

The immediate Achilles' heel of this challenge is that it fails to consider seriously the possibility that federalism and subsidiarity might reduce the perils it otherwise astutely identifies. In addition, it occludes the unsettling fact that many decisions are *already* being made by powerful states and privileged private interests affecting billions of people over which most of them have little say: when China or the US refuses to cut back on emissions contributing to global warming, or a handful of large Western banks pursues irresponsible policies resulting in a worldwide economic catastrophe, they are decisively shaping the lives of countless people who never had a chance to participate in making them. From the perspective of the politically and socially excluded, one person/one vote in a humongous world-wide polity with billions of citizens even now would represent significant improvement. Globalization's forward march means that its chances of doing so will likely increase in the future. The criticism also implicitly treats geography as an historical constant, misleadingly inferring that the relationship between a global government and ordinary people necessarily must be plagued by a sense of extreme distance. Yet this nexus is a socially variable one determined by historically alterable experiences of space and time. In the early US, for example, it took members of Congress many days to reach Washington, and information about its deliberations just as long to get back home. Today citizens can switch on their televisions and watch live broadcasts of congressional hearings and key votes, while firing off electronic messages to their representatives in a mere nanosecond.

The point is not that global democracy can rely on an easy technological fix (for example, computerized referenda), but instead that we should avoid rigidly excluding the possibility of dramatic shifts in how we experience and interact with government. If worldwide political authorities acted effectively to secure basic rights and preserve the peace, citizens would likely come to identify with them, just as our historical predecessors gradually transferred loyalties from local to national political entities in part because of the effectiveness with which the latter performed vital tasks. Like nationally based democracy, global democracy will need to implement political and social devices capable of counteracting political alienation and successfully linking individual citizens to federal institutions. However, to exclude *a priori* the chance of doing so merely because of large numbers or geographical distance misses some of the more interesting lessons of modern democratic political development.

World State Means Class Rule by the Poor

On a planet divided by stunning material inequalities, where billions of people struggle just to get by, world government would supposedly lead to a massive redistribution of economic resources from the rich to poor. Facing destitution, the poor will rush to transform the world state into an instrument of class tyranny: as democracy's manifold opponents ominously predicted for centuries, it would then indeed mean unharnessed class domination by the poor. In addition, world government threatens sound economic policy by inviting the desperate masses to punish prosperous and productive peoples and national communities.

In its crudest form, this argument seems untenable. First, it is by no means normatively self-evident that democracy should *not* permit significant economic redistribution. What's so bad about millions of children no longer facing starvation or debilitating diseases from which rich peoples no longer suffer? Second, a federal global polity constructed along liberal democratic lines would necessarily include familiar institutional checks against popular majorities. Even in class-divided countries like India, revealingly, democracy has not allowed the poor to swamp the well-to-do with unreasonable policy demands. As an empirical point, notwithstanding the anxieties of its conservative critics, democracy at the national level has rarely generated demands for massive redistribution. So there are at least some reasons for believing that similar anxieties are likely to prove as overheated at the global as they have at the national level.

When formulated in a more subtle fashion, the criticism is less easily discarded. As a number of Progressive Realists worried, no supranational society or global community was likely to buttress social and political integration amid stunning inequalities, material or otherwise.[10] Successful statehood presupposes the more-or-less automatic performance of certain underlying social activities which rest implicitly on a modicum of reciprocity and material equality, or at least a sufficiently shared sense of justice. If the rich and otherwise privileged can consistently pretty much get what they want and evade common rules (e.g. taxation laws), the poor and socially vulnerable will come to question government's legitimacy. At crucial junctures, they may fail to defend the political order, or simply evade common rules by their own devices. Materially divided societies oftentimes lack a sufficiently robust sense of common justice or the common good. Without them, the fragile and complex formal as well as informal devices whereby political and social integration are supposed to take place become imperiled. Substantial empirical evidence already shows that inequality corrodes trust and divides "government from citizens, rich from poor, minority from majority" within nation states (Wilkinson and Pickett, 2009: 51). Unless checked at the global level, it will prevent a viable political order from emerging there.

On an even more immediate note, it is unclear why rich and powerful countries would ever join a global federal system likely to be dominated by the poor. Even the most popular politician in the wealthy countries of the North would be committing political suicide by seriously advocating, for example, that core functions of social and economic policy today be handed over to a democratized and reformed United Nations, in which poor and populous countries were given the right to determine their economic fate.

These are serious worries. However, at least one response deserves consideration.

Not altogether dissimilar from the expectations of Progressive Realism, a host of functionalist-style international organizations, focusing on concrete policy tasks tackled by creative institutional means (for example, the IMF, WTO, or International Labor Organization [ILO]), have already deepened humankind's sense of a shared social and economic fate. Within the United Nations, many specialized agencies to some extent designed in a functionalist spirit (Claude, 1971: 378–408; also, Groom and Taylor, 1975), have helped do so as well. In part because of such developments, global society is more mature than it was when mid-century Progressive Realists chronicled its limitations. Even if today it still offers too insecure a foundation for full-scale world government, only the most one-sided analysis of global law and institutions could miss the advances that have occurred in the last fifty years or so. Whatever the blind spots of existing discourse about "global governance without government," its enthusiasts have convincingly described the far-reaching ways in which important policy and legal functions are now exercised at levels beyond the nation state.

So recent historical experience tentatively suggests that well-designed institutional reforms might contribute to the deepening of supranational society, and perhaps the achievement of one in which explosive class and social divisions had been reduced. If one looks at recent trends in global economic regulation, however, it is hard to avoid the conclusion that they have taken an overwhelmingly *neoliberal* character, with the emphasis placed on reducing trade barriers, opening up markets, limiting state regulation, and encouraging the free flow of capital across borders (Reinicke, 1998). The most important functionalist-style institutions at the global level (for example, WTO and IMF) remain neoliberal bastions. Even if such global bodies have helped cement the foundations of an emerging global society, they have insufficiently contributed to countering material inequalities which not only breed injustice and disorder but also impede progress towards an integrated supranational society.

In this context, one present-day Cosmopolitan reform proposal meshes well with Progressive Realism. Held advocates the "opening up of functional international government organizations (such as the WTO, IMF, and World Bank) to public examination and agenda setting," to be undertaken perhaps by elected supervisory bodies, in part as a way of guaranteeing their accountability to a sufficiently broad range of social and economic perspectives (2004: 112). Held hopes that their predominant neoliberal orientation could in this way be checked by identifiably social democratic policies. In a parallel spirit, many activists, labor organizations, and even some major national governments have argued for outfitting the WTO and NAFTA (North American Free Trade Agreement) with strict "social clauses" in order to create enforceable institutional mechanisms making them more responsive to the needs of workers and the socially vulnerable (Cabrera, 2004: 128–42). The underlying motivation seems twofold. First, there is no reason why the negative externalities of economic globalization have to be disproportionately borne by the poor and working classes. Second, given their institutionally developed character and obvious centrality to the existing economic order, such bodies are the best place to start guaranteeing that international economic functionalism undertakes necessary *social* – and perhaps even social-democratic – correctives to the reigning market orthodoxy. Elsewhere I have argued that the ILO offers important opportunities for achieving improved global labor and social standards. Unlike the WTO and IMF, it already provides substantial representation to organized labor, possesses tremendous practical experience and organizational know-how in labor and social policy, and rests on well-tested decision making procedures for navigating the waters of both global pluralism and a complex global economy. Despite its present weaknesses, one of our oldest functionalist global institutions provides a potential basis for pursuing reform (Scheuerman, 2008: 47–68).

One might legitimately squabble about the details of such proposals as well as their immediate political viability. For our limited purposes here, I merely suggest that the possibility of concrete institutional steps capable of reducing global material inequality should not be dismissed out of hand. There is simply no sound basis for excluding the long-term prospect of a less divided global economy and thereby a thicker supranational society. For this reason as well, world government remains a potentially desirable institutional aim, albeit one whose minimal social and economic presuppositions still need to be built.

World Statehood as an Empty Illusion

Walzer once heatedly described the pursuit of world government as akin to

> the withering away of the state or the administration of things or the millennial kingdom or the end of time; we can imagine it any way we please; it is an empty vision; it provides no practical guidance. (1986: 239)

As we have seen, hard-headed mid-century Realists thought otherwise. Hopefully, I have succeeded in this chapter in buttressing their views against intemperate and dismissive accounts of world statehood.

Yet an additional point still needs to be made against the accusation that the dream of world government "provides no practical guidance" to political actors. In fact, the Progressive Realist model of global reform gains support from astute recent analysts of the United Nations.

Few scholars are as familiar with the UN as the US political scientist Thomas Weiss, arguably the planet's leading expert on it. In his provocative

What's Wrong with the United Nations and How to Fix it (2009), Weiss offers a refreshingly balanced and clear-headed view of the UN, according to which we need to acknowledge its undeniable accomplishments, while simultaneously conceding that in its present form it remains inadequate to some key responsibilities of global governance. Weiss is rightly skeptical of utopian proposals to revolutionize the UN overnight, let alone immediately jettison it for some novel (and purportedly superior) form of global government in which the nation state suddenly disappears. Instead, he thoughtfully sketches out a series of down-to-earth institutional reforms aimed at enhancing the UN's ability to do its job. Perhaps the biggest dilemma facing it today, Weiss argues, is a sprawling and excessively decentralized organizational structure, where key activities are duplicated, rival bureaucratic units compete inefficiently, and policy endeavors are exercised in unison with non-UN bodies in ways that sometimes dilute their administrative capacities. An astonishingly feudalistic and polyarchical system which too often has a hard time completing even simple undertakings, the UN is overdue for an organizational shake-up, even at the risk of rattling powerful – as well as less powerful – national governments.

So what is to be done? The UN's unwieldy decision making and administrative structures require far-reaching consolidation and centralization, overlapping and competing jurisdictions have to be reorganized, and perhaps most importantly, the international civil service should be reinvigorated. Too often, Weiss shows, administrative incompetence and ignorance even of standard operating procedures keep the UN from successfully managing relatively uncontroversial tasks. If this is beginning to sound reminiscent of some of the arguments put forth earlier in the present volume, it probably should: Weiss wants the UN to pursue initially modest – yet potentially consequential – organizational reforms in the direction of global statehood (Weiss, 2009: 215–33) The UN's failure to complete even some of those responsibilities presently assigned to it is attributable to failures to instantiate familiar prerequisites of modern statehood: most importantly, an effective civil service, operating in a hierarchically organized bureaucracy in which officials possess clear responsibilities and can be held accountable.

Weiss' proposals dovetail with Progressive Realism's gradualist vision of a long march towards world statehood. Even if it remains a distant goal, the idea of world government can provide sensible guidelines to practical-minded reformers. The real "empty vision" is an institutionally conservative faith in a Westphalian system that supposedly can shape global affairs for eternity. Even if only our distant offspring will perhaps first enjoy its fruits, world government represents both a viable and potentially attractive alternative.

CONCLUSION: A NIEBUHRIAN PRESIDENT?

Whether or not Ernie and Connie should now join (or more likely: refound) their local chapter of the World Federalists will have to be left to the judgment of readers who have patiently made it to this advanced stage in our marathon. At the very least, I hope that those among you who subscribe to Cosmopolitanism or other reformist theories will have found my efforts to revitalize the neglected legacy of Progressive Realism useful. As for Neorealists, perhaps you will now be more open to the possibility of a cogent and hard-headed vision of global reform, building on the best of the Realist tradition while admitting the need for institutional imagination and a robust political ethics. Maybe you will even reconsider your knee-jerk hostility towards the idea of world government.

At first look, the revisionist account of Realism provided above faces an immediate obstacle: key figures in the last Bush Administration, as well as some prominent intellectual apologists, appealed to Realism in order to legitimize its disastrous foreign policies. One of the Administration's main global architects, Condoleezza Rice, not only periodically described herself as a Realist, but also referred appreciatively to the ideas of Morgenthau and others, while the right-wing publicist Charles Krauthammer tried to marshal the belligerent forces of what he dubs "democratic Realism" in order to justify the Bush Administration's aggressive policies against the so-called "existential enemy, the enemy that poses a mortal threat to freedom," namely "Arab–Islamic Totalitarianism" (Felix, 2002: 93–4; Krauthammer, 2004).

Of course, Realism is a complex and multi-sided intellectual tradition. Even so, it remains difficult to see how the Bush Administration's knee-jerk enmity to international law and morality, brazen attempt to discredit the United Nations, and shocking sacrifice of basic human rights (e.g. the torture ban) can be plausibly described as having built on mid-century Realist ideas. Its hubristic view of US power and reckless faith in the transformative potential of military force assaulted Realist political ethics and its emphasis on the foreign policy virtues of humility, moderation, and prudence. Even if the neoconservatives who dominated the Bush Administration possessed the *Realpolitiker*'s instinctive appreciation for the harsh game of power politics, they discarded not only the politically progressive reformist impulses motoring mid-century Realism, but also its balanced views about a host of complex moral, legal, and political matters.

Neoconservatives opportunistically pick and choose from the Realist canon, reducing complex arguments to cynical homilies, in order to dress their unpalatable views in an appealing intellectual costume. They misleadingly transform humanitarian figures like Morgenthau and Niebuhr into allies not only against so-called foreign "existential enemies," but also domestic social reforms akin to those once sought by Realists. Although more remains to be said about the complicated nexus between Realism and Neoconservatism, there is no question that the Bush Administration assaulted Progressive Realism's most valuable contributions (Mearsheimer, 2005; Schmidt and Williams, 2008).

What then of President Barack Obama's apparent embrace of Niebuhr's Christian Realism? Although his policies are being predictably shaped by many factors, Obama has described Niebuhr as "one of my favorite philosophers," and as widely reported by journalists and political commentators in the blogosphere and elsewhere, a number of his public utterances have directly echoed Niebuhrian themes.[1] After receiving the Nobel Prize, Obama's acceptance speech borrowed heavily from Niebuhr.[2] While acknowledging the imperfection of human nature and the perils of naive political visions blind to its ugliest attributes, Obama insisted that we not abandon the hopeful expectation "that the human condition can be perfected." Following in the footsteps of Niebuhr's analysis of Gandhi, he respectfully criticized defenders of a nonviolent path to social change for ignoring harsh truths about a political universe where recourse to violence remains tragically unavoidable. Nonviolence distorts the tough choices political actors and especially political leaders "sworn to protect" their countries must make. Yet Obama simultaneously praised them for holding onto an ideal of universal love capable of inspiring reform:

> The non-violence practiced by men like Gandhi and King may not have been practical or possible in every circumstance, but the love that they preached – their fundamental faith in human progress – that must always be the North Star that guides our journey.

Nor does the inevitability of tragic choices represent "a call to cynicism – it is a recognition of history; the imperfections of man and the limits of reason." Following Niebuhr, Obama's speech outlined the contours of a political ethics sensitive to the terrible paradoxes of political action in a violent world, while also sympathetically describing international organization and law as invaluable steps in the right direction. Despite their existing limitations, they reduce the necessity of political violence and contribute to the "gradual evolution of human institutions." Again echoing left-leaning mid-century Realism, the President correctly noted that true security cannot "exist where human beings do not have access to enough food, or clean water, or the medicine and shelter they need to survive." The successful growth of global institutions ultimately depends on social reform and the elimination of extreme poverty.

Not surprisingly perhaps, President Obama has moved rapidly to reaffirm the US commitment to the UN and international law, becoming the first US executive to chair a meeting of the Security Council, and at least initially promising to close Guantanamo Bay and end the heinous torture policies of his right-wing predecessor. Even more ambitiously, he has embraced the goal of a non-nuclear world, taking steps to stem the tide of nuclear proliferation. Like mid-century Progressive Realists, he rightly sees it – and not the mostly mythical "Arab–Islamic totalitarianism" identified by the neocons – as the main threat to human survival.[3] He has also acknowledged that climate change now represents an equally frightening threat to humankind. Obama has not only broken with the Neanderthal-like global warming denialism of his Republican predecessors, but has pushed – unfortunately, with little success thus far – for the United States to take some belated steps to reduce it.

Though perhaps the most eloquent among them, Obama is hardly the first major US (or, for that matter, UK) politician to appeal to Niebuhr.[4] To be sure, the relationship between the President's impressive rhetoric and his apparent readiness to compromise in the face of obstinate political opponents has left even erstwhile enthusiasts frustrated: his Niebuhrian sensitivity to the unavoidability of tough political trade-offs has perhaps made him *too* quick to seek political common ground with critics on a host of divisive domestic and foreign issues. From the perspective of Progressive Realism, one might also legitimately criticize heightened US military involvement in Afghanistan, as well as the fact that US anti-terror policy continues to evince some disturbing disdain for international law. Although Obama initially seemed to abandon the dangerous rhetoric of a "war on terror," continuities with the Bush Administration's counterterrorism policies have been more far-reaching than his normatively appealing language sometimes reveals.[5] Even if the theological currents which occasionally shape his rhetoric stem in part from Niebuhr's forward-looking agenda, one might also worry that they inadvertently help undermine liberal models of religious toleration already under assault in the United States by the religious right.

Interestingly, Obama's political thinking has been inspired especially by the senior and increasingly cautious Niebuhr, and not the young radical firebrand of the 1930s and 1940s.[6] Despite the frenzied attacks of his right-wing critics, Obama is no socialist: his view of capitalism is less critical than mid-century Progressive Realism's. Even though his stubborn pursuit of health care reform would surely have gladdened the hearts of his Progressive Realist predecessors, his social and economic views are more conventional than theirs. Not surprisingly, he has hesitated before proposing far-reaching social and economic experiments that may be necessary, as they were during the New Deal, to humanize and stabilize the US (and global) political economy. Significantly, Niebuhr's comparatively moderate views from the 1950s and 1960s were formulated in a political context very different from that in which Obama now operates. Mainstream US conservatives then accepted the rudiments of the welfare and regulatory states; both Democrats and Republicans supported a relatively robust United Nations and believed that the United States should lead the way in reforming international law. The Reagan Revolution – now represented by stunningly retrograde figures like Sarah Palin – subsequently destroyed the bipartisan political and social consensus that encouraged the aging Niebuhr to jettison his radical views and embrace left-liberal positions associated with the Democratic Party.

If commitments to the welfare state and a reformist vision of global governance are again to become ascendant, however, we probably need many more radical firebrands like the young Niebuhr. Without their heavy lifting, Obama's version of center-left Christian Realism may simply end up offering the US body politic a reliable antidote *at the wrong time*. When administered incorrectly, even otherwise useful medicines can prove counterproductive.

So Obama's selective endorsement of Niebuhr provides grounds for cautious optimism as well as real concern. Unfortunately, both Obama's conservative and leftist critics continue to downplay its complex dynamics. On the right, the *NY Times* columnist David Brooks has frequently commended Obama for taking Niebuhr's political legacy seriously (2007; 2009). Yet he consistently obscures its reformist and indeed potentially leftist impulses, reducing Niebuhr's Christian Realism to a staid middle-of-the-roadism, a theologically minded political philosophy which serves as a stand-in for the contemporary median US voter. What gets lost is that even in his most circumspect moments, Niebuhr sought a substantial (and expanding) welfare state as well as relatively significant global reforms. Not surprisingly perhaps, Brooks has also accused Obama of committing intellectual treachery against Christian Realism, at one point absurdly describing the President's middle-of-the-road economic stimulus package as an abrogation of the Realist virtues of humility and modesty (Tippett, 2009). Unlike Brooks, however, Niebuhr never conflated Christian humility with public policy centrism: Christian political ethics was consistently married to left-liberal and sometimes radical policy preferences. In reality, precisely when deviating from Brooks' rigidly centrist political script, Obama has at least *begun* to offer an inkling of what a rigorous real-life version of Progressive Realism might look like.

On the left, readers of the *New Left Review* were recently confronted with an astonishingly congruent view of Niebuhr. Tariq Ali dismisses Niebuhr as a "pastor of Cold War consciences," while Gopal Balakrishnan pretty much ignores Niebuhr's radical political impulses, seeing in him little more than a political opportunist who caved into the conformist pressures of the Cold War (Ali, 2010: 115; Balakrishnan, 2010: 211–21).[7] Neither writer seems to possess more than a cursory knowledge of Niebuhr's ideas, or even consider it worth their time actually discussing them: why bother doing so when one already knows that they represent an apology for US imperialism? Like Brooks, they interpret Niebuhr as a political centrist, and since they also see Obama as his disciple, they promptly relegate Obama to the latest in a long line of postwar liberal sell-outs to US imperialism. "I told you so!" they smugly shout at those who hoped for more from the 2008 elections than Obama's relatively cautious center-left presidency.

Yet this view of the Niebuhr–Obama nexus seems at least somewhat one-sided. As I have argued in this volume, Progressive Realism offers a surprisingly fertile theoretical resource for critical-minded students of global politics. To his credit, Niebuhr always highlighted the ways in which the voice of conscience encouraged each of us to take resolute political action in the face of injustice. Rather than wait for Obama to change the world for us, let us start doing so on our own.

If I am not mistaken, Progressive Realism provides an excellent starting point for thinking about why and how we need to do so.

NOTES

___

Preface

1 Although my account differs in ways to be discussed in the text, let me give proper credit where credit is due: I have been inspired by a fascinating recent book by Campbell Craig (2003) on Realist reformism.
2 Eric Posner's rational choice-inspired critique of "global legalism" in fact points implicitly to the necessity of ambitious varieties of postnational statehood. Unfortunately, Posner fails to follow this path because he uncritically endorses a dismissive view of world government (2009: 8–10).

Introduction: Meet the Progressive Realists

1 Ernie's answer is derived from many Cosmopolitan critics (Archibugi, 2008: 126–31; Beitz, 1979: 11–50; Caney, 2005; Doyle, 1997: 106; Habermas, 2006: 166–8; Held, 1995: 74–5; Jones, 1999: 114–15). It overlaps with other conventional accounts of Realism as well (Clinton, 2007; Donnelly, 2000; Freyberg-Inan, 2004; Griffiths, 1992; Haslam, 2002; Rosenberg, 1994; Spegele, 1996; Wight, 1992).
2 I have learned a great deal from a growing body of excellent recent scholarship on Realism that has similarly challenged conventional preconceptions (Bell, 2009; Booth, 1991; 2008; Cox 2000; Cozette, 2008a; 2008b; Craig, 2003; Murphy, 2001; Murray, 1997; Lebow, 2003; Oren, 2009; Schou Tjalve, 2008; Sylvest, 2008; Williams, 2005; Williams, 2007). From the older (vast) literature, Smith (1986) remains indispensable. For recent attempts to enlist Realism for the cause of a progressive US foreign policy, see Brown (2009) and Lieven and Hulsman (2006).
3 The masculinist language here is justified since the early Realists were all in fact men.

4   The literature abounds with attempts to provide definitions of "classical" Realism. Like Ernie, many associate it with an institutionally conservative and anti-reformist theory resting on a pessimistic view of human nature. Yet not all mid-century Realists, for example, built directly on philosophical anthropology. The "classical" Realists whom I will categorize as Progressive Realists in fact supported global reform, at least as a long-term aspiration; some of them (e.g. Carr and Schuman) did not base their reflections on a theory of human nature, and even those who did (i.e. Morgenthau and Niebuhr) argued that it was by no means excessively pessimistic. Revealingly, the term "Realism" was used in a number of different ways even by mid-century thinkers who ultimately embraced it. For example, Morgenthau did not offer a cogent definition of "Realism" until the 2nd edition (!) of *Politics Among Nations* (1954: 4–13), using the term in a number of different ways during the course of his long career (Scheuerman, 2009). Niebuhr repeatedly distanced himself from what he critically described as a "too consistent Realism," or amoral power politics; Wolfers similarly distanced himself from the term (1962: 81–102).

5   On Carr, see (Cox, 2000; 2001a; Haslam, 2000; Jones, 1998; Linklater, 1997); on Morgenthau (Frei, 2001; Murray, 1997; Scheuerman, 2009; Thompson and Myers, 1984; Williams, 2005; Williams, 2007); on Niebuhr's political thinking (Fox, 1985; Lovin, 1995; McKeogh, 1997; Merkley, 1975; Meyer, 1988; Warren, 1997).

6   One might also add Kennan's widely read *American Diplomacy: 1900–50* (1951) to this list of canonical texts. Kennan, however, was ultimately an intellectual conservative, notwithstanding his growing hostility to US nuclear policy and calls late in his career for dramatic shifts to it (Mayers 1988; Stephanson 1989). More important, his theoretical contributions – like Lippmann's – were limited.

7   Martin Wight's pamphlet *Power Politics* (1946) can be aptly described as Realist. Yet Wight soon distanced himself from Realism and joined arms with Hedley Bull to define – in some opposition to Realism – the "English School" of international politics. In *International Theory: The Three Traditions* (1992) Wight unfortunately helped popularize the misleading view of Realism as fundamentally Machiavellian and/or Hobbesian.

8   Admittedly, some of the thinkers whom I have chosen not to discuss mesh nicely with elements of the story I will try to tell. So Lippmann, for example, began his career as a socialist, as did Wight. Both Wight and Butterfield were also theologically motivated. Yet they all became relatively conservative intellectual and political figures.

9   The biographical details that follow are drawn from many sources. On Herz see (Hacke and Puglierin, 2008; Herz, 1984; Puglierin, 2008); Morgenthau (Frei, 2001; Scheuerman, 2009; Thompson and Myers, 1984); Niebuhr (Bingham, 1961; Fox, 1985; Merkley, 1975); for Schwarzenberger (Steinle, 2002; 2004). On Schuman, see especially (Bucklin, 2001; Oren, 2003:116–21; also: Gosnell, 1981; Barnett, Burns, MacGregor, and Green, 1981). For Wolfers, see Winks (1987: 40–3) and especially the many documents available at the Yale University Archives.

10   Nor do I mean to deny that at least some of their ideas were politically and institutionally conservative. Yet the left-leaning and reformist impulses outweigh conservative elements.

11   The term is likely to seem jolting given Realism's somewhat undeserved conservative reputation. Yet Booth (1991) and Howe (1994) have similarly dubbed Carr a "utopian Realist," and Richard Falk (1997) has described Carr and others as representatives of "critical Realism," characterized chiefly by its appreciation for the central place of historical and structural change in international relations. See also Murphy (2001).

12   See, for example, Herz (1984: 100) and Schuman (1941: 198–260) who, though no lawyer, at times could wax enthusiastic about the League even after its demise.

13   It later became the London Institute of World Affairs.

14   Niebuhr's *Moral Man and Immoral Society* (1932) was preoccupied to an oftentimes forgotten extent with the question of violent vs. non-violent strategies for social change.

15   See the excellent discussion by Paul Merkley, who rightly notes: "Reading Tillich [in the 1930s], Niebuhr made the great political discovery of his life: religious Marxism" (1975: 79). Tillich's advocacy of what he had called "faithful" or "belief-ful Realism" was likely one source of Niebuhr's embrace of the term (Tillich, 1956 [1932]). On Tillich's socialism, see his (1977 [1933]) volume. Wolfers employed the term "believing Realism" on at least one occasion, contrasting it to cynical versions of Realism, on the one hand, and irresponsible utopianism, on the other (1940). Niebuhr's relatively long-standing commitment to radical politics in the 1930s and 1940s gets downplayed both by conservatives (Brooks, 2009) eager to embrace his legacy and radicals (Balakrishnan, 2010) unhappy with his shift towards left-liberalism during the Cold War. Unfortunately, Guilhot (2010) also misses the politically progressive impulses behind Realist political theology.

16   See the extensive correspondence between Wolfers and Tillich at the Yale University Archives (Wolfers Collection, Box 3, Folder 37).

17   See his (1926) article in *The World Tomorrow*, a US-based left-Christian journal, for which Niebuhr served as a contributing editor, and Normas Thomas – longterm US Socialist Party presidential candidate – was the first editor.

18   Carr can be included here as well. Yet he came relatively late to socialism (Haslam, 1999; Cox, 2001a). Friedrich Hayek recognized the socialist roots of Realism, but only in order to dismiss its contributions to international thought (1994 [1944]: 204–8, 252–53). For more on Hayek, see Chapter 2 of this volume.

19   See the short essay for an English-language student publication published by the (ecumenical) World Student Christian Federation (Wolfers, 1927).

20   Unfortunately, Carr and Schuman periodically succumbed to the irresponsible political illusion that Soviet Russia, despite its ugly warts, was a fundamentally positive force for historical change. On Carr's analysis of the Soviet Union, see Conquest (1999) and Davies (2000; also, 1984). I do not discuss

Carr's work on Soviet Russia because it transcends the scope of this study. For the record, I think it possible to salvage some elements of Carr's version of Progressive Realism without having to reproduce his poor political judgment about the USSR or, for that matter, German appeasement, which he supported in the 1930s. Where I think Carr's version of Progressive Realism may have rendered him vulnerable to dangerous political illusions will be noted (see Chapter 1 this volume). Schuman's fellow-traveling is documented by O'Neill (1982) and Warren (1966). His dissertation (1928) was published by International Publishers, a publisher tied to the Communist Party. In 1932, he signed off on a public statement (with John Dos Passos, Sherwood Anderson, and other radicals) endorsing the Communist Party candidacy of William Z. Foster (League of Professional Groups for Foster and Ford, 1932), though he later oddly denied ever having been aware of having done so. In the 1930s, he was involved in left-wing and anti-fascist organizations with links to the Communist Party. For his defense of a socialist collectivism shaped by Western liberal values, see (1941a, 694–95). Despite his express commitment to a socialism based on liberal individualism, he praised the Soviet experiment (1930; 1936b), and even defended the Stalinist Show Trials and the prosecution of Trotsky (1937b). The latter argument generated fiery critical responses from anti-Stalinists like Sidney Hook (1937; also, Trager, 1940). On the eve of the Nazi–Soviet Non-Aggression Pact, he signed (with Max Lerner, I. F. Stone, and Dashiell Hammett) an open letter in *The Nation* describing the Soviets as having worked "unceasingly for a peaceful international order," and praising them for "steadily expanding democracy in every sphere" (cited in Oshinsky, 1983: 94). He praised Stalin's statesmanship in the context of the Non-Aggression Pact, though he then quickly proceeded to criticize the subsequent Soviet invasion of Finland (1939b; 1939c). Edward Shils – who knew the young Schuman from the University of Chicago in the 1930s – is right to describe him as having then been a communist fellow-traveler (2000: 108). Even his postwar textbook on Soviet politics (1946a) was by no means free of some of the familiar traits of mid-century US left-wing fellow traveling (Chamberlin, 1946). In 1948 he served on the platform committee for the ill-fated candidacy of the left-wing Progressive Party candidate, Henry Wallace (MacDougall, 1965). As with Carr, my attempt to salvage Progressive Realism entails no endorsement or apology for Schuman's fellow-traveling. Although some will surely disagree, it is possible to resuscitate elements of Schuman's Realism as well without being forced to follow his errors of political judgment. Indeed, features of Progressive Realism as reconstructed here – in particular, its demanding political ethics – provide rich resources for criticizing political misjudgments of this type.

21   While those Progressive Realists who were non-Jews (i,e., Carr, Niebuhr, Schuman, Wolfers) secured prestigious academic posts with relative facility (Carr began at Aberystwyth before ultimately landing at Cambridge; Niebuhr spent most of his career at the Union Theological Seminary in New York; Schuman began at the University of Chicago before becoming a professor at

Williams College; Wolfers was named to the Yale faculty shortly after leaving Germany, and gained an endowed chair in 1949), their Jewish émigré colleagues only did so with great difficulty. Ultimately, Morgenthau became a professor at the University of Chicago, but only after having been treated badly at the University of Kansas City; Herz began at Howard University before teaching at the City University of New York; Schwarzenberger was not named to a professorship at the University of London until 1962.

22   During the Second World War, Schuman assisted the war effort as an employee of the Federal Communication Commission, where he analyzed German radio broadcasts. His political past provided an easy target for political conservatives bent on demonstrating the scope of left-wing influence in the federal government (Brinson, 2004: 77, 101–3). Although queried in great detail by the House Un-American Activities Committee about his youthful political involvements, he quickly fell out of the scope of its witch hunt (US Congress, 1943). Schuman provided a spirited response in the *American Political Science Review* (1943) questioning the legality of the hearings: "The candid observer can scarcely escape the conclusion that Congress has here violated basic principles of the Constitution and the Bill of Rights" (829). In 1950, Senator McCarthy included Schuman on his list of "Reds" who had allegedly infiltrated the State Department, even though Schuman had merely given one (unpaid) talk there (in 1946) (Oshinsky, 1983: 125–6). Unfortunately, Schuman was by no means the only prominent US political scientist in the 1930s and 1940s who harbored illusions about the Soviets (Oren, 2003: 47–125).

23   Wolfers was reportedly close to Dean Acheson, Secretary of State under Harry Truman, and subsequently an academic player in the Democratic Party's attempt to formulate a liberal anti-communist alternative to Eisenhower's conservative foreign policies. (Acheson was a Yale graduate and later a member of the university's governing Yale Corporation). Wolfers served as a conduit between Yale and the State Department, which he apparently visited on a biweekly basis, while coordinating a Wednesday luncheon seminar through Yale's Institute for International Studies at which State Department matters were discussed. He also seems to have served as an academic link to the Washington intelligence community: his sister-in-law, who also lived in New Haven for awhile, reportedly was an OSS agent (Winks, 1987: 40–3, 325).

24   Niebuhr helped found the liberal Americans for Democratic Action, of which Morgenthau was also a member. Morgenthau was a member as well of the Academic Committee on Soviet Jewry, the Kurdish-American Society, Council for a Livable World, National Council for Civic Responsibility, SANE [The Committee for a Sane Nuclear Policy], and Turn Toward Peace (Lebow, 2011).

25   See, for example, the pamphlet Schuman wrote for the organization Another Mother for Peace (1969), entitled *Why a Department of Peace*. Schuman opposed the Vietnam War, and was a vocal member of the Williams College faculty in protesting it.

26 Those Progressive Realists motivated by deep moral and indeed religious impulses – Morgenthau, Niebuhr, Schwarzenberger, and Wolfers – were consistently critical of the Soviet Union.
27 The myth of hegemonic interwar "idealism" has, however, now been pretty much discredited (Wilson, 1998).
28 For the case of Niebuhr see, for example, the early essays collected in Chrystal (1977).

1 Why (Almost) Everything You Learned About Realism is Wrong

1 Although generally neglected, the concept of international society is pivotal for Progressive Realism, as we will see in Chapter 3.
2 The socialist background here is especially evident in an early essay by Wolfers (1923; also, 1924). But it can be detected elsewhere, for example: Schuman (1941b: 113).
3 Unfortunately, we cannot consider the matter of whether this interpretation of Machiavelli (or Hobbes) is an accurate one. Admittedly, Realists sometimes operated with one-dimensional readings of canonical writers.
4 Wolfers characterized Carl Schmitt as a representative of this tradition, which he described as culminating in Nazism (1962: 52–3). Archival materials show that Wolfers was not only familiar with Schmitt's work during the Weimar era, but frequently criticized it – for example – at a public forum at the Berlin Hochschule für Politik in 1932 (Arnold Wolfers Collection, Box 17, Folder, Yale University Archives). See also his criticisms of Schmitt's conception of the politics in (Wolfers, 1928: v–lx). On Morgenthau's exchange with Schmitt, see Scheuerman (1999: 225–51). I now believe that I overstated Schmitt's influence on Morgenthau there.
5 Though rarely noted in the secondary literature, the Kantian overtones to Morgenthau's moral views are striking.
6 The critical comments are innumerable, but for examples from a handful of major works see (1941: 25, 70–1, 100, 121, 218; 1943, 240–1, 249).
7 Carr clearly dismissed Niebuhr's theological view of history, which Niebuhr considered essential to sound political ethics (Carr, 1962: 96, 144).
8 On Carr's enthusiasm for appeasement, see Haslam (1999: 57–80) and Cox (2001a). Carr deleted many of the offending passages from the original 1939 edition of *Twenty Years' Crisis* (Cox, 2001b). His enthusiasm for the Soviets is most alarming in *The Soviet Impact on the Western World* (1947), yet it can be found elsewhere as well.
9 Both were credited by Carr with "the outstanding achievement of modern realism," namely its grasp of the fact that thought and ethical standards "are historically conditioned, being both products of circumstances and interests and weapons framed for the furtherance of interests" (1964 [1939]: 68). Carr described Marx's key discovery as the idea that "every mode of thought is the product of the social conditions of the age in which it is born" (1934: vii).

10 In striking contrast to Morgenthau, Niebuhr, and Wolfers, and even less so than Carr, Schuman was relatively uninterested in the theoretical and moral complexities of political ethics. At least in the 1930s and 1940s, he conveniently closed his eyes to the ugliest features of Soviet communism. In a piece for *The New Republic,* he described the Nazi-Soviet Non-Aggression Pact as a "work of diplomatic genius worthy of a Medici, a Richelieu, or a Bismarck," in short, as a masterful stroke of *Realpolitik* on Stalin's part (1939b: 159). When the Soviets subsequently attacked Finland, he then criticized their "blind brutality, as devoid of political intelligence as of legal and moral scruples" (1939c: 290). As one critic of his fellow-traveling tendencies has noted, Schuman was "hard to pin down. In one mood he despised moralizers, in another he moralized" (O'Neill: 1982: 28). The theoretical source of this tension was that Schuman was more willing than most other Progressive Realists to concede that Machiavelli offered a productive starting point for making sense of the existing international system: Machiavellian *Realpolitik* constituted a central feature of the (sad) international status quo; "Machiavellian detachment" was described by him as a praiseworthy "effort to delve beneath phraseology to underlying realities," and thus to cut through the "idealistic verbiage" that masked unsettling truths about international anarchy and power politics (1933: viii). At the same time, Schuman advocated the replacement of international anarchy and *Realpolitik* by a world government: *Realpolitik* may have been a necessary feature of international anarchy, but it could and should be jettisoned for a normatively superior alternative (1933: 823–54). In the final analysis, Schuman – like other Progressive Realists – condemned *Realpolitik*. So even his praise for Stalin's statesmanship was ultimately hemmed in by an important qualification: a new global political and social order should soon replace the need for power politics "beyond sentiment" (1939b: 159). Not surprisingly perhaps, Schuman oscillated confusedly between praising *Realpolitiker* – including, at least for a while, Stalin – and "moralizing" in defense of a global alternative.

11 See Chapter 2 this volume.

12 See also his critique of Kennan's idea of the national interest, where he notes that national "egotism is not the cure for an abstract and pretentious idealism" (1951: 139).

13 Of course, one will find such nostalgia in Progressive Realism. See, for example, Morgenthau (1954: 511–17). However, it would be a mistake to permit such nostalgic elements to overshadow other features of the story.

14 In part because his religious orientation made him skeptical of the hubristic impulses of Soviet communism, Niebuhr consistently criticized many facets of Stalinism in the 1930s and of the postwar era as well. On Niebuhr's significant role in the anti-communist orientation of postwar US liberalism, and the resulting splits on the US left, see (Kleinman, 2000).

15 Herz described survival but also pity as fundamental instincts (1951: 1–16).

2   Realists Against the Nation State

1   The literature, of course, is massive, but for helpful overviews see Breuilly (2006), Calhoun (2007), Canovan (1996), Delanty and O'Mahony (2002), as well as now-classic discussions by Anderson (1991), Deutsch (1962), Gellner (1992), and Smith (1971).

2   Carr similarly noted that the "old conception of national character based on biological differences" had been exploded. Yet "differences of national character arising out of different national backgrounds of society and education are difficult to deny" (1962: 38). Like Morgenthau, he tried to hold onto a plausible version of the idea of national character.

3   Morgenthau's analysis here (1954: 96–101) mirrors Arendt's discussion of the origins of "mass society" (1951).

4   See Chapter 3.

5   In this assessment, the fundamental dynamics of modern nationalism, and not a specific political ideology (e.g. liberalism or communism) *per se*, leads political leaders to identify their parochial interests with those of humanity at large, and to conflate national power aspirations with humankind's highest moral aspirations. Unfortunately, Morgenthau and others are often misunderstood on this point: modern (universalistic) *liberalism* may in fact aggrandize the missionary and potentially imperialistic impulses of modern foreign policy, but its roots are deeper.

6   See Chapter 3 this volume.

7   Niebuhr's language anticipated Harvey and other recent social theorists when he described contemporary society's "instruments of production, transport and communication" as having "reduced the space-time dimensions of the world to a fraction of their previous size" (1944: 158).

8   On this debate, see Hirst and Thompson (1996), as well as Held, McGrew, Goldblatt, Perraton (1999).

9   This claim gains support from recent scholars who point out that "[t]he pre-1914 system was ... genuinely international, tied by efficient long-distance communications and industrialized means of support" (Hirst and Thompson, 1996: 9).

10   Carr sometimes waxed enthusiastic about the Soviets (1947). However, at least in *Conditions of Peace* (1942), one finds positive comments about the New Deal and its (idiosyncratic) attempt to overcome the classical liberal state/society divide (1942: 71, 75, 96–7). Michael Cox reports that Carr visited the US in 1938 and even had tea at the White House with First Lady Eleanor Roosevelt (2001a: xxxiii), and asked his publisher to send the White House a complimentary copy of *Conditions of Peace* (1942).

11   For Hayek's own polemical response to Carr, whom he described as one of a number of dangerous "totalitarians in our midst," see (1992 [1944]: 204–8). Obviously, fundamental theoretical and normative differences separated the free-market Hayek from the socialist Carr. For Hayek, any idea of regionally based economic organization was, rather oddly and unconvincingly,

tied to Carl Schmitt's fascist vision of a Nazi *Grossraum* [Greater Region]. In contrast, Carr criticized Nazi models of a unified European economy while still wanting to hold open the possibility of a regionally based economic order.

12 Such "continental Keynesianism" has at least some supporters today (Hirst and Thompson, 1996: 163–4).

13 The question of the relationship between Carr's 1930s support for German appeasement – analyzed ably by Haslam (1999: 57–80) and Cox (2001a; 2001b) – and his underlying international theory is complex. Many reasons led Carr to support appeasement, including the plausible view that the Versailles Treaty had treated the Germans poorly. His growing awareness that small nation states were no longer viable also played a role. However, appeasement conflicted with Carr's *own* express commitment to multinational political and social orderings that would 1) struggle to achieve greater social and economic equality and 2) do proper justice to national identity, albeit in novel institutional ways. The Nazis, of course, sought neither.

14 See, for example, Miller (1995).

3 Realist Global Reformism

1 Progressive Realists were not alone in seeing the Second World War as proof of the necessity of far-reaching international reform. See, for example, Willkie (1966 [1943]), presidential candidate for the Republican Party in 1940 and, more generally, Deudney (2007: 193–243) and Partington (2003) who emphasize the importance of H. G. Wells to mid-century debates on international reform.

2 *International Politics: An Introduction to the Western State System* (New York: McGraw Hill and Co., 1933) went through seven editions, with the last one appearing in 1969. Revealingly, its title was changed – in accordance with Schuman's increasingly ardent reformist orientation – to *International Politics: The Western State System in Transition* (1941).

3 On Niebuhr's evolving views during the 1930s and 1940s, see Merkley (1975: 63–180) and Fox (1985: 142–223). Schuman described his own position as "Liberal" in his heavily Marxist study of the Weimar Republic (1937a: x–xi).

4 Mark Mazower points out that such ideas "for a formal Anglo-American Union to guarantee democratic solidarity" were "mooted briefly in the critical early months of the war" by many others as well (2009: 59). As we will see, Schwarzenberger also endorsed such a union.

5 Although in hindsight somewhat naive, his early embrace of what social scientists later described as the "convergence thesis" clearly helped motor his enthusiasm for world government. It was maintained by Schuman well into the 1960s, with Stalin's death and the rise of Khrushchev confirming his faith (1958; 1962; 1967).

6 Beyond the key pieces cited below, Niebuhr offered frequent editorial remarks – and stunningly numerous book reviews – dealing with the topic for journals

like *Christianity and Crisis, Christianity and Society*, and *Radical Religion*. See also Niebuhr (1943: 284–6).

7 The appeal to Hume and Burke became explicit, for example, in Niebuhr (1959: 56–7). See also the interesting book by Crane Brinton (1948), whose views oftentimes mirrored Niebuhr's.

8 The same tension plagued Wolfers' occasional reflections on the topic. Although conceding that "[e]xponents of world government are not necessarily utopians for hoping that peoples and governments someday will commit an act of radical self-abnegation and abdicate as sovereign entities in favor of a world state," and admitting that a world state could prove advantageous, he similarly noted that its fundamental social presuppositions had yet to be realized (1962: 93; also, 55–6, 58, 64, 93, 130–5). Furthermore, this was unlikely to happen in the foreseeable future: "Can anyone imagine the United States and the Soviet Union subordinating themselves voluntarily to an authority over which their chief opponent might come to exercise supreme control?" (1962: 131). Unfortunately, Wolfers had even less to say about how such presuppositions might be achieved, other than mentioning the more-or-less conventional efforts of statesmen and diplomats to reduce international tensions. Morgenthau similarly argued that sound diplomacy was essential for the "mitigation and minimization" of intense global political conflict. Traditional diplomacy could help ward off nuclear conflict and buy humanity time to develop a more mature world community (1954: 505). As we will see, however, Morgenthau supplemented this argument with more far-reaching calls for constructive international reform.

9 Niebuhr's final writings occasionally reverted to the defensive position that a universal political community, however desirable and perhaps necessary, conflicted with humankind's deeply rooted parochialism and tribalism. Our failure to achieve a mature global order was simply a reminder of the congenitally flawed character of human existence. For the believing – and now more pessimistic – Christian, the apparent unfeasibility of a world polity merely provided "a final revelation of the incongruity of human existence," whose tragic nature revealed itself in the unsettling fact that human beings needed a world polity yet were unlikely to achieve it (1965: 83). "Perhaps we are fated, for some centuries at least, to live in a situation in which the global community appears to be a necessity because of the interdependence of nations, but an impossibility because there are not enough organic forces of cohesion in the global community." Unfortunately, "[p]erhaps there will *never* be enough of these factors" (1959: 266; my emphasis).

10 These views closely paralleled Morgenthau's (Scheuerman, 2009: 117–22).

11 Craig (2003: 86–92) plausibly suggests that Niebuhr by the early 1960s became more open towards the possibility of far-reaching global reforms. However, in one of Niebuhr's final works (see footnote 9), he expressed some skepticism (Niebuhr, 1965).

12 On Carr's economic ideas, see Rich (2000).

13 A point, by the way, neglected even by superb commentaries on Carr's wartime proposals (Linklater, 2000; Haslam, 1999; Haslam, 1999, 81–118).

The secondary literature on functionalism is large, but it fails to investigate the relationship to Realism (Ashworth and Long, 1999; Groom and Taylor, 1975). One exception is the valuable book by Booth and Wheeler (2008).

14   For instance, the New Dealers never attempted to secure the welfare state by expressly amending the US Constitution.

15   See Chapter 1 this volume.

16   Many other reasons for the neglect of Carr in the postwar US should be noted: he was already hard at work on his massive (and quite respectful) account of the Soviet Revolution. Unlike others in his Realist cohort, he had no interest in trying to cultivate influence among Cold War foreign policy elites. Also, he pretty much abandoned international theory after the mid 1940s. Interestingly, Schuman – whose political proclivities most closely mirrored Carr's – also became an increasingly marginal figure to US political science.

17   Perhaps Morgenthau's view here was closer to that of Niebuhr, who at one juncture noted that the mutual loyalties essential to global community were "difficult but not impossible" in the face of "great disproportions of power and fortune" (1955: 20).

18   For a helpful recent discussion of Tönnies and his legacy for sociological discussions about the idea of community, see Gertenbach, Laux, Rosa, Strecker (2010). Like the young Schwarzenberger, Tönnies was a member of the German SPD.

19   An irritated Morgenthau noted the excessively "idealistic" overlap here with Schuman in an early review of *Power Politics* (Morgenthau, 1942).

20   Schwarzenberger's Atlantic Union echoed Schuman's earlier wartime proposals. Interestingly, Morgenthau also briefly toyed with the possibility of a free-world supranational association of liberal democratic states that might begin to break the ties between national statehood and the monopoly on violence by putting control of nuclear weapons into their joint hands (1960: 308–9).

21   Carr had also alluded to the excesses of an "idealistic view of functional internationalism" which "failed to take account from the outset ... the unsolved issue of power" (Carr, 1967 [1945]: 50–1).

22   In 1948 the ill-fated left-wing Progressive Party presidential candidate Henry Wallace's platform included a world government plank. Schuman not only served on the platform committee, but reportedly penned the relevant sections (McDougall, 1965: 564). Significantly, Niebuhr (and later Morgenthau) were active in the anti-communist Americans for Democratic Action, a liberal organization critical not only of the Wallace candidacy but of its close ties to communists and fellow travelers. This partisan political dispute undoubtedly colored the theoretical differences separating the adamant one-worlder Schuman, on the one hand, from the more cautious Morgenthau and Niebuhr, on the other. Still, it would be a mistake to associate the "One World" movement in the late 1940s with the far left; many of its defenders were political conservatives (Wooley, 1988). The Soviet Union, by the way, was generally critical of calls for world government, taking them as a Trojan horse for Western imperialism. Schwarzenberger's skepticism about functionalism, by

the way, may also have had immediate political motivations. In the debate on European unity in the late 1940s and early 1950s, the British Labor Party tended to push for functionalist-style integration in opposition to calls for a European federal union. As Schuman noted in an insightful piece written at the time, "Laborite distrust of Churchill" (who served again as Prime Minister starting in 1951) as well as "Socialist doubts of the viability of any federation dominated by Continental conservatives championing 'capitalism'" played significant roles in Labor's functionalist European discourse (Schuman, 1951: 736–7). Schwarzenberger's argument can be read as an implicit critique of the Labor Party position on European unification: he shared Labor's policy preferences, but seems to have believed that federalism – and especially an Atlantic Union – ultimately remained the best way to advance them.

23 But not radical politics altogether, as when he described the US as drifting "in the direction of total militarism and the garrison state" (1952a: 207). Schuman remained a critic of capitalism, though he now rejected ambitious visions of economic planning (1952a: 307).

24 Schuman relied on Robert Hutchins' (1949: 105–6) argument here. In some ways, Schuman's views fall neatly within the gambit of mainstream one-world thought (see Lent, 1955).

25 Morgenthau was a great admirer of this proposal in part because of its functionalist heritage (Scheuerman, 2009: 152–55). Its failure does not seem to have tempered his sympathies.

26 But see the interview with Morgenthau and Niebuhr (1967). However, no new ground was broken there.

27 See Chapters 4 and 5 this volume.

28 See Chapter 5 this volume.

29 Kissinger seemed to commit precisely that error Niebuhr had warned about in his critique of the theologian Karl Barth: the belief in a dramatic and perhaps insurmountable impasse between human existence and a transcendent God made it difficult to locate moral and political action sufficiently within real-life history (Merkley, 1975: 68–74).

30 The only exception I can find to the overwhelmingly anti-reformist tenor of Kissinger's thought is a short 1961 piece in which he concedes the ongoing "breakdown of the nation state" and then – primarily as a way of strengthening NATO – advocates a loose "Atlantic confederacy" in which the US, UK, and France would be required to share with other NATO members the right to "determine the circumstances in which nuclear weapons would be released" (1961: 19). Kissinger did not advance this position, however, as Secretary of State under either Presidents Nixon or Ford. In contrast to Progressive Realism, the essay shows no interest in postnational political organization as a way of advancing social reform, for example, or improving the odds that humankind might survive the nuclear age by advancing towards world statehood: Kissinger's Atlantic confederation was exclusively a device for strengthening the nuclear capacities of NATO against the Soviets. Although strategic concerns obviously also sometimes motivated Progressive Realists, they typically took a backseat in the reformist arguments recalled here.

31 As Craig perceptively shows, however, Waltz's theory rests implicitly on many normative – and oftentimes institutionally conservative – preferences of its own.

32 See, for example, the debate between Sagan and Waltz (2003) on nuclear proliferation. As Sagan shows, the experience of Cold War nuclear deterrence cannot be easily reproduced; nuclear proliferation poses many profound threats.

33 See also Coates (2000) for a critique of Zolo.

4 What Cosmopolitans Can Learn from Progressive Realism

1 For example, Held (2004), as well as Habermas' cosmopolitan model and especially his social-democratic vision of a reformed EU (2001).

2 A position, by the way, which Kissinger apparently considered "idealistic" (Morgenthau, 1973).

3 Think, for example, of longstanding US political hostility to social and economic rights.

4 Held's proposals have been widely discussed at great length by many scholars; I will not cover familiar territory here. For important recent endorsements see Linklater (1998) and Caney (2005: 148–88).

5 For Held's ambitious list of short-term measures, see (1995: 279–80).

6 For a critical discussion, see Thaa (2001). Like Cosmopolitanism, Communitarianism is a complex position drawing on a multiplicity of philosophical sources. For an excellent discussion see Forst (2002).

7 A subtle (and also more cautious) defense of the communitarian critique of global democracy is provided by Chris Brown (1995a; 1995b), who concedes the possibility of wider varieties of political community beyond the nation state, while employing some core communitarian intuitions to deflate naive progressivist models of global reform. Brown's position overlaps with my reconstruction of Progressive Realism in some ways, though it differs by taking much more communitarian baggage onboard.

8 See also Chapter 5 this volume.

9 See Deutsch (1969; 1970), as well as Deutsch, Burrell, Kann, Lee, Lichterman, Lindgren, Loewenheim, Van Wagenen (1957). For recent attempts to revitalize Deutsch's theoretical agenda, see Adler and Barnett (1998); Booth and Wheeler (2008: 183–90). Progressive Realists occasionally cited Deutsch's work. Unfortunately, they failed to engage it properly.

10 For a subtle version of the republican position, see Bellamy and Castiglione (1998).

11 A mistake to which even democratic theorists as impressive as Robert Dahl (1999) and Ingeborg Maus (2006) perhaps succumb.

12 This theoretical lacuna also plagues Nielsen (1988).

13 This type of argument, by the way, is still made for Switzerland by many global reformers (Brunkhorst, 2008: 494). However, it rests on a historical misreading of the (idiosyncratic) Swiss case.

14   For the crucial theoretical statement on "governance without government" see Rosenau and Czempiel (1992).

15   For an important exception to the anti-statism of contemporary cosmopolitanism, see the excellent critique by Marchetti (2008) as well as the sensible book by Höffe (1999). For an extreme version of anti-statist Cosmopolitanism see Dryzek (1999).

16   See, for example, Bohman (2007), or any of the many writings of the German critical theorist Hauke Brunkhorst, who clearly has influenced Habermas in this context. For more on Brunkhorst's thinking, see below (3).

17   Although describing the European Union as a "regional state," Vivien Schmidt in fact endorses crucial elements of the postsovereignty thesis (2006).

18   These are curious examples since they arguably underline the fragilities of loose political confederation. The US under the Articles of Confederation is widely considered a failure since its collapse produced a more centralized federal republic in 1787. The German confederation faced a different fate: it was replaced by Bismarck's (vastly more centralized) German Empire. As for Switzerland, it has been a federal state since the mid-nineteenth century, prior to which it was plagued by incessant violence and disorder.

5   What Other Global Reformers Can Learn from Progressive Realism

1   There are, of course, other contemporary proponents of far-reaching global reform. But in my view the four approaches discussed here are among the most creative and fruitful.

2   Thus the title of her most important book (2004b).

3   She did, however, unfortunately endorse the disastrous invasion of Iraq (2003).

4   However, readers will look in vain for a sufficiently critical analysis of the global capitalist political economy, a flaw – by the way – plaguing many of the reform models discussed in this chapter. Slaughter's astonishingly positive account of the global financial regulatory system is particularly troubling in light of its recent collapse and the ensuing worldwide economic crises.

5   There are some interesting parallels here to Daniel Deudney's republican reform model (see below). Like Deudney, Slaughter seems to think that global reform can rest satisfied with a highly decentralized as well as non-statist global system, in which mechanisms of popular control for federal or "global" matters – as in Deudney's eulogistic account of antebellum America (where, for example, US Senators were chosen by state legislatures, and not directly chosen by voters) – are at best relatively indirect.

6   Unfortunately, Slaughter ultimately offers a truncated interpretation of the idea of global deliberative equality: it requires nothing more than "clear criteria for participation [in government networks] that will be fairly applied" (2004b: 246), or, alternately, that "all government networks should be open to any government officials who meet specified criteria or conditions of

membership" (2004b: 259). Formulations of this type support a technocratic reading of her work.

7 For recent attempts to update especially Bull's framework, see also Little and Williams (2006).

8 The crucial (and highly influential) text here is Wight (1992), which misconstrued Realism.

9 Compare here with Held (1995: 136–40) as well as Buzan (2004: 202–3).

10 Acceptance of this point, by the way, hardly requires accepting the naive and anachronistic endorsements of state planning offered by Carr or Schuman, for example. For an interesting recent attempt to defend a vision of planning appropriate to contemporary conditions see Giddens (2009: 91–128).

11 He thought that the social as well as moral homogeneity of this group had been badly undermined in the twentieth century, however.

12 As demonstrated in an excellent book by Nicholas Wheeler (2000).

13 The answer to this quagmire, as Andrew Hurrell rightly suggests, may be to formulate a model of postnational governance that emphasizes the possibility of shared *procedures* rather than *values* (2006: 212–14). Admittedly, this theoretical move still raises many tough questions.

14 This is a theme, for example, in Bull (1977).

15 Niebuhr and Schuman barely make appearances in his otherwise astonishingly detailed discussion of twentieth-century international thought; Carr is grouped unsympathetically – and without sufficient evidence – alongside reactionary German geopoliticians like Karl Haushofer. Like Hayek, Deudney sees mid-century models of regionalization as congenitally linked to the far right.

16 A somewhat odd claim since Wells – as Deudney himself notes – sometimes offered a technocratic vision of political order.

17 Deudney breaks here as well with other recent republican international thinkers who more accurately describe republican government as necessarily "hierarchical and coercive" (Onuf, 1998: 7). His main thesis, by the way, was anticipated in some ways by the controversial German author Ernst Jünger (1980 [1960]).

18 See in a related vein Pettit (2000).

19 In fairness, he perhaps concedes this point when he describes the US as having institutionalized a "recessed" form of popular sovereignty. Nonetheless, this matter does not trouble him as much as it should.

20 Here as well, mid-century Realists typically gave expression to a superior – and more balanced – range of views about US policy.

21 This is a hugely complicated theoretical matter. For Wendt's subtle discussion of the relationship between ideas and power, see especially (1999: 92–138). One important difference between him and Progressive Realists is that some of the latter (i.e. Carr) thought that only a critically oriented theory of ideology (along the lines attempted by Karl Mannheim) could make sense of the nexus between ideas and norms, on the one hand, and social relations of power, on the other. In my view, a properly reformulated critique of ideology (where ideas would of course be interpreted as much more than the mere "superstruc-

ture" of underlying power interests) need not deny the constructivist insight that in international politics (as in other areas of social life) "ideas all the way down" are crucial. Yet a theory of ideology – which Wendt seems to lack – would place those ideas in a somewhat more critical light than he does.

22   In fairness, Wendt mentions Nazism and Bolshevism as examples of the dangers of this teleological view of history and its implications for political action (2003: 529). My criticism here echoes Shannon (2005), who worries about the lack of agency in Wendt's model of world state formation. See also Checkel's earlier criticism in a related vein (1998: 340–42). For Wendt's attempt to respond see (2005).

6   Who's Afraid of the World State?

1   In a similar vein, see Craig (2003; 2008). I have also relied below on some fine recent discussions of world government: (Cabrera, 2004, 2010; Etzioni, 2001; Heater, 1996; Höffe, 1999; Horn, 1996; Lu, 2006; Marchetti, 2008; Tamir, 2000).
2   See especially Chapters 4 and 5 this volume.
3   See Chapters 4 and 5.
4   Progressive Realists also typically endorsed far-reaching egalitarian social reforms, along the lines of a robust welfare state and even more ambitious socialist-style experiments. Wisely, however, they seemed unsure about the complicated question of whether such policies might be pursued at the global level, or best left at the regional or perhaps even national levels.
5   See Chapter 1.
6   Similarly, one of the most eloquent recent defenses of world government comes from Yael Tamir, erstwhile theoretician of "liberal nationalism" (2000).
7   In fairness, Walzer has recently tempered his early enthusiasm for the Wilsonian vision (2004: 171–92).
8   See Chapter 2 this volume.
9   For an exhaustive account of Kant's huge role in modern thinking about international organization see Eberl (2008).
10   To be sure, they understandably debated how much material equality was required by a viable supranational society. See Chapters 4 and 5 this volume.

Conclusion: A Niebuhrian President?

1   The comment was made in a now famous conversation with the *NY Times* columnist David Brooks. For the details see Tippett (2009).
2   Quotations that follow are taken from an online version available at: *http:// www.nytimes.com/2009/12/11/world/europe/11prexey.text.html*
3   This, by the way, seems to have enraged contemporary Realists less faithful to the legacy of mid-century left-leaning Realism than Obama.
4   In the US Adlai Stevenson, Hubert Humphrey, Jimmy Carter, and Bill Clinton are among those who have publicly praised Niebuhr; in the UK, Denis Healy,

Tony Benn, and Richard Crossman mentioned his influence (McKeogh, 1997: 1). In recent years, some prominent journalists – including *New Republic* editor Peter Beinart – have also turned to Niebuhr for inspiration. A devastating critique of their efforts to retool Niebuhr for the battle against terrorism is provided by Bacevich (2006).

5   For example, the US continues to practice rendition: some detainees are sent to countries where they may be subject to severe abuse and perhaps torture. The Administration has also approved controversial and probably unconstitutional "drone" attacks on US citizens based abroad and suspected of terrorism. Despite Obama's early promise to close "Gitmo," it remains open. Moreover, the Administration has made it clear that some of its detainees may remain there indefinitely. Others are now being tried before highly flawed and rightly controversial military commissions which have been legitimately criticized by human rights organizations.

6   Obama provided a blurb for a recent University of Chicago reissue of Niebuhr's *The Irony of American History* (1952), one of Niebuhr's politically most cautious late works. However, some of his comments show clear marks of the more radical *Moral Man and Immoral Society* (1932).

7   Unfortunately, there is a long history of hostile leftist misreadings of Niebuhr. For example: Williams (1980: 183).

REFERENCES

Abizadeh, Arash (2005). Does Collective Identity Presuppose an Other? On the Alleged Incoherence of Global Solidarity. *American Political Science Review* 99 (1): 45–60.

Adler, Emmanuel and Barnett, Michael (eds) (1998). *Security Communities*. Cambridge: Cambridge University Press.

Ali, Tariq (2010). President of Cant. *New Left Review* (61): 99–116.

Alston, Philip (1997). The Myopia of Handmaidens: International Lawyers and Globalization. *European Journal of International Law* (3): 435–48.

Alvarez, Jose (2001). Do Liberal States Behave Better? A Critique of Slaughter's Liberal Theory. *European Journal of International Law* (12): 183–246.

Anderson, Benedict (1991). *Imagined Communities: Reflections on the Origin and Spread of Nationalism*. London: Verso.

Archibugi, Daniele (2008). *The Global Commonwealth of Citizens*. Princeton: Princeton University Press.

Arendt, Hannah (1951). *The Origins of Totalitarianism*. New York: Harcourt Brace and Jovanovich.

(1970). *On Violence*. New York: Harcourt Brace and Jovanovich.

(1972). *Crises of the Republic*. New York: Harcourt Brace and Jovanovich.

Aron, Raymond (1966). *Peace and War: A Theory of International Relations*, Richard Howard and Annette Baker Fox (trans.). New York: Doubleday.

Ashley, Richard (1981). Political Realism and Human Interests. *International Studies Quarterly* (25): 204–36.

Bacevich, Andrew (2006). The American Political Tradition. *The Nation* (10 July) http://www.thenation/com/doc/20060717/bacevich.

Barnett, Vincent M., Burns, MacGregor, James, and Green, Fred (1981). Frederick L. Schuman: At Williams College. *PS* (14): 807–8.

Ashworth, Lucian and Long, David (eds) (1999). *New Perspectives on International Functionalism*. New York: St Martin's.

Balakrishnan, Gopal (2010). Sermons on the Present Age. *New Left Review* (61): 211–21.

Beitz, Charles W. (1979). *Political Theory and International Relations*. Princeton: Princeton University Press.

Bell, Duncan (ed.) (2009). *Political Thought and International Relations: Variations on a Realist Theme*. Oxford: Oxford University Press.

Bellamy, Richard and Castiglione, Dario (1998). Between Cosmopolis and Community: Three Models of Rights and Democracy within the European Union. In *Re-Imagining Political Community: Studies in Cosmopolitan Democracy*, Daniele Archibugi (ed.). Stanford: Stanford University Press, 152–78.

Benhabib, Seyla (2006). *Another Cosmopolitanism*. Berkeley: University of California Press.

Bingham, June (1961). *Courage to Change: An Introduction to the Life and Thought of Reinhold Niebuhr*. New York: Charles Scribner's and Sons.

Bohman, James (2007). *Democracy Across Borders: From Demos to Demoi*. Cambridge, US: MIT Press.

Booth, Kenneth (1991). Security in Anarchy: Utopian Realism in Theory and Practice. *International Affairs* (67): 527–45.

      (2008). Navigating the "Absolute Novum": John H. Herz's Political Realism and Political Idealism. *International Relations* (22): 510–26.

Booth, Kenneth and Wheeler, Nicholas J. (2008). *The Security Dilemma: Fear, Cooperation and Trust in World Politics*. New York: Palgrave.

Breuilly, John (2006). Introduction. In Gellner, *Nations and Nationalism*. Ithaca: Cornell University Press, pp. xiii–liii.

Brinson, Susan (2004). *The Red Scare, Politics, and the Federal Communications Commission, 1940–1960*. Westport, CT: Praeger.

Brinton, Crane (1948). *From Many One: The Process of Political Integration; The Problem of World Government*. Cambridge, US: Harvard University Press.

Brooks, David (2007). Obama, Gospel and Verse. *New York Times* (26 April).

      (2009). Obama's Christian Realism. *New York Times* (15 December): A15.

Brown, Chris (1995a). International Political Theory and the Idea of World Community. In *International Relations Theory Today*, Ken Booth and Steve Smith (eds). University Park: Penn State University Press, pp. 90–109.

      (1995b). International Theory and International Society: The Viability of the Middle Way? *Review of International Studies* 21: 183–96.

Brown, Seyom (2009). *Higher Realism: A New Foreign Policy for the United States*. New York: Paradigm.

Brunkhorst, Hauke (2003). Verfassung ohne Staat? Das Schicksal der Demokratie in der europäischen Rechtsgenossenschaft. *Leviathan* (31): 530–43.

      (2004). A Polity without a State? European Constitutionalism between Evolution and Revolution. In *Developing a Constitution for Europe*, Erik Oddvar Eriksen, John Erik Fossum and Agustin Jose Menendez (eds). London: Routledge, pp. 88–105.

      (2005). *Solidarity: From Civic Friendship to Global Legal Community*. Cambridge, US: MIT Press.

(2008). State and Constitution: A Reply to Scheuerman. *Constellations* (15): 493–501.

Bull, Hedley (1969). The *Twenty Years' Crisis* Thirty Years On. *International Journal* (24): 625–38.

(1977). *The Anarchical Society: A Study of Order in World Politics*. New York: Columbia University Press.

Buzan, Barry (2004). *From International to World Society? English School Theory and the Social Structure of Globalization*. Cambridge: Cambridge University Press.

Cabrera, Luis (2004). *Political Theory of Global Justice: A Cosmopolitan Case for the World State*. New York: Routledge.

(2010). World Government: Renewed Debate, Persistent Challenges. *European Journal of International Relations* (16): 315–37.

Calhoun, Craig (2003). The Class-Consciousness of Frequent Travellers: Towards a Critique of Actually Existing Cosmopolitanism. In *Debating Cosmopolis*, Daniele Archibugi (ed.). London: Verso, pp. 86–116.

(2007). *Nations Matter: Culture, History, and the Cosmopolitan Dream*. London: Routledge.

Caney, Simon (2005). *Justice Beyond Borders: A Global Political Theory*. Oxford: Oxford University Press.

Canovan, Margaret (1996). *Nationhood and Political Theory*. Cheltenham, UK: Edward Elgar.

Carr, E. H. (1934). *Karl Marx: A Study in Fanaticism*. London: J. M. Dent.

(1942). *Conditions of Peace*. London: Macmillan.

(1947). *The Soviet Impact on the Western World*. New York: Macmillan.

(1949). The Moral Foundations for World Order. In *Foundations for World Order*. Denver: University of Denver Press, pp. 53–76.

(1951). *The New Society*. London: MacMillan.

(1950–78). *A History of Soviet Russia*, Vols I-14. London: MacMillan.

(1962). *What is History?* New York: Alfred Knopf.

(1964 [1939]). *The Twenty Years' Crisis, 1919–1939*. New York: Harper and Row.

(1967 [1945]). *Nationalism and After*. London: MacMillan.

(2003b [1949]). Rights and Obligations. In *From Napoleon to Stalin and Other Essays*. New York: Palgrave, pp. 11–18.

(2003b [1953]). Karl Mannheim. In *From Napoleon to Stalin and Other Essays*. New York: Palgrave, pp. 177–83.

Castells, Manuel (1996). *The Rise of the Network Society*. Oxford: Blackwell's.

Chamberlin, William H. (1946). Academic Dr Jekyll and Mr Hyde. *New Leader* (16 March): 13.

Chase-Dunn, Christopher (1990). World-State Formation: Historical Processes and Emergent Necessity. *Political Geography Quarterly* (9): 108–30.

Checkel, Jeffrey (1998). The Constructivist Turn in International Relations Theory. *World Politics* (50): 324–48.

Chrystal, William (ed.) (1977). *Young Reinhold Niebuhr: His Early Writings, 1911–1931*. New York: Pilgrim Press.

Claude, Inis L. (1962). *Power and International Relations*. New York: Random House.

Coady, C. A. J. (2008). *Messy Morality: The Challenge of Politics*. Oxford, UK: Clarendon Press.

Coates, Tony (2000). Neither Cosmopolitanism Nor Realism: A Response to Danilo Zolo. In *Global Democracy: Key Debates*, Barry Holden (ed.). London: Routledge, pp. 87–102.

Cohen, Jean L. (2008). A Global State of Emergency or the Further Constitutionalization of International Law: A Pluralist Approach. *Constellations* (15): 456–84.

Conquest, Robert (1999). Agit-Prof. *The New Republic* 221 (1 November): 32–7.

Cox, Michael (2001a). Introduction. In Carr, *Twenty Years' Crisis*. New York: Palgrave, pp. ix–lviii.

(2001b). From the First to the Second Edition of *The Twenty Years' Crisis*: A Case of Self-Censorship? In Carr, *The Twenty Years' Crisis*. New York: Palgrave, pp. lxxii–lxxxii.

(ed.) (2000). *E. H. Carr: A Critical Appraisal*. New York: Palgrave.

Cozette, Murielle (2008a). Reclaiming the Critical Dimension of Realism: Hans J. Morgenthau on the Ethics of Scholarship. *Review of International Studies* (34): 5–27.

(2008b). What Lies Ahead: Classical Realism on the Future of International Relations. *International Studies Review* (10): 667–79.

Craig, Campbell (2003). *Glimmer of a New Leviathan: Total War in the Realism of Niebuhr, Morgenthau, and Waltz*. New York: Columbia University Press.

(2008). The Resurgent Idea of World Government. *Ethics and International Affairs*. 22(2): 133–42.

Dahl, Robert (1999). Can International Organizations Be Democratic? A Skeptic's View. In *Democracy's Edges*, Ian Shapiro and Casiano Hacker-Cordon (ed.). Cambridge: Cambridge University Press, pp. 19–36.

Davies, R. W. (1984). "Drop the Glass Industry": Collaborating with E. H. Carr. In *New Left Review* 145 (May–June): 56–70.

(2000). Carr's Changing Views on the Soviet Union. In *E. H. Carr: A Critical Appraisal*, Michael Cox (ed.). New York: Palgrave, pp. 91–108.

Delanty, Gerard and O'Mahony, Patrick (2002). *Nationalism and Social Theory*. London: Sage.

Deudney, Daniel (2007). *Bounding Power: Republican Security Theory from the Polis to Global Village*. Princeton: Princeton University Press.

Deutsch, Karl (1962). *Nationalism and Social Communication*. Cambridge: MIT Press.

(1969). *Nationalism and its Alternatives*. New York: Alfred Knopf.

(1970). *Political Community at the International Level*. New York: Archon Books.

Deutsch, Karl, Burrell, Sidney, Kann, Robert, Lee, Maurice, Lichterman, Martin, Lindgren, Raymond, Loewenheim, Francis, and Van Wagenen, Richard (1957).

Political Community and the North Atlantic Area: International Organization in the Light of Historical Experience. Princeton: Princeton University Press.

Dickson, Peter W. (1978). *Kissinger and the Meaning of History*. Cambridge: Cambridge University Press.

Donnelly, Jack (2000). *Realism and International Affairs*. Cambridge: Cambridge University Press.

Doyle, Michael (1983). Kant, Liberal Legacies, and Foreign Affairs. Parts 1 and 2. *Philosophy and Public Affairs* (12): 205–54, 323–53.

(1997). *Ways of War and Peace*. New York: Norton.

Dunne, Tim (1998). *Inventing International Society*. New York, Palgrave.

(2000). Theories as Weapons: E. H. Carr and International Relations. In *E. H. Carr: A Critical Appraisal*, Michael Cox (ed.), pp. 217–33.

Dryzek, John S. (1999). Transnational Democracy. *Journal of Political Philosophy* (7): 30–51.

Epp, Roger (1991). *The Augustinian Moment in International Politics: Niebuhr, Butterfield, Wight and the Reclaiming of a Tradition*. Aberystwyth: University of Wales, International Politics Research Paper, No. 10.

Erskine, Toni (2008). *Embedded Cosmopolitanism: Duties to Strangers and Enemies in a World of "Dislocated Communities"*. Oxford: Oxford University Press.

Falk, Richard (1987). *The Promise of World Order: Essays in Normative International Relations*. Philadelphia: Temple University Press.

(1995). *On Humane Governance: Towards a New Global Politics*. Cambridge: Polity.

(1997). The Critical Realist Tradition and the Demystification of State Power: E. H. Carr, Hedley Bull, and Robert W. Cox. In *Innovation and Transformation in International Studies*, Stephen Gill (ed.). Cambridge: Cambridge University Press, pp. 39–55.

Federalist Papers (1961). Ed. Clinton Rossiter. New York: New American Library.

Felix, Antonia (2002). *Condi: The Condoleezza Rice Story*. New York: Newmarket.

Forst, Rainer (2002). *Contexts of Justice: Political Philosophy Beyond Liberalism and Communitarianism*. New York: University of California Press.

Fox, Richard Wightman (1985). *Reinhold Niebuhr: A Biography*. Ithaca: Cornell University Press.

Frei, Christoph (2001). *Hans J. Morgenthau: An Intellectual Biography*. Baton Rouge: Louisiana State University Press.

Freyberg-Inan, Annette (2004). *What Moves Man: The Realist Theory of International Relations and Its Judgment of Human Nature*. Albany, NY: Suny Press.

Fuller, Lon (1964). *The Morality of Law*. New Haven: Yale University Press.

Funk, Albrecht (2003). The Monopoly of Legitimate Violence and Criminal Policy. In *International Handbook of Violence Research*, Wilhelm Heitmeyer and John Hagan (eds). Dordrecht: Kluwer, pp. 1057–75.

Gellner, Ernest (1992). Nationalism Reconsidered and E. H. Carr. *Review of International Studies* (18): 285–93.

(2006). *Nations and Nationalism*. Ithaca: Cornell University Press.

Gertenbach, Lars, Laux, Henning, Hartmut, Rosa, and Strecker, David (2010). *Theorien der Gemeinschaft*. Hamburg: Junius.

Giddens, Anthony (2009). *The Politics of Climate Change*. Cambridge: Polity.

Glaser, Charles L. (1994–5). Realists as Optimists: Cooperation as Self Help. *International Security* (19): 50–90.

Gosepath, Stefan and Merle, Jean-Christoph (eds) (2002). *Weltrepublik. Globalisierung und Demokratie*. Munich: C. H. Beck.

Gosnell, Harold F. (1981). Frederick L. Schuman: The Chicago Years. In *PS* (14): 806–7.

Griffiths, Martin (1992). *Realism, Idealism and International Politics: A Reinterpretation*. London: Routledge.

Groom, A. J. R. and Taylor, Paul (eds) (1975). *Functionalism: Theory and Practice in International Relations*. New York: Crane, Russak, and Co.

Guilhot, Nicolas (2010). American Katechon: When Political Theology Became International Relations Theory. *Constellations* (17): 224–53.

Habermas, Jürgen Haben (2001). *The Postnational Constellation*. Cambridge, US: MIT Press.

(2006). *The Divided West*. Cambridge: Polity.

Hacke, Christian and Puglierin, Jana (2008). John H. Herz: Balancing Utopia and Reality. *International Relations* (22): 367–82.

Halliday, Fred and Rosenberg, Justin (1998). Interview with Kenneth Waltz. *Review of International Studies* (24): 371–86.

Harvey, David (1989). *The Condition of Postmodernity*. Oxford: Blackwell's.

Haslam, Jonathan (1999). *The Vices of Integrity: E. H. Carr, 1892–1982*. London: Verso.

(2002). *No Virtue Like Necessity: Realist Thought in International Relations Since Machiavelli*. Cambridge: Cambridge University Press.

Hayek, F. A. (1994 [1944]). *The Road to Serfdom*. Chicago: University of Chicago Press.

Heater, Derek (1996). *World Citizenship and Government: Cosmopolitan Ideas in the History of Western Political Thought*. New York: St Martin's.

Held, David (1995). *Democracy and the Global Order: From the Modern State to Cosmopolitan Governance*. Stanford: Stanford University Press.

(2004). *Global Covenant: The Social Democratic Alternative to the Washington Consensus*. Cambridge: Polity.

Held, David, McGrew, Anthony, Goldblatt, David, and Perraton, Jonathan (1999). *Global Transformations: Politics, Economics and Culture*. Stanford: Stanford University Press.

Herz, John (1951). *Political Realism and Political Idealism*. Chicago: University of Chicago Press.

(1959). *International Politics in the Atomic Age*. New York: Columbia University Press.

(1976). *The Nation State and the Crisis of World Politics*. New York: David McKay.

(1978). Legitimacy: Can we retrieve it? *Comparative Politics*. 10 (317–43).

(1984). *Vom Überleben. Wie ein Welbild entstand. Autobiographie.* Düsseldorf: Droste Verlag.

Hirst, Paul and Thompson, Grahame (1996). *Globalization in Question.* Cambridge: Polity.

Höffe, Otfried (1999). *Demokratie im Zeitalter der Demokratisierung.* Munich: Beck.

Hoffmann, Stanley (1978). *Primacy or World Order: American Foreign Policy Since the Cold War.* New York: McGraw Hill.

Holden, Barry (ed.) (2000). *Global Democracy: Key Debates.* London: Routledge.

Honig, Jan Willem (1996). Totalitarianism and Realism: Hans Morgenthau's German Years. In *Roots of Realism,* Benjamin Frankel (ed.). *New York: Frank Cass,* pp. 218–313.

Hook, Sidney (1937). Liberalism and the Case of Leon Trotsky. *Southern Review* (3): 267–82.

Horn, Christopher (1996). Philosophische Argumente für den Weltstaat. *Allgemeine Zeitschrift für Philosophie* (21): 229–51.

Horton, Walter Marshall (1934). *Realistic Theology.* New York: Harper and Brothers.

Howorth, J. Being and Doing in Europe since 1945: Contrasting Dichotomies of Identity and Efficiency. In *Why Europe?* J. Andrews (ed.). Basingstoke: Palgrave, 2000, pp. 85–96.

Howe, Paul (1994). The Utopian Realism of E. H. Carr. *Review of International Studies* (20): 277–97.

Howse, Robert (2007). Review of Slaughter, *A New World Order. American Journal of International Law* 101(1): 231–34.

Hutchins, Robert M. (1949). The Constitutional Foundations for World Order. In *Foundations for World Order.* Denver: University of Denver Press, pp. 95–114.

Hurrell, Andrew (2006). The State of International Society. In *The Anarchical Society in a Globalized World,* Richard Little and John Williams (eds). New York: Palgrave, pp. 191–215.

Ikenberry, G. John and Slaughter, Anne-Marie (2006). *Forging A World of Liberty Under Law: US National Security in the 21st Century* (Princeton: Princeton Project on National Security).

Jachtenfuchs, Markus (2006). Das Gewaltmonopol. Denationalisierung oder Fortbestand? In *Transformation des Staates?,* Stephan Leibfried and Michael Zürn (eds). Frankfurt: Suhrkamp, pp. 69–91.

Jaspers, Karl (1961). *The Future of Mankind,* E. B. Ashton (trans.). Chicago: University of Chicago Press.

Jones, Charles (1998). *E. H. Carr and International Relations: A Duty to Lie.* Cambridge: Cambridge University Press.

(1999). *Global Justice: Defending Cosmopolitanism.* Oxford: Oxford University Press.

Jünger, Ernst (1980 [1960]). Der Weltstaat. In *Sämtliche Weke,* Vol. 7. Stuttgart: Klett-Cotta, pp. 481–526.

Kant, Immanuel (1970). *Kant's Political Writings,* H. S. Reiss (ed.). Cambridge: Cambridge University Press.

Kennan, George (1951). *American Diplomacy, 1900–1950.* Chicago; University of Chicago Press.

Kissinger, Henry (1951). *The Meaning of History: Reflections on Spengler, Toynbee and Kant.* Cambridge, US: Harvard University, Department of Government, Senior Thesis.

    (1954). The Conservative Dilemma: Reflections on the Political Thought of Metternich. *American Political Science Review* (48): 1017–30.

    (1957). *A World Restored: Metternich, Castlereagh and the Problems of Peace 1812–22.* Boston: Houghton Mifflin.

    (1961). For an Atlantic Confederacy. *The Reporter* (2 February): 16–20.

    (1968). The White Revolutionary: Reflections on Bismarck. *Daedulus* (97): 888–924.

Kleinman, Mark L. (2000). *A World of Hope, a World of Fear: Henry A. Wallace, Reinhold Niebuhr, and American Liberalism.* Columbus, Ohio State University Press.

Koskenniemi, Martti (2001). *The Gentle Civilizer of Nations: The Rise and Fall of International Law 1870–1960.* Cambridge: Cambridge University Press.

Kratochwil, Friedrich (2010). How (Il)liberal is the Liberal Theory of Law/ Some Critical Remarks on Slaughter's Approach. *Comparative Sociology* (9): 120–45.

Krauthammer, Charles (2004). "Democratic Realism: An American Foreign Policy for a Unipolar World" (Irving Kristol Lecture, 12 February 2004, American Enterprise Institute, Washington, DC) (www.aei.org/include/pub-printasp?pubID =19912).

Layne, Christopher (2006). *The Peace of Illusions: American Grand Strategy from 1940 to the Present.* Ithaca: Cornell University Press.

League of Professional Groups for Foster and Ford (1932). *Culture and Crisis.* New York: Workers Library Publishing.

Lebow, Richard Ned (2003). *The Tragic Vision of Politics: Ethics, Interests and Orders.* Cambridge: Cambridge University Press.

    (2011). German Jews and American Realism. *Constellations* (forthcoming).

Lebow, Richard Ned and Stein, Janice Gross (1994). *We All Lost the Cold War.* Princeton: Princeton University Press.

Lent, Ernest S. (1955). The Development of United World Federalist Thought and Policy. *International Organization* (9): 486–501.

Levinson, Sanford (2006). *Our Undemocratic Constitution.* Princeton: Princeton University Press.

Lieven, Anatol and Hulsman, John (2006). *Ethical Realism: A Vision for America's Role in the World.* New York: Pantheon.

Linklater, Andrew (1997). The Transformation of Political Community: E. H. Carr, Critical Theory and International Relations. *Review of International Studies* (23): 321–8.

    (1998). *The Transformation of Political Community.* Cambridge: Polity.

(2000). E. H. Carr, Nationalism and the Future of the Sovereign State. In *E. H. Carr: A Critical Appraisal*. Michael Cox (ed.), pp. 234–57.

Linklater, Andrew and Suganami (2006). *The English School of International Relations: A Contemporary Reassessment*. Cambridge: Cambridge University Press.

Little, Richard (2003). The English School vs. American Realism: A Meeting of Minds or Divided by a Common Language. *Review of International Studies* (29): 443–60.

(2007). *The Balance of Power in International Relations: Metaphors, Myths and Models*. Cambridge: Cambridge University Press.

Little, Richard and Williams, John (eds) (2006). *The Anarchical Society in a Globalized World*. New York: Palgrave.

Lovin, Robin W. (1995). *Reinhold Niebuhr and Christian Realism*. Cambridge: Cambridge University Press.

Lu, Catherine (2006). World Government. In *Stanford Encyclopedia of Philosophy*; available at *plato.stanford.edu/entries/world-government/*.

MacDougall, Curtis D. (1965). *Gideon's Army*. New York: Marzani and Munsell.

Macintosh, D. C. (ed.) (1931). *Religious Realism*. New York: MacMillan.

McKeogh, Colm (1997). *The Political Realism of Reinhold Niebuhr: A Pragmatic Approach to Just War*. New York: St Martin's Press.

Mangone, Gerard J. (1951). *The Idea and Practice of World Government*. New York: Columbia University Press.

Mann, Michael (1993). *The Sources of Social Power: The Rise of Classes and Nation states, 1760–1914*. Cambridge: Cambridge University Press.

Mannheim, Karl (1985 [1936]). *Ideology and Utopia*. New York: Harcourt Brace and Jovanovich.

Marchetti, Raffaele (2008). *Global Democracy: For and Against*. London: Routledge.

Maus, Ingeborg (2006). From Nation state to Global state, or the Decline of Democracy. *Constellations* (13): 465–84.

Mayers, David (1988). *George Kennan and the Dilemmas of US Foreign Policy*. Oxford: Oxford University Press.

Mazower, Mark (2009). *No Enchanted Palace: The End of Empire and the Ideological Origins of the United Nations*. Princeton: Princeton University Press.

Mearsheimer, John (1994). The False Promise of International Institutions. *International Security* (19): 5–49.

(2001). *The Tragedy of Great Power Politics*. New York: Norton.

(2005). Hans Morgenthau and the Iraq War: Realism Versus Neoconservatism (*www.opendemocracy.net/democracy-americanpower/morgenthau_2522.jsp*) (19 May 2005).

Merkley, Paul (1975) *Reinhold Niebuhr: A Political Account*. Montreal: McGill-Queen's University Press.

Meyer, Donald (1988). *The Protestant Search for Political Realism, 1919–1941*. Middletown, Ct.: Wesleyan University Press.

Miller, David (1995). *On Nationality*. Oxford: Oxford University Press.

Mitrany, David (1946). *A Working Peace System*. London: National Peace Council.

(1975). *The Functional Theory of Politics*. London: Martin Robertson.

Mollov, M. Benjamin (2002). *Power and Transcendence: Hans J. Morgenthau and the Jewish Experience*. Lanham, MD.: Lexington Books.

Morgan, Glyn (2005). *The Idea of a European Superstate*. Princeton: Princeton University Press.

Morgenthau, Hans (1929). *Die international Rechtspflege, ihr Wesen und ihre Grenzen*. Leipzig: Universitätsverlag von Robert Noske.

(1940). Positivism, Functionalism, and International Law. *American Journal of International Law* (34): 260–84.

(1942). Review of *Power Politics* by George Schwarzenberger. *American Journal of International Law* (36): 351–52.

(1944). The Limitations of Science and the Problem of Social Planning. *Ethics* (54): 174–85.

(1945a). The Machiavellian Utopia. *Ethics* (55): 145–47.

(1945b). The Scientific Solution of Social Conflicts. In *Approaches to National Unity*. Lyman Bryson, Louis Finkelstein, and Robert MacIver (eds). New York: Harper and Brothers, pp. 419–37.

(1946). *Scientific Man Vs. Power Politics*. Chicago: University of Chicago Press.

(1948a). The Political Science of E. H. Carr. *World Politics* (1): 127–34.

(1948b; 1st edn). *Politics Among Nations: The Struggle for Power and Peace*. New York: Alfred Knopf.

(1948c). The Twilight of International Morality. *Ethics* (58): 79–99.

(1949). National Interest and Moral Principles in Foreign Policy: The Primacy of the National Interest. *American Scholar* (18): 207–12.

(1951). *In Defense of the National Interest*. New York: Alfred Knopf.

(1954; 2nd. edn). *Politics Among Nations: The Struggle for Power and Peace*. New York: Alfred Knopf.

(1956). Has Atomic War Really Become Impossible? In *Bulletin of Atomic Scientists* 12 (January): 7–9.

(1958). *Dilemmas of Politics*. Chicago: University of Chicago Press.

(1960). *The Purpose of American Politics*. New York: Alfred Knopf.

(1962a). Another Legacy of Hiroshima: The Partially Scientific Mind. *Bulletin of Atomic Scientists* 18 (June): 34–6.

(1962b). Death in the Nuclear Age. In *The Restoration of American Politics*. Chicago: University of Chicago Press, pp. 19–25.

(1962c). The Influence of Reinhold Niebuhr in American Political Life and Thought. In *Reinhold Niebuhr: A Prophetic Voice in Our Time*, Harold Landon (ed.). Greenwich, CT.: Seabury, pp. 97–116.

(1962d). The Intellectual and Political Functions of a Theory of International Relations. In *The Decline of Democratic Politics*. Chicago: University of Chicago Press, pp. 62–78.

(1966). Introduction. In Mitrany, *A Working Peace System*: Chicago: Quadrangle Books.

(1970). *Truth and Power: Essays of a Decade, 1960–70*. New York: Praeger.

(1972). *Science: Servant or Master?* New York: Meridian Books.

(1973). The Danger of Détente. In *New Leader* 56 (Oct 1, 1973): 7.

(1975). Explaining the Failures of US Foreign Policy: Three Paradoxes. In *The New Republic* (11 October): 16–21.

(1979). *Human Rights and Foreign Policy*. New York: Council on Religion and International Affairs.

Morgenthau, Hans and Niebuhr, Reinhold (1967). The Ethics of War and Peace in the Nuclear Age. *War/Peace Report* 7 (February): 3–8.

Mouffe, Chantal (2000). *The Democratic Paradox*. London, Verso.

Murphy, Cornelius (1999). *Theories of World Governance: A Study in the History of Ideas*. Pittsburgh: Duquesne University Press.

Murphy, Craig (2001). Critical Theory and the Democratic Impulse: Understanding a Century-Old Tradition. In Richard Wyn Jones, *Critical Theory and World Politics*. Boulder: Lynne Rienner, pp. 61–76.

Murray, Alastair (1997). *Reconstructing Realism: Between Power Politics and Cosmopolitan Ethics*. Edinburgh: Keele University Press.

Navari, Cornelia (1995). David Mitrany and International Functionalism. In *Thinkers of the Twenty Years' Crisis: Inter-War Idealism Reassessed*, David Long and Peter Wilson (eds). Oxford: Clarendon Books, pp. 214–31.

Niebuhr, Reinhold (1932). *Moral Man and Immoral Society*. New York: Charles Scribner's Sons.

(1934) *Reflections on the End of an Era*. New York: Charles Scribner's Sons.

(1935). *An Interpretation of Christian Ethics*. New York: Harper and Brothers.

(1940). *Christianity and Power Politics*. New York: Charles Scribner's Sons.

(1941). *The Nature and Destiny of Man. Volume I. Human Nature*. New York: Charles Scribner's Sons.

(1942). The Problem of Power. *The Nation* (10 January 1942): 42–4.

(1943). *The Nature and Destiny of Man. Volume II. Human Destiny*. New York: Charles Scribner's Sons.

(1944). *The Children of Light and the Children of Darkness*. New York: Charles Scribner's Sons.

(1946). The Russian Adventure. *The Nation* (23 February 1946): 232–4.

(1951). Editorial Notes. *Christianity and Crisis* 11(18): 138–9.

(1952). *The Irony of American History*. New York: Charles Scribner's Sons.

(1953a). *Christian Realism and Political Problems*. New York: Charles Scribner's Sons.

(1953b). Christian Faith and Social Action. In *Christian Faith and Social Action*. John A Hutchinson (ed). New York: Charles Scribner's Sons, pp. 225–43.

(1955). Moral Implications of Loyalty to the United Nations. *Motive* (October): 17–20.

(1959). *The Structure of Nations and Empires*. New York: Charles Scribner's Sons.

(1965). *Man's Nature and His Communities*. New York: Charles Scribner's Sons.

[1967a [1942]. Plans for World Reorganization. In *Love and Justice: Selections from the Shorter Writings of Reinhold Niebuhr*. D. B. Robertson (ed.), pp. 206–13.

(1967b [1943]. The Possibility of a Durable Peace. In *Love and Justice: Selections from the Shorter Writings*, pp. 196–200.

(1967c [1943]). American Power and World Responsibility. In *Love and Justice: Selections from the Shorter Writings*, pp. 200–6.

[1967d [1945]. The San Francisco Conference. In *Love and Justice: Selections from the Shorter Writings*, pp. 213–15.

[1967e] [1953]. Can We Organize the World? In *Love and Justice: Selections from the Shorter Writings*, pp., 216–17.

Niebuhr, Reinhold and Schuman, Frederick (1942). The Federation of the Free/No Adequate Blueprint. *The Nation* (24 January 1942): 103.

(1946). Professor Schuman Protests/Dr Niebuhr Replies. *The Nation* (30 March 1946): 383.

Nielsen, Kai (1988). World Government, Security, and Global Justice. In *Problems of International Justice*, Steven Luper-Foy (ed.). Boulder: Westview, pp. 263–82.

Obama, Barack (2009). Nobel Acceptance Speech (11 December) [http:www.nytimes.com/2009/12/11/world/Europe/11prexy.text.html.]

Occhipinti, John D. (2003). *The Politics of EU Police Cooperation*. Boulder: Lynn Rienner.

O'Neill, William L. (1982). *A Better World – The Great Schism: Stalinism and the American Intellectuals*. New York: Simon and Schuster.

Onuf, Nicholas (1998). *The Republican Legacy in International Thought*. Cambridge: Cambridge University Press.

Oren, Ido (2003). *Our Enemies and US: America's Rivals and the Making of Political Science*. Ithaca: Cornell University Press.

(2009). The Unrealism of Contemporary Realism: The Tension between Realist Theory and Realists' Practice. *Perspectives on Politics* (7): 283–301.

Osborn, Ronald (2009). Noam Chomsky and the realist Tradition. *Review of International Studies* (35): 351–70.

Oshinsky, David M. 1983. *A Conspiracy So Immense: The World of Joe McCarthy*. New York: Free Press.

Outhwaite, William (2008). *European Society*. Cambridge: Polity.

Partington, John S. (2003). *Building Cosmopolis: The Political Thought of H. G. Wells*. Aldershot: Ashgate.

Pells, Richard (1973). *Radical Visions and American Dreams: Culture and Social Thought in the Depression Years*. New York: Harper.

(1985). *The Liberal Mind in a Conservative Age*. Middletown, CT: Wesleyan University Press.

Pentland, Charles (1973). *International Theory and European Integration*. New York: Free Press.

Pettit, Philip (2000). *Republicanism: A Theory of Freedom and Government*. Oxford: Oxford University Press.

Pogge, Thomas (1988). Moral Progress. In *Problems of International Justice*, Steven Luper-Foy (ed.). Boulder: Westview Press, pp. 283–304.

(1994). Cosmopolitanism and Sovereignty. In *Political Restructuring in Europe: Ethical Perspectives*, Chris Brown (ed.). London: Routledge, 89–122.

Posner, Eric (2009). *The Perils of Global Legalism*. Princeton: Princeton University Press.

Preuss, Ulrich (2002). Entmachtung des Staates? In *Weltrepublik, Globalisierung und Demokratie*, Stefan Gosepath and Jean-Christophe Merle (eds). Munich: Beck, pp. 99–110.

Puglierin, Jana (ed.) (2008). *International Relations* [special issue on John Herz] 22:4.

Rawls, John (1999). *The Law of Peoples*. Cambridge, US: Harvard University Press.

Reinicke, Wolfgang (1998). *Global Public Policy: Governing Without Government?* Washington, DC: Brookings.

Rich, P. (2000). E. H. Carr and the Quest for Moral Revolution in International Relations. In *E. H. Carr: A Critical Appraisal*. Michael Cox (ed.), pp. 198–216.

Rice, Daniel (2008). Reinhold Niebuhr and Hans Morgenthau: A Friendship with Contrasting Shades of Realism. *Journal of American Studies* (42): 255–91.

Rittberger, Volker and Zangl, Bernhard (2000). *International Organization: Polity, Politics and Policies*. New York: Palgrave.

Rosanvallon, Pierre (2000). *The New Social Question: Rethinking the Welfare State*. Princeton: Princeton University Press.

Rosenau, James N. and Czempiel, Ernst-Otto (eds) (1992). *Governance Without Government: Order and Change in World Politics*. Cambridge: Cambridge University Press.

Rosenberg, Justin (1994). *The Empire of Civil Society: A Critique of the Realist Theory of International Relations*. London: Verso.

Ruggie, John Gerard (1993). Territoriality and Beyond: Problematizing Modernity in International Relations. In *International Organization* (47): 139–74.

Sagan, Scott and Waltz, Kenneth (2003). *The Spread of Nuclear Weapons: A Debate Renewed*. New York: Norton.

Scheuerman, William E. (1999). *Carl Schmitt and the End of Law*. Lanham, Md.: Rowman and Littlefield.

(2004). *Liberal Democracy and the Social Acceleration of Time*. Baltimore: Johns Hopkins University Press.

(2006). Globalization. In *Stanford Encyclopedia of Philosophy* (http://plato.stanford.edu/entries/globalization)

(2008). *Frankfurt School Perspectives on Globalization, Democracy, and the Law*. London: Routledge.

(2009). *Hans Morgenthau: Realism and Beyond*. Cambridge: Polity.

Schmalz-Bruns, Rainer (2007). An den Grenzen der Entstaatlichung. Bemerkungen zu Jürgen Habermas' Modell einer "Weltinnenpolitik ohne Weltregierung". In *Anarchie der kommunikativen Freiheit*, Peter Niesen and Benjamin Herborth (eds). Frankfurt: Suhrkamp, pp. 269–93.

Schmidt, Brian (2005). Competing Realist Conceptions of Power. *Millennium: Journal of International Studies* (33): 523–49.

Schmidt, Brian and Williams, Michael (2008). The Bush Doctrine and the Iraq War: Neoconservatives Vs. Realists. *Security Studies* (17): 1–30.

Schmidt, Vivien A. (2006). *Democracy in Europe: The EU and National Polities.* Oxford: Oxford University Press.

Schmitt, Carl (1996 [1932]). *The Concept of the Political*, George Schwab (trans.). Chicago: University of Chicago Press.

Scholte, Jan Aart (2000). *Globalization: A Critical Introduction.* New York: St Martin's.

Schuman, Frederick (1928). *American Policy Toward Russia Since 1917: A Study of Diplomatic History, International Law and Public Opinion.* New York: International Publishers.

(1930). The Soviets. *The New Republic* (28 May); 51–2.

(1931). *War and Diplomacy in the French Republic: An Inquiry into Political Motivations and the Control of Foreign Policy.* New York: McGraw Hill.

(1932). The Ethics and Politics of International Peace. *International Journal of Ethics* (42): 148–62.

(1st. edn, 1933). *International Politics: An Introduction to the Western State System.* New York: McGraw Hill.

(1935) *The Nazi Dictatorship: A Study in Social Pathology and the Politics of Fascism.* New York: Alfred Knopf.

(1936a). Fascism: Nemesis of Civilization. *Southern Review* (2): 126–32.

(1936b). Liberalism and Communism Reconsidered. *Southern Review* (2): 326–38.

(1937a). *Germany Since 1918* (New York: Henry Holt, 1937).

(1937b). Leon Trotsky: Martyr or Renegade? *Southern Review* (3): 51–74.

(1939a). *Europe on the Eve: The Crisis of Diplomacy, 1933–39.* New York: Alfred Knopf.

(1939b). Machiavelli in Moscow. In *The New Republic* (29 November): 158–60.

(1939c). Machiavelli Gone Mad. In *The New Republic* (27 December): 290.

(1941a). *Design for Power: The Struggle for the World.* New York: Alfred Knopf.

(3rd edn. 1941b). *International Politics : The Western State System in Transition.* New York: McGraw Hill.

(1941c). *Night Over Europe: The Diplomacy of Nemesis, 1939–40.* New York: Alfred Knopf.

(1943). "Bill of Attainder" in the Seventy-Eighth Congress. *American Political Science Review* (37): 819–29.

(1944). Dr Guerard's Delusion *Antioch Review* (4): 496–500.

(1945). The Dilemma of the Peace-Seekers. *American Political Science Review* (39): 12–30.

(1946a). *Soviet Politics, at Home and Abroad.* New York: Alfred Knopf.

(1946b) Toward the World State. *The Scientific Monthly* (63): 5–19.

(1951). The Council of Europe. *American Political Science Review* (45): 724–40.

(1952a). *The Commonwealth of Man: An Inquiry into Power Politics and World Government*. New York: Alfred Knopf.

(1952b) International Ideals and the National Interest. *Annals of the American Academy of Political and Social Sciences* (280): 27–36.

(1955). UN: The First Decade. *The Nation* (30 July): 98.

(1958). How Many Worlds? *New Republic* (3 February): 13–16.

(1962). *Russia Since 1917. Four Decades of Soviet Politics*. New York: Alfred Knopf.

(1967). *The Cold War: Retrospect and Prospect*. Baton Rouge: Louisiana University Press.

(1969). *Why a Department of Peace*. Beverley Hills: Another Mother for Peace.

Schwarzenberger, George (1939). Rule of Law and the Disintegration of the international Society. *American Journal of International Law* (33): 56–77.

(1st, edn, 1941). *Power Politics: An Introduction to the Study of International Relations and Post-War Planning*. London: Jonathan Cape.

(1943a). Jus Pacis Ac Belli? Prolegomena to a Sociology of International Law. *American Journal of International Law* (37): 460–79.

(1943b). The Three Types of Law. *Ethics* (53): 89–97.

(1951). *Power Politics: A Study of International Society*. New York: Praeger.

(1957). *Atlantic Utopia: A Practical Utopia?* London: Federal Educational Trust.

(1963). Federalism and Supranationalism in the European Communities. In *Current Legal Problems: A Symposium on English Law and the Common Market*. London: Stevens and Sons, pp. 17–33.

(1964). *Power Politics: A Study of World Society*. New York: Praeger.

(1965). Beyond Power Politics? In *The Year Book of World Affairs*. London: Stevens and Sons, pp. 23–34.

(1973). *Civitas Maxima?* Tübingen: Mohr.

Shannon, Vaughn P. (2005). Wendt's Violation of the Constructivist Project: Agency and Why a World State is *Not* Inevitable. *European Journal of International Relations* (11): 581–87.

Shaw, Martin (1994). *Global Society and International Relations*. Cambridge: Polity.

(2000). *Theory of the Global State: Globality as an Unfinished Revolution*. Cambridge: Cambridge University Press.

Shils, Edward (2000). *A Fragment of a Sociological Autobiography*. New Brunswick: Transaction.

Slaughter, Anne-Marie (1995). International Law in a World of Liberal States. *European Journal of International Law* (6): 503–38.

(1997). The Real New World Order. *Foreign Affairs* (76): 183–97.

(1999–2000). Judicial Globalization. *Virginia Journal of International Law* (40): 1103–24.

(2000). Governing the Global Economy Through Government Networks. In *The Role of Law in International Politics*. Michael Byers (ed.). Oxford: Oxford University Press, pp. 177–206.

(2003). Good Reasons for Going Around the UN. *New York Times* (18 March 2003): A33.

(2004a). Global Government Networks, Global Information Agencies, and Disaggregated Democracy. In *Public Governance in the Age of Globalization*. Karl-Heinz Ladeur (ed.). Aldershot: Ashgate, pp. 121–56.

(2004b). *A New World Order*. Princeton: Princeton University Press.

(2007). *The Idea That is America*. New York: Basic Books.

(2009). America's Edge: Power in a Networked Age. *Foreign Affairs* (88): 94–113.

Smith, Anthony (1971). *Theories of Nationalism*. New York: Harper and Row.

Smith, Michael (1986). *Realist Thought from Weber to Kissinger*. Baton Rouge: Louisiana State University Press.

Snyder, Glenn H. (2002). Mearsheimer's World – Offensive Realism and the Struggle for Security. In *International Security* (27): 149–73.

Söllner, Alfons (1987). German Conservatism in America: Morgenthau's Political Realism. *Telos* (72): 161–72.

Somek, Alexander (2011). From the Rule of Law to the Constitutionalist Make-over: Changing European Conceptions of Public International Law. *Constellations* (17) [in press].

Spegele, Roger (1996). *Political Realism in International Theory*. Cambridge: Cambridge University Press.

Steinle, Stephanie (2002). *Völkerrecht und Machtpolitik. Georg Schwarzenberger (1908–1991)*. Baden-Baden: Nomos Verlag.

(2004). Georg Schwarzenberger (1908–1991). In *Jurists Uprooted: German-speaking Émigré Lawyers in Twentieth-century Britain*. Jack Beatson and Reinhard Zimmerman (eds). Oxford: Oxford University Press, pp. 663–80.

Stephanson, Anders (1989). *Kennan and the Art of Foreign Policy*. Cambridge, US: Harvard University Press.

Stirk, Peter (2005). John H. Herz: Realism and the Fragility of the International Order. *Review of International Studies* (31): 285–306.

Sylvest, Casper (2008). John H. Herz and the Resurrection of Classical Realism. *International Relations* (22): 441–55.

Tamir, Yael (2000). Who's Afraid of the Global State? In *Nationalism and Internationalism in the Post-Cold War Era*, Kjell Goldmann, Ulf Hannerz, and Charles Westin (eds). London: Routledge, pp. 216–43.

Tan, Kok-Chor (2004). *Justice Without Borders: Cosmopolitanism, Nationalism and Patriotism*. Cambridge: Cambridge University Press.

Taylor, Paul (1975). Introduction. In Mitrany, *The Functional Theory of Politics*, ix–xxv.

Thaa, Wolfgang (2001). Lean Citizenship: The Fading away of the Political in Transnational Democracy. *European Journal of International Relations* (7): 503–23.

Thelen, Mary Frances (1946). *Man as Sinner in Contemporary American Realistic Theology*. Morningside Heights, NY: King's Crown Press.

Thompson, Kenneth (1960). *Political Realism and the Crisis of World Politics*. Princeton: Princeton University Press.

(2007). Reinhold Niebuhr: A Personal Reflection and Political Evaluation. In *The Realist Tradition and Contemporary International Relations.* David W. Clinton (ed.). Baton Rouge: Louisiana State University Press, pp. 1–23.

Thompson, Kenneth and Myers, Robert J. (eds) (1984). *Truth and Tragedy: A Tribute to Hans J. Morgenthau.* New Brunswick, NJ: Transaction Books.

Tillich, Paul (1956 [1932]). *The Religious Situation.* H. Richard Niebuhr (trans.). New York: Meridian Books.

(1977 [1933]). *The Socialist Decision.* Franklin Sherman (trans.). New York: Harper and Row.

Tippett, Krista (2009). Speaking of Faith: Preserving World and Worlds (Transcript of National Public Radio Program with E. J. Dionne and David Brooks) [http://speakingoffaith.publicradio.org/programs/2009/obama-theology].

Tjalve, Vibeke Schou (2008). *Realist Strategies of Republican Peace: Niebuhr, Morgenthau, and the Politics of Patriotic Dissent.* New York: Palgrave.

Tomlinson, John (1999). *Globalization and Culture.* Cambridge: Polity.

Trager, Frank (1940). Frederick L. Schuman: A Case History. *Partisan Review* (7): 143–51.

US Congress (1943). *Investigation of Un-American Propaganda Activities in the United States: Hearings Before a Special Committee on Un-American Activities, House of Representatives, Seventy-Eighth Congress, First Session,* Vol. 7 [Tuesday 30 March 1943]: 3087–3192

Voskuil, Dennis N. (1988). Neo-orthodoxy. In *Encyclopedia of American Religious Experience,* Vol. II, Charles H. Lippy and Peter W. Williams (eds). New York: Charles Scribner's Sons, pp. 1147–57.

Waltz, Kenneth (1959). *Man, the State, and War.* New York: Columbia University Press.

(1979). *Theory of International Politics.* New York: McGraw Hill.

(2008). *Realism and International Politics.* New York: Routledge.

Walzer, Michael (1986). The Reform of the International System. In *Studies of War and Peace,* Oyvind Osterud (ed.). Oslo: Norwegian University Press, pp. 227–40.

(2004). *Arguing About War.* New Haven: Yale University Press.

Warren, Frank (1966). *Liberals and Communism: The "Red Decade" Revisited.* Bloomington: Indiana University Press.

Warren, Heather A. (1997). *Theologians of a New World Order: Reinhold Niebuhr and the Christian Realists, 1920–1948.* New York: Oxford University Press.

Weber, Max (1994 [1919]). The Profession and Vocation of Politics. In *Political Writings,* Peter Lassman and Ronald Speirs (eds). Cambridge: Cambridge University Press, pp. 309–69.

Weiss, Thomas (2008). *What's Wrong with the UN and what can we do about it?* Cambridge: Polity.

Wendt, Alexander (1992). Anarchy is What States Make of It: The Social Construction of Power Politics. *International Organization* (46): 391–425.

(1999). *Social Theory of International Politics.* Cambridge: Cambridge University Press.

(2003). Why a World State is Inevitable. *European Journal of International Relations* (9): 491–542.

(2005). Agency, Teleology, and the World State: A Reply to Shannon. *European Journal of International Relations* (11): 589–98.

Wheeler, Nicholas J. (2000). *Saving Strangers: Humanitarian Intervention in International Society*. Oxford: Oxford University Press.

(2008). 'To Put Oneself into the other Fellow's Place': John Herz, the Security Dilemma and the Nuclear Age. *International Relations* (22): 493–509.

Wight, Martin (1946). *Power Politics*. London: Royal Institute of International Affairs.

(1992). *International Theory: The Three Traditions*. New York: Holmes and Meier.

Williams, Michael C. (2005). *The Realist Tradition and the Limits of International Relations*. Cambridge: Cambridge University Press.

(ed.) (2007) *Realism Reconsidered: The Legacy of Hans J. Morgenthau in International Relations*. Oxford: Oxford University Press.

Williams, William Appleman (1980). *Empire as a Way of Life*. New York: Oxford University Press.

Wilkinson, Richard and Pickett, Kate (2009). *The Spirit Level: Why More Equal Societies Almost Always do Better*. London: Allen Lane.

Willkie, Wendell (1966 [1943]). *One World*. Urbana: University of Illinois Press.

Wilson, Peter (1998). The Myth of the "First Great Debate". *Review of International Studies* (24): 1–16.

Winks, Robin (1987). *Cloak and Gown: Scholars in the Secret War, 1939–61*. New York: William Morrow and Co.

Wittner, Lawrence (1993). *One World or None: A History of the World Nuclear Disarmament Movement Through 1953*. Stanford: Stanford University Press.

Wolfers, Arnold (1923). Macht und Gemeinschaft in der Weltpolitik. *Blätter für Religösen Sozialismus* (4): 21–8.

(1924). *Die Aufrichtung der Kapitalherrschaft in der abendländischen Geschichte*. Philosophical Faculty, University of Giessen, Doctoral Dissertation.

(1926). How Can Democracy Be Saved? *The World Tomorrow* (9): 256–58.

(1927). Can the Anti-Spiritual Elements in the Capitalistic System Be Changed? In *The Student World* (October): 306–11.

(1928). Vorwort. In *Probleme der Demokratie* (Berlin: Schriftenreihe der Deutschen Hochschule für Politik), pp. v–lx.

(1962). *Discord and Collaboration: Essays on International Politics*. Baltimore: Johns Hopkins University Press.

(1964 [1940]). Armistice Day Address. In *Yale Alumni Review* (4)8: 5.

Zolo, Danilo (1997). *Cosmopolis: Prospects for World Government*. Cambridge: Polity.

(2002). *Invoking Humanity: War, Law and Global Order*. London: Continuum.

INDEX